Carly's Voice

BREAKING THROUGH AUTISM

ARTHUR FLEISCHMANN
with CARLY FLEISCHMANN

A Touchstone Book

Published by Simon & Schuster

New York   London   Toronto   Sydney   New Delhi

Touchstone
A Division of Simon & Schuster, Inc.
1230 Avenue of the Americas
New York, NY 10020

First Touchstone trade paperback edition September 2012

TOUCHSTONE and colophon are registered trademarks of Simon & Schuster, Inc.

For information about special discounts for bulk purchases,
please contact Simon & Schuster Special Sales at 1-866-506-1949
or business@simonandschuster.com.

The Simon & Schuster Speakers Bureau can bring authors to your live event. For
more information or to book an event contact the Simon & Schuster Speakers
Bureau at 866-248-3049 or visit our website at www.simonspeakers.com.

Designed by Ruth Lee-Mui

Manufactured in the United States of America

11   13   15   17   19   20   18   16   14   12

Library of Congress Cataloging-in-Publication Data

Fleischmann, Arthur.
Carly's voice : breaking through autism /
Arthur Fleischmann with Carly Fleischmann.
p.   cm.
"A Touchstone book."
1. Fleischmann, Carly, 1995–   2. Fleischmann, Arthur.   3. Autistic children—
Ontario—Toronto—Biography.   4. Parents of autistic children—Ontario—
Toronto—Biography.   5. Autism in children—Treatment—Case studies.   6. Autistic
children—Education—Case studies.   7. Communication—Study and teaching—Case
studies.   8. Voice output communication aids—Case studies.   9. Toronto (Ont.)—
Biography.   I. Fleischmann, Carly, 1995–   II. Title.
RJ506.A9F587 2012
618.92'858820092—dc23
[B]   2011032733

ISBN 978-1-4391-9414-0
ISBN 978-1-4391-9415-7 (pbk)
ISBN 978-1-4391-9416-4 (ebook)

*For those who have not yet found their inner voice
and those who will help them do so.*

Although the world is full of suffering,
it is full also of the overcoming of it.

—*Helen Keller*

Prologue

It was the end of the day. Two of my business partners were slumped in the stylishly uncomfortable club chairs across from my desk. I was leaning back with my feet up.

"That was an awful meeting," I observed.

"We were terrible," said one partner.

"We talked way too much. Blah, blah, blah," said the other.

"At one point," I said, "I thought, 'Oh my God, who's talking so much? I'm so bored.' Then I realized it was *me*."

We laughed. The three of us had just wrapped up a business meeting with a prospective client, one we didn't really want. As a fledgling ad agency, however, we only ate what we killed in those early days, and we shot at most anything that moved.

"There will be plenty of other opportunities," I concluded with a shrug as I stood to signal that it was day over, time to go home.

I left the office, a place of hipness and friendly banter—which my assistant had dubbed "the epicenter of love"—and climbed into my car.

As I headed home to our comfortable house in a central Toronto neighborhood, I was probably listening to The Fray or Creed blasting on the stereo and singing. With the windows and sunroof open, I could enjoy the warm evening air. As I cut through the Annex, then up University Avenue through Yorkville, I wondered how I could view Toronto as such a beautiful, livable city and my wife could view it as so *not*. Then again, she grew up in Toronto and saw it through a different lens. As someone who grew up in a suburb but always preferred the city, I appreciated Toronto's cosmopolitan charm.

The sun had started sinking, casting a golden light. The summer colors were fading, coming to the end of their all-too-short season. But the dying maple leaves found one more blast of energy and painted a palette of gold and red on the trees lining the streets.

I arrived home and parked my car in the driveway that extended to the back of the house, noting that my wife, Tammy, was out. This was not unusual on a weekday evening. Typically, one of the kids had an activity, or Tammy had an appointment or an errand to run. Before entering the house, I stopped to survey our little dollop of tranquility outside our back door: a cedar fence that surrounded the small, vibrant garden; a limestone patio; and a lawn that had kept its vigor well, considering the lateness of the season. I paused on the back porch for a moment, listening to the babble of the waterfall I installed that summer, and steeled myself with a deep exhale.

The back door into the kitchen was unlocked. This *was* unusual, but not alarming. We lived in a tidy and well-groomed neighborhood of old brick homes, with well-groomed neighbors that kept to themselves. The kitchen, which we had recently renovated, was orderly and calm. Our nanny had already fed the kids and cleaned up dinner.

"Hey," I called into the den to my preteen son playing on his

Xbox. He grunted a response. I dropped my satchel and called up the stairs "Helloooo," with just enough sarcasm to elicit a "Hi" from one of my twin seven-year-old daughters, Taryn.

"Where's Carly?" I yelled to our nanny over the sound of the bath filling. I asked this question instinctively and nearly as frequently as I inhaled.

"Isn't she in her room?" she replied from the washroom.

"Oh shit," I said.

I ran from bedroom to bedroom. Down the stairs, through the living room, dining room, and den, and into the basement in what can only be described as one continuous swoop through the house. But I knew I wouldn't find her here. The house was too quiet. It lacked her frenetic energy that usually electrified every room. For a brief moment the four of us—our nanny, my son, my daughter, and I—faced each other at the landing. Carly was gone.

We stood staring at one another. If she's not here, then where is she? "Who saw her last?" I asked. I was not assessing blame, but merely fumbling my way through detective work.

"She was sitting on her bed while I filled the bath," replied our nanny. She had a slow calm about her that could test my patience. But she had always been so dedicated to Carly and to our family, so tolerant of the challenging tasks of helping to raise a little girl with severe autism. In this role, many personality quirks could be overlooked.

As I dashed back down to the kitchen, the evening light was fading rapidly through the bay window behind the kitchen table. Although we lived in a large, active city, Carly's life was tightly prescribed. There were only a few places we took her on foot in our neighborhood. Almost instinctively, I bolted through the back door and down the street. There was a small park several blocks away. We had been going there on warm nights after dinner ever since we moved to the neighborhood, when the girls were one year old.

Before they could walk the distance, we would push them in their twin stroller, drawing the attention of passersby. Though I rolled my eyes at women cooing at my two sweet-faced twins in their adorable outfits, I secretly enjoyed the attention.

Swinging on park swings was one of Carly's favorite pastimes; she seemed to find the whooshing of air in her face relaxing. And having her contained by a child swing was a relief after a long day of work.

I was horrified at the thought that I might find her there. She would have had to cross several busy city blocks in the twilight. I was equally horrified by the possibility that I might *not* find her there. This was both my plan A and plan B. We lived only several streets over from a large main avenue lined with stores and restaurants. Toronto is a grid of streets, each one spawning another. If she wasn't at the park, there was no telling where she might be.

I ran the four or five blocks, oblivious to traffic. I was winded with anxiety. My little girl was seven. She should know better than to leave the house without an adult. She should be afraid of being alone in the dark or out among strangers. But Carly did not know these things. It seemed to us that there were a great many things she should have known but didn't.

As I rounded the corner, I saw a woman standing by her bicycle, transfixed by a strange sight. A little girl, my little girl, stood near the swing set. She was naked except for her sport sandals. The dress she had been wearing sat in a ball on the ground. Carly stood rigid-limbed, making short jerking, bowing movements from the waist like a short-circuiting robot.

"Oh, thank God," I heard myself breathe. But I did not feel the relief of a parent being reunited with a kid who had wandered off to see a shiny toy at the mall. I knew that I could not merely scold Carly and hope she would learn a lesson. Carly seemed to have no fear and no conscience. My wife and I couldn't take a breath without knowing exactly where she was. One lapse in scrutiny and here we were—Carly, in the park, naked, at dusk, alone. I felt happy to have found her, but I also felt the crush of frustration and desperation, knowing that this would not be a onetime near-catastrophe. It was just a moment in our lives. And we would have many more.

As I ran toward Carly, the woman asked, "Are you her father? Thank goodness!" She sounded the way I should have felt. "I didn't know what to do," she exclaimed, now sounding almost guilty. But this should not be her guilt.

I already had my standard-issue explanation, so well-rehearsed it's a verbal tic. "Carly has autism." Three short words must suffice to explain a tome of weird behaviors and limitations. It's shorthand for Carly-is-different-she-acts-in-odd-ways-she-loves-taking-off-her-clothes-especially-if-what-she-is-wearing-has-a-spot-of-water-on-it-she-likes-repetitive-motion-like-that-of-the-swing-she-doesn't-speak. We didn't know what Carly knew and what she was incapable of knowing. She made odd movements and sounds and covered her ears when it was noisy. She cried often. And she never, ever stopped moving. Never.

In one motion I picked up Carly's dress and pulled it over her head. With little hope it would have any impact on future flights, I told Carly, "You can't just leave the house, Carly. You scared me. And you must keep your clothes on when you're outside." I wanted to say, "Stop this. Stop scaring the shit out of me. Stop creating havoc every five minutes. Stop being so needy. I love you, but stop."

But I didn't. Instead, I thanked the woman for staying with my daughter. She repeated that she didn't know what to do or whom to call. I could see she was happy to escape this situation. She was not unsympathetic, but I could see gratitude in her eyes that this was not her life; that she could extract herself from this pathetic situation and ride home to her family. She'd have a hell of story to tell her kids that night.

I took Carly by the hand. She did not resist or melt down into one of her usual tantrums. Perhaps there was hope that she was aware that what she did was wrong? I can always hope. "We'll come back to the park tomorrow, Carly," I said as we walked toward home. I repeated over and over that she must only leave the house with an adult. Please, let her learn this lesson.

Back home I sighed, "I found her." Tammy was home by then. Taryn was in the bath, and I sent Carly upstairs with our nanny to join her. I explained everything to my wife, who closed her eyes and dropped her head. We didn't need to discuss this any further. It was just one more reminder of the challenges we faced.

The next day, my wife called a home-security company and had a chiming alarm installed so we would know when the door had been opened.

Upstairs, I heard the bath running again. The *bleep bleep bleep bleeps* told me that Matthew was back to defeating the warlords. The air conditioning hummed. Everything was back to the way it should be. Our house was filled with all the normal evening sounds heard in all the other normal houses on our normal block.

But this was not a normal house.

This was Carly's house.

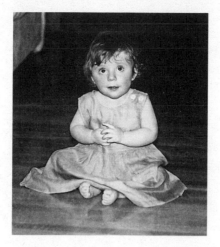

Part I

❧

Chaos Is Born

There is no education like adversity.
—*Benjamin Disraeli*

1

In the Eye of the Storm

A news reporter once asked me to describe our a-ha moment with Carly. He wanted to understand that blinding flash of insight we had had about our daughter. I thought for a moment before replying, "There never has been a moment like that. Carly has always just been Carly."

From the moment our daughters were born on a gray morning in January 1995, both my wife and I knew which twin—Twin A or Twin B—was going to grow up to live the life of Carly, and which would become Taryn. Call it intuition or cosmic intervention, but one baby just *was* a Carly.

After the unsettled time around the birth of our son four and a half years earlier, we were elated to close the book on trauma and start a new life with our enlarged family. Matthew had been born during the grieving period for Tammy's mother, who had died suddenly just months before his birth.

Having the twins had not come easily. Creating life was not an issue for Tammy; sustaining it had been. After three miscarriages in the years after Matthew was born, we were about to break the curse. We looked forward to a fresh start. Quid pro quo; we were *owed* that much.

"How many bedrooms do you have?" Tammy's obstetrician-gynecologist had asked her cryptically five months earlier, during the summer of 1994.

"Three," Tammy replied.

"You might want to consider four," Dr. Amonkwa said.

It seemed that the Clomid, progesterone, and aspirin that he had prescribed had broken the cycle of lost babies and parental despair. Rather than one child, Tammy was pregnant with twins. Other doctors had told us that perhaps more children were not meant to be. But we, and in particular Tammy, seldom took "perhaps not" at face value.

After careful monitoring for the rest of the nine months, Tammy gave birth to our daughters. We considered naming them after the drugs that made their successful birth possible, but Clomid and Progesterone Fleischmann would have been cruel.

Our older twin and middle child arrived at 7:38 a.m., and her little sister, Taryn, fourteen minutes later. Carly had been the feisty one in utero, clamoring to get here. But once she arrived, she seemed to take a look around and say, "Oh, wrong place." This world would never be in step with our little girl. Within weeks of her birth, Carly took on a startled and cranky look, one that matched her demeanor.

Taryn was peaceful and elegant with a cap of dark hair and a quizzical expression. But Carly arrived blotchy and patchy and looking surprised. From the prenatal medical records, there was little to suggest that the fraternal twins would have such different fates. Tammy's medical chart indicated that the delivery of the girls was "spontaneous, vaginal, and uncomplicated," much like the act of their creation had been. After a week in the hospital, we bundled our tiny new-potato-like parcels into furry winter baby buntings and brought them home to our modest Toronto house.

The next six months were a bleary, sleep-deprived period of normalcy. As normal as a household can be with three children under five, two of whom eat every three hours, twenty-four hours a day. Tammy and I would plod up the steep, narrow staircase to our bedroom around 9:00 p.m., lugging two babies and six mini-bottles of formula. Frighteningly, all six portions would be consumed before 5:00 a.m. the next morning, each feeding followed by the requisite diaper change.

Tired as I felt, I couldn't fail to smile at the two little swaddled lumps. Carly and Taryn slept in a large woven basket that we placed atop a low dresser that Tammy had been lugging through life since college. It was stained a puzzling shade of green and had more sentimental than aesthetic value. Now tucked into an alcove in our bedroom, it served as a pedestal on which our daughters started their lives.

The two girls had spent nine months pressed together in Tammy's womb and felt completely natural being tucked in tightly, snuggled closely. We made a conscious effort from the start to give them unique identities, refraining from dressing them the same or referring to them as "the twins," but rather as Carly and Taryn. Yet, they were two halves of the same whole and would lie together, reaching out and touching each other, practically hugging. How were we to know that one day they would grow to be like the front and back cover of a book—matching opposites—with so much separating them?

Since dinner parties were out of the question (not that they happened often before the girls' arrival), we covered our dining room table with a large pad and plastic tablecloth for changing the babies when downstairs. Tammy's friend Sue would come over on Sunday afternoons and help us with laundry. While Tammy simultaneously fed the two babies, Sue and I would cook as much food as we could squeeze into our freezer for the week ahead. The first months were a blur of laundry, poo, spit-up, quiche, and lasagna. But Tammy was happy to have a family after the false starts and dying hopes. I have scores of photographs of the early days, each of us taking turns holding both babies. We both seem to have a tired but amazed expression, as if to say, "How'd this happen?"

Life took on a chaotic rhythm that was made manageable by the arrival of our nanny, Mari. Mari had recently moved from St. Lucia to join her sisters and cousins; one sister worked as a nanny for a friend of ours. She took to our daughters immediately, a broad, open smile spreading across her usually serious face whenever she saw the two girls. Although a very quiet person, Mari exuded confidence in running our household—a thankless task we were more than happy to relinquish. For the next twelve years she would buttress our family and steadfastly help care for all three of our children and home. Tammy and Mari divided the never-ending tasks of Matthew's school and after-school activities and the seemingly endless work required to keep Carly and Taryn fed and clean. Tammy and I took a divide-and-conquer approach from the start, something that would stand us in good stead in the years to come.

My career had me at the office by 8:00 a.m. and seldom home before 7:00 p.m. Nevertheless, after work I did my best to focus on Matthew—to be sure he wasn't left out. We had been warned that boys in particular could get regressive when new babies come into the house. I recall my brother more as a tormentor when he was nine or ten. He once tried to feed me cat food and put pepper in my sister's chocolate pudding. On other occasions, he would hide under my bed or in the closet at night until the lights were out, then jump out and scream. Ghouls really do exist, at least until they become teenagers. Eventually, even little boys outgrow their wickedness.

Not knowing what to expect, I assumed Matthew might continue in the family tradition since he had his rambunctious tendencies. A year or two before the girls were born, we had bought a book titled *Raising Your Spirited Child* to help us understand why even the smallest thing, like an itchy tag at the neck of his shirt, could set off a full-blown tantrum. He was a rigid kid who vacillated between playful sweetness and the terrible twos that had overstayed their welcome.

While Mari and Tammy bathed the girls, I would eat dinner with Matthew. Then, in the warming spring evenings, I would take him to the park. As we walked, I often reflected on how Matthew's infancy was also anything but ordinary.

Always a snorty eater, in the fall of 1990 when Matthew was eight months old, we had to rush him to the emergency room, barely able to breathe. After several days in the hospital while the doctors ran tests, we were told Matthew had been born with a double aortic arch. The vessels carrying blood to and from his heart were wrapped around his trachea and windpipe, literally strangling him like jungle vines choking a tree.

But Matthew was a trooper and rebounded from surgery quickly. Five years later, Matthew loved to hear how he had been a brave patient, how he was giggling and laughing within days of his operation. He wore his scar as a badge of honor. "You have no trouble eating now," I joked with him. "Remember the time when you were two and Mom and I caught you taking an ear of corn out of the garbage after dinner?" Tammy and I had been washing dishes, and, upon hearing Matthew making noises of gastronomical bliss, found him smiling up at us as he finished an ear of corn that had been scraped from a plate into the garbage.

By late spring, the girls were sleeping through the night; Matthew was on a schedule; and Tammy and I even got an hour or two of quiet time before bed. We felt like we had gotten off the dirt road and onto the open highway. We traded a sedan for a minivan and ventured out on day trips and visits to friends, always lugging the girls, an oversized twin stroller, a huge diaper bag, and our rambunctious five-year-old son who ran circles around us making sounds like the Indy 500.

Before their first birthday, however, we began to see Carly and Taryn heading in different directions. Our first challenges with Carly were innocuous enough. Tubes in her ears to relieve the heavy fluid buildup one month. A few tests with audiologists to be sure the infections hadn't compromised her hearing the next. Tammy and I could handle this level of intervention. Lots of kids had tubes put in their ears. It was as common as diaper rash. Just by looking at her, however, we knew that Carly had deeper issues than goopy ear canals.

While Taryn's skin had smoothed into creamy baby softness, Carly's often had a ruddy, chapped look. Taryn's eyes seemed to giggle almost from birth, while Carly often wore a dozy gaze. And while Taryn was making headway at crawling, pulling herself up, and achieving all the other milestones of a toddler, Carly languished on her back. The biggest difference between the girls, however, was their personality. Taryn was happy and peaceful; Carly cried incessantly, earning her the nickname Cryly.

Our pediatrician did not seem particularly alarmed, but after the experience we had had with Matthew, Tammy and I were on full alert. We were referred to a physiotherapist at the Hospital for Sick Children, the first of what would become a legion of specialists. When it was clear that one appointment per week would not get Carly moving, Tammy enrolled her in a private clinic. Three times a week Tammy brought Carly to physical therapy, where they would tediously coax Carly from lying to sitting, and from sitting to butt-shuffling across the floor.

❧

Excerpt from progress report, Play and Learn Integrated Nursery Program, *January 4, 1996:*

J. Spitz, Coordinator

SUMMARY AND RECOMMENDATIONS

At 10 months of age Carly has shown some delays in her language, gross motor, auditory attention and memory, self-help and socialization skills. Frequent ear infections with fluid in the middle ear may certainly have impacted her language and auditory attention and memory skills. She appears to have some generalized low tone which may be impacting upon her gross motor skills at this time. Therapy input seems to be appropriately managed through the two therapists seeing Carly at this time. This gives Carly intensive focus on motor development at this time. Carly and her mother have begun the weekly parent and child program at Play and Learn. Through this program we can target specific skills through a play approach. As well, home visits can commence at the family's convenience to provide other suggestions of activities that will enhance Carly's development. She will be reassessed in six months.

Just after Taryn's and Carly's first birthday, we had to acknowledge that Tammy's obstetrician had been right. We needed a bigger house. Our dining room, which hadn't been used for eating since the girls arrived, was filled with toys and scooters. Our kitchen, barely large enough to be described as "eat-in," required that we eat dinner in shifts. And the two small bathrooms were always a traffic jam.

With three children instead of the planned two, we scrapped the idea of sending Matthew to private school and in the winter of 1996 found a house in a leafy section of the city near excellent public schools, parks, and stores. If not exactly a dream home, given our budget (which we overshot), it was more house than we had hoped for, and compared with our cramped quarters, it was a mansion. Four bedrooms, a den on the main floor, and a finished basement for a playroom. No more tripping over fire trucks and sit-on turtles with wheels. "They'll carry me out of here in a body bag," I told Tammy.

This was to be our house for life. I sought a measure of serenity in a home to counterbalance my rapid-fire job and rough-and-tumble family. Despite the awareness that Carly and Taryn were developing on diverging paths, I was confident we were starting something new and exciting. I had recently changed jobs, joining a hot new ad agency that had recently opened in Toronto. I was given a significant role in running a large portion of the agency's flagship beer account. With my newly enlarged family and a house in a great neighborhood with good schools, I was feeling pretty pleased with myself.

But as the professional side of my life took off, my home life was about to slip into quicksand. Tammy was anxious about the growing chasm between the two girls. "Something's off," she said. I chalked it up to her vigilant nature and refused to put it on my "to worry about" list. Nevertheless, my wife began exploring play groups that would be ideally suited to both girls. Taryn needed the stimulation to match her extroverted personality; Carly needed it to pull her out of her sluggishness. For the next year, the months between the girls' first and second birthdays, they went to what was clinically termed an "integrated early intervention program." For several hours, several days a week the girls would go to a center resembling a cross between a kindergarten room and a kid's birthday party. There they would encourage Carly to use her hands, paint, and play like the "integrated kids"—those more like Taryn. There are still pictures of Carly, smiling, covered in finger paint festooning a wall in our basement. But these playful pictures captured only moments in time. As soon as Carly was home, she would sit on the floor of our den rocking back and forth, humming to herself, and ignoring the world around her. Play was not something that came naturally to our daughter.

One of the instructors at Carly's program told us, "You have to stay in her face." Specialized workers, originally paid for by insurance and then later out of our own wallet when benefits ran out, would arrive at the house with jangly toys and oversized Raggedy Ann dolls. For hours they would sit on the floor of our den or the playroom with an exaggerated cheerfulness, encouraging Carly to follow instructions, take items from one hand and pass it to another, and play like other two-year-olds. Carly mainly stared up at them with a look that was a mixture of wonder and boredom. Taryn, on the other hand, was already off to play dates with friends.

After mornings at preschool, Tammy spent the afternoons making the rounds at medical facilities and hospitals. Sometimes I would take time off work to join her. The next four years would feel like an incarceration in a house of mirrors. One doctor unable to explain Carly's lack of progress would send us on to another, who then pointed us in another direction.

Step 1: Wait in beige-and-gray waiting room filled with toys you don't want child to touch for fear of infection by flesh-eating disease. Little worry for us, however, as Carly ignored pretty much everything. Depending on the type of doctor (neurologist, audiologist, geneticist, developmental pediatrician), exchange sympathetic looks with other parents of kids who appear equally (but seldom as severely) out of step with the world as Carly. Note: If at doctor such as ear, nose, and throat, avoid sidelong glances of other parents who stare at Carly secretly thanking God their child is playing with flesh-eating-diseased-Playskool-firehouse while Carly sits on the floor and rocks back and forth.

Step 2: Admission to claustrophobic examining room with the assurance that doctor will be along shortly (what's the medical definition of *shortly*?) and the taking of medical history by the resident or intern ("Can't you just read the notes from the previous eight doctors? *You* tell *me* what's wrong.").

Step 3: Repeat the medical history when the specialist finally arrives just as Carly is completely losing it, screaming at the top of her lungs and attempting to fling herself from the stroller, tethered by a waist strap; stare up at the pensive, twisted face of the doctor as he/she reads through a four-inch-thick chart.

Step 4: The perfunctory physical examination of eyes, ears, pelvis, back, limbs, and joints while Carly writhes and screams, making said examination even more perfunctory. Think to self, "What can poking at our daughter uncover that the millions of dollars in scans and blood tests failed to reveal?" A physical exam cannot possibly give us any insight into what's wrong with Carly.

Step 5: The raised eyebrow and sympathetic arm touch by doctor as we're sent on our way to see another special specialist. On occasion, stop to pick up requisition for additional blood work or scans of head or random body part.

Step 6: Repeat and repeat and repeat until numb.

The momentum of appointments, play groups, and therapy was accelerating at an alarming rate. The notes, papers, and schedules of doctors' consultations taped to our refrigerator were elbowing out Matthew's and Taryn's artwork and magnetic letters. There were weeks where Tammy had at least one doctor or therapist's appointment every day. We referred to these years as the Fix Carly Years. Both Tammy and I have backgrounds in business and marketing; we are career problem solvers. We hunched our shoulders to the gristmill and pushed. In particular, Tammy took this on as a mission. In the evenings, she would recount the conclusions from an appointment I had missed, though I confess many of the details washed over me. Months melted into a slurry, with little to show for it. On paper, anyway, Carly was perfectly healthy.

Carly became known as "the enigma of the Hospital for Sick Children" by the team of doctors who had followed her. She had been assigned the label GDD (global developmental delay) because she was missing most of her developmental milestones such as walking, talking, playing, and following basic instructions. Later they added pervasively developmentally delayed—a broad term for a spectrum of conditions such as autism because of her lack of eye contact, social engagement, and speech. But there was no underlying cause for these conditions. Carly's lack of speech development was particularly confounding. It would be several years before her inability to make more than garbled sounds would be diagnosed as apraxia—a motor-planning deficiency in which the muscles in her mouth failed to obey the directions from her brain. We could find no ailment to cure or person to blame for Carly being so *Carly*. Our naïveté about what lay ahead was a blessing; we refused to be discouraged. *Delayed* had an optimistic ring. I reasoned that planes and trains that were delayed would eventually arrive. In fact, many of the doctors' reports told us that they expected gains. Her pediatrician noted that with Carly, it was like being on a ladder: She would move up, but we just didn't know to where.

It took months of intensive MEDEK, a particularly draconian form of physiotherapy, to coax Carly into walking on her own, which she would finally do just after her second birthday. In addition to therapy appointments at a local clinic, therapists came to the house to teach Carly how to hold a cup, move items from one hand to another, and work on her fine motor skills—all the things most children intuitively learn. When a therapist wasn't persuading Carly into a standing position or encouraging her to put pegs in holes, stack blocks, or thread a spool with string, Mari was. While Taryn played, Carly worked; she worked harder than most adults.

At times, the girls were not so very different. On occasion, Carly could be all smiles and giggles. The sisters would roll around like oversized puppies on their bedroom floor, Taryn hugging her sister and saying, "Oh Carly, oh Carly," in that one-way conversation we'd all learned to have with her. Carly giggled from the attention. From a very young age, Taryn reacted to her sister with good humor and empathy. I sat on the den floor and would take turns bouncing them on my knees, singing the children's song "The Grand Old Duke of York." But while Taryn would gleefully yell, "More, more Grappa Dupa Yorp" when I finished the rousing chorus, Carly would burst into tears until I started up again. "Again for Carly," Taryn would say, providing her sister's voice. Taryn was protective of her sister, guarding Carly as if she were a prized possession. Only on rare occasions when Carly would grab food or a toy away did Taryn scold her with a furrowed brow.

Often, while Taryn would play with her Barbies, Polly Pockets, or coloring books, Carly would sit nearby holding yet another developmental discovery toy we had purchased in the hopes of engaging her. She would not play, per se, but rather turn the toy over as if to check its country of origin and scratch at the imprinted bottom surface. Her nails would trace over the embossed words like she was reading Braille, but her eyes told me she was elsewhere. Often she would put her tiny index finger into the screw holes that held the brightly colored plastic pieces together.

When not holding a toy, Carly would stare at her hands and wriggle her fingers as if she were meeting them for the first time. "Carly's doing fingie," Matthew would say. I would look on, encouraging her to press the green button to illuminate the green light, or to stack the colored cups. I could not enter her world, whatever world it was, and fruitlessly called her into mine.

Try as we did to encourage Carly to entertain herself, even for a few minutes, the only acts she would spontaneously engage in were rocking and banging. Pressing her heels deep into the mattress of her bed or the cushions of her favorite overstuffed chair in the den, Carly would lift herself to near-standing and then slam back with full force. All the while, she would drone *ahhhh ahhhh ahhhh*—as soothing to us as nails on a chalkboard—and stare into space. If uninterrupted, her methodical, vertebrae-shattering ritual could go on for hours. Despite best efforts to redirect her or at least cushion the blows, she ultimately wore holes in the chair and broke her solid oak bed so often that it eventually required steel-reinforcing bars. This much we knew: Carly had strong core muscles. If nothing else, she likely would never have a bad back.

Excerpt from psychologist's assessment, February 2, 1997:

Dr. M. Mary Karas

DIAGNOSTIC IMPRESSIONS

Carly is only 25 months old. Yet with increasing awareness of the characteristics of the PDDs, one can offer a provisional diagnosis consistent with her behavior profile. Although she presents with the main characteristics of the developmental delay, she also presents many features of the PDDs. She is resisting change, is affectively isolated and has no functional communication other than through elementary gestures. She is quite unaware of danger and seems to have a vague awareness of the characteristics of the people around her . . .

SUMMARY

The psychological testing revealed that Carly is delayed in a number of developmental areas consistent with a diagnosis of PDD since she seems to represent with greater delay in the area of language than intellectual abilities. Carly's developmental delay is at present the major consideration, but her parents' and caregivers' awareness of her meeting many of the criteria for Autistic Disorder should also be of relevance to programming efforts for her. The fact that she grows up with a highly competent co-twin make her delays more evident to her parents and may have a more adverse effect on them than had she been a singleton. On the other hand, her sister should provide a role model for her to stimulate as well as play companion. The fact that Carly enjoys her play and games with her sister reflects this benevolent influence of Taryn on Carly.

Fifteen years later I looked through the color-coded medical files and remembered how much I had forgotten. True, Tammy had maintained the frontline role of investigator in attempting to unearth the causes of our daughter's issues; I worked to pay for that which insurance or socialized medicine would not. But I was not completely absent. Doctors' clinical notes refer to my presence at appointments I have long since purged from my memory. I have little recollection of the consultations with geneticists, neurologists, audiologists, dieticians, physical therapists, occupational therapists, developmental pediatricians, and psychologists that would become a full-time occupation for Tammy. And after all that, after years of blood tests, skin biopsies, metabolic studies, MRIs, evoked potentials, hearing tests, and God recalls what else, we knew only this: Carly was, as her developmental pediatrician stated in her notes, *complicated*.

Scanning the doctors' notes reminded me of all the things that Carly *wasn't*. Most parents have a long list of comical stories from their children's early years. Once I lay sprawled across our bed, grabbing five minutes of quiet while the twins napped. Just as I dozed off, Matthew pounded through the bedroom like Napoleon invading Italy, chanting "stinky farty butt, stinky farty butt," and knocked over a framed photograph balanced on the nightstand. When he noticed what he'd done, he contritely stammered, "I'll fish stick," meaning to say "fix it."

Taryn made us laugh with her independence and vivacity. Taking toys out of the closet, she would settle on the floor at our feet and happily play for hours. She always maintained a sense of humor where her sister was concerned. Once Carly was lying naked on our bed after a bath; perhaps she was three or four. Taryn picked up one of Tammy's credit cards that was on the nightstand and pretended to swipe it in the crevice between Carly's buttocks, announcing, "I'll pay with credit." She and Tammy laughed so hard tears streamed down their cheeks.

A few minutes later, Taryn came back into our room and dropped her pajama pants to reveal a Tootsie Roll poking out from her bottom. She squealed, "I have a fudgy butt!" before falling to the floor in gales of laughter. Perhaps I should have been concerned about my children's scatological preoccupation, but it provided such comic relief that we encouraged it.

Even Taryn's sassiness had an innocent sweetness to it. She once called her nursery school teacher *missy*. "My name is *Miss Whittington*," the young woman corrected her. "Okay, Missy Miss Whittington," Taryn said with a giggle. Even at three she had a comic's sense of timing.

But I cannot think of any such memories of Carly.

The pages that document the first years of Carly's life are an inventory of inabilities. "Working with Carly was hard," noted her developmental pediatrician upon our first consult. "I got her to sit at the table and take objects I offered to her, but she was unable to stack cubes or put pegs in a pegboard. She did not respond to any language cues. I heard some consonant babble, but no isolated words." Even a year later, after hours of intervention, Dr. Stephensen, a developmental pediatrician we saw regularly, noted that "I still find Carly a bit of an enigma, but one cannot deny that she has gotten a thorough workup with so many consultants involved."

Even when Carly did acquire skills, they were often used in ways that reminded me that she was distinct from her brother and sister. Once she learned to walk, she immediately began to run—generally headlong into dangerous situations like a busy street. Once she found the joy in grabbing objects, she began flinging them—a plate of food or a cup of juice. I came to appreciate Mari more and more. After dinner, she would sweep and mop up the pounds of food Carly had flung (had she actually eaten anything?) and take the girls out for a walk to the park.

For the hour they were out, the house was reasonably quiet. Matthew's best friend lived across the street, so the two were inseparable after school. Tammy would be at her desk plodding through the reams of forms the government creates to discourage those of us in need of help from applying for it. And I could sit quietly, read the paper, and eat in silence for thirty minutes and ready myself for when Mari left for the night and Carly was gearing up for round two. Not exactly a family meal, but we were making the best of our distorted reality.

Perhaps we've never felt an a-ha moment with Carly because her progress was overshadowed by her challenges. She finally learned to walk and, in a fashion, feed herself. She could utter a few bleary words such as *mama* and *cackah*, meaning cracker, or *ooce* for juice. Even these approximations for language would soon evaporate like steam. By four years old, she was not toilet trained and would awake in the middle of the night and remain volcanic for hours. No sooner up, she would strip off her pajamas (a skill in itself, her developmental pediatrician reminded us), rip off her diaper, and jump about her room barking *ahhhh ahhhh ahhhh*. And then rock. Always the incessant rocking. The rocking became the manifestation of everything I hated about Carly's condition. It was irritating, destructive, and unstoppable. "Ssshhhh," I would say, but it came out more like, "Stop, God damn it." In some ways it was best that Carly couldn't speak; my expletives were often free-flowing.

Taryn, who shared the room with Carly, somehow slept through it. Either that or she had learned the first lesson of growing up as the sibling of a disabled child: Lay low. Tammy's and my exhaustion and frustration from the Sisyphean task of remaking the bed, reclothing Carly, and tucking her in left us in a perpetual short-tempered state.

Tammy spent hours searching for someone who could help dissipate the hurricane that was our daughter. We couldn't find anyone up to the task, much less a cure. What simple solution could there be to stop a thirty-pound child from hurtling her body full force against a wall? We learned to improvise and tackle bits and pieces at a time. One night I came in to kiss Carly good night and found Mari had put Carly in a tight-fitting Lycra bathing suit over her diaper. "She has trouble taking it off and she seems to like it," Mari explained. We had read that some kids like Carly were comforted by the sensation of snugness. Besides, if she couldn't remove the bathing suit, she couldn't remove the diaper. It was a novel solution that we used until Carly became fully toilet trained—a skill she finally mastered when she turned five. At least foraging in the dark for her pull-ups and her pajamas was a thing of the past. Getting her to sleep through the night would be something that would take another seven years, however.

In addition to being diagnosed with severe autism and oral apraxia by her developmental pediatrician, Carly had been identified as having moderate to severe developmental delay at the age of two. It was a broad and general expression that has replaced the abhorrent term *retarded* and is used when doctors can't identify any specific condition. "Carly has no specific etiology," is how they put it. Several years later, I Googled *etiology*. I learned that it was of Greek origin and meant "the study of why things occur or the reasons why things exist." Greeks used myths to explain phenomena they couldn't rationalize. For all the answers we'd gotten as to why Carly was as she was, a myth would have been as useful.

I didn't blame the doctors for their lack of specificity. How could I? Carly couldn't engage in many of the diagnostic tests they tried. She didn't follow multistep instructions or tasks nor could she speak to explain what was going on inside her body. On occasion she cooed when held and cuddled by Tammy and me, and often giggled and laughed with her sister. Most of the time she was content to be adrift in her own world, sitting on the periphery of ours.

As we dragged her from doctor to clinic to lab and back again, day after day, it occurred to us perhaps we were merely trying to label and identify *her*. How many more needle pricks would we make her endure? Sleepless nights with electroencephalogram leads attached to her little sweaty head? Evoked potential, hearing, and sight exams? Skin and muscle biopsies? The repetitive narrative of providing oral history to each subsequent doctor, nurse, and resident was enough to make us want to call it quits. Through her early childhood, we had learned nothing that was helping her come back to us, nothing that made her play with other children or even play meaningfully by herself, nothing that would help her noisy mouth form intelligible words. We had diagnoses, but little insight into what could be done to help Carly escape the whirlpool.

We were beginning to feel that enough was enough and decided there would be no more physical suffering on account of science. "If it's just information for information's sake and no cure will come from it, then it's time to stop," Tammy said to me one evening, her body slumped on the couch, defeat on her tear-streaked face. We no longer held out hope that we would discover a specific part of Carly that was broken and could be easily fixed. Global developmental delay, pervasive developmental delay, autism, oral-motor apraxia—all conditions, but none of them specific ailments. Had she had cancer, we'd have known what to do. Had she incurred brain damage or had a stroke, we would understand her condition. But Carly's affliction was like a blob of mercury: visible and dense and real, but try to grab it and it jumped from our grasp.

Despite what doctors described in her medical records as "valiant efforts by her caring and deeply committed parents," we would never receive an a-ha moment, much as we craved one. One dead-end street led to another. Somehow, life had to move on. Our other kids were growing and developing. We were running out of referrals and recommendations. And while our medical system is public in Canada, many of our therapies and consults were beyond coverage and had pushed our credit line to the brink. "I feel like there's a button in her brain we just need to switch on," Tammy said. But that button would remain out of sight, out of reach. In our hearts, we had hoped to find a magic pill that would turn Carly into someone else; someone who could speak, play, and be with us. But that folly had to come to an end. It's not that we would give up on our daughter, but it was time to stop asking *why*, and start asking *now what?*

Excerpt from clinical genetics report, October 12, 1997:

Dr. D. Shaet, Division of Clinical Genetics

Developmental milestones are delayed but have improved . . . she does not like laying on her stomach and to move she shuffles on her buttocks. Carly's fine motor skills are delayed but she acquitted many milestones during the last year. She improved her pincer grasp but does not like to touch objects and does not pile blocks. She makes no attempts to put a puzzle together and does not scribble.

Regarding language, she has difficulties both in receptive and expressive language . . . she does not follow more than a one-step command. Carly interacts with her sister frequently, but not other children. . . .

The investigations done so far have failed to reveal any specific diagnosis. I explained to the parents that I doubt if we will be able to further delineate her condition. However, we wish to continue following her every 2 years and would like to be updated of her growth, development and of any medical/neurological investigation done . . .

Sincerely,
D. Shaet, MD, FABMG, FCCMG, FRCPC
Division of Clinical Genetics
CC: file, Dr. I. Tine (Neurology), Dr. D. Stephensen (Developmental Pediatrics), Dr. J. Kobayashi (Neurology), Dr. M. Goldstein (Pediatrician)

A Recurring Dream

I am dreaming a dream I've had many times since Carly was born. The two of us are sitting in the kitchen. Or maybe it's the den. We are talking. Carly is talking. She's teasing me about something.

"How do you like my haircut?" I ask her.

"It looks like your head got caught in a food processor," she deadpans.

I wake up laughing out loud.

Then I roll over on my side and cry.

2

⚜

Red Lentils and Chemo

In the winter of 1996–1997, we had come to realize that the terrible twos for Carly would be nothing like those we had experienced with Taryn and Matthew. We struggled to find ways to cope with her sleeplessness, bleating, and crying; her inability to walk, play, or approximate the beginnings of language. Rather than enjoying Carly's childhood, we were consumed by the tedious task of pushing her from one doctor to the next. While we had a clear diagnosis of autism and developmental delay, there was no clarity on the best way to educate or care for our daughter.

Raising three kids—a seven-year-old and two two-year-olds—is challenging in an ideal situation. That one of the two-year-olds didn't walk, talk, or show any interest in play made for a tedious existence. There were only so many times I could take them to the zoo, where we could push Carly in her stroller while Matthew bounded ahead and Taryn clutched my hand and waddled alongside.

We were also faced with Carly's bouts of inexplicable sobbing. As she sat on the floor, her face would twist up like she was in pain and she would shriek for hours. She would raise her arms to be picked up, but once held, squirm to be put down. At first, my heart would break. Tammy and I took turns trying to comfort her. Over time, as doctor after doctor could find no cause for physical pain, frustration took over.

At a stage where most young mothers who didn't work outside the house were beginning to enjoy play dates and walks to the park with their two-year-olds, Tammy's full-time job was to scamper down the rabbit hole of doctors and therapy appointments in search of an answer to the puzzle that was our daughter. It was little surprise to me that the quest to find the broken link inside Carly's brain would leave Tammy wan and without energy.

Tammy's exhaustion, however, was extreme. She would fall asleep any time she wasn't physically moving. Palm to cheek, sitting up, Tammy dozed while helping Matthew with homework, at the movies, reading the newspaper. Even stress and noise couldn't keep her awake; she drifted off sitting in a straight-backed metal chair next to the MRI scanner in which Carly (screaming, of course) was having a head scan.

Then Tammy began to cough. It invaded her body with such force that she would vomit. Her physician put her on rounds of antibiotics to no effect. Nor could the respirologist find anything out of the ordinary. It dragged on for months. We probably should have been more mindful at the time, but when lost in the woods, even Little Red Riding Hood didn't notice she was chatting with a wolf.

During a quick visit to a friend in New Jersey, Tammy felt a lump in her groin and her throat closed in fear. Her mother had passed away suddenly from cancer less than six months after we had moved back to Toronto from New York in 1989. Her grandmother similarly died in her mid-fifties. Tammy wondered if this was the family legacy.

She went to see her physician first thing Monday morning upon returning home from her visit with her friend. After the exam, Tammy was sent down the hall for an ultrasound of her pelvis. Technicians aren't supposed to comment on their findings—good or bad news is to be dispensed by the physician. Tammy shivered from the look of concern on the woman's face. The moment the ultrasound sensor rolled over her groin, Tammy felt it hit speed bumps and knew it wasn't good.

Rushing back to her doctor, she pleaded with the secretary to get the test results immediately rather than be put in the queue and forced to wait an agonizing week. Feeling sick and tired is bad enough without adding terror of the unknown. Not liking what the ultrasound showed, the physician sent Tammy immediately to a surgeon for a consult and biopsy. More waiting. New agonizing.

Even before excising the tissue sample, the surgeon calmly told Tammy he expected to find cancer based on the size and shape of the lymph node. Preemptively, he booked an appointment for her with an oncologist at one of Canada's top cancer hospitals.

The test results confirmed the surgeon's suspicion and after several meetings with an oncologist, Tammy was diagnosed with lymphoma. She would need chemotherapy. Immediately. Our lives, already one long doctor's appointment, were about to get worse. I wondered if calm and happiness could ever worm its way back in.

I was beginning to feel like Haiti. Or Sri Lanka. A place where natural disasters just start coming and don't have the good sense to stop. The minutes and hours that followed the diagnosis are gone to me now. How we got through the next few days is a complete blank. In fact, the next year would be a hazy maze of appointments and treatment and emotional exhaustion.

With all of our energy going into Tammy's treatment and daily life, there was little left for scouring websites and following up on leads to find suitable programs for Carly. We knew enough from the reading Tammy had done that "early intervention"—therapy and programming—was the key to long-term success with kids with autism. But there was no manual, no organization or expert who could put together a comprehensive plan of action. It all fell on Tammy to coordinate.

We were fortunate enough to have been referred to a physiotherapist named Esther Gold when Carly was one year old. The woman both had a private practice and worked part-time for Northland, a school for children with special needs.

"You should see if they have a spot for Carly," Esther told us. "She could receive her physio *and* all of the other therapy she needs—and you wouldn't have to run all over the city to get it."

Just as Tammy was beginning chemo, we begged our way into the already overcrowded school, finding that one of the positive side effects of having cancer is the kindness it can evoke from others.

As Tammy focused her efforts on her treatment, maintaining a positive state of mind through yoga and relaxation classes, and caring for three kids, Carly began a daily regimen of physiotherapy, speech-language therapy, music and art therapy, and social skills development at Northland. Not a typical childhood experience, but one that allowed us to feel some relief that we were doing the best we could for our daughter. She would be taught everything that just comes naturally to most kids. We rejoiced at small wins such as her learning how to hold a sippy cup, sit still on a chair for ten minutes during music time, and sort blocks by color.

During this time at Northland, we were introduced to Barb Nash-Fenton, the speech-language pathologist who would become Carly's teacher, advocate, and confidante. Fourteen years later, as I look back on Carly's early years, I realize how life comes down to happenstance. If we had not met Esther, would we have heard about Northland? If not for Tammy's cancer, would the school's director have had the empathy to find a spot for Carly? And if not for Northland, most certainly we would not have met Barb, who would become a pillar in our life in the coming years.

In fact, through the year, we would learn that Tammy's cancer had as great an effect on others as it did on her. We came to realize that we all reflect our own fears and faith in how we treat friends and relatives experiencing life-threatening illness, but in the weeks that would come, Tammy learned to quickly put aside those who couldn't handle her illness.

Along with those in our life who couldn't cope with our complex saga came others of amazing kindness and selflessness. Often, these were people of whom we had few expectations—sometimes complete strangers. At first it felt awkward when a neighbor of a friend would offer to drive carpool or cook dinner for us. "Oh, we're fine, thanks," I'd say. Quickly I learned that these people were not offering out of obligation but rather out of a real desire to help, a need to make a difference. Turning them down was as selfish as it was foolish. At the time, my father-in-law was dating a woman who did some part-time catering. Throughout the summer and fall of 1997, Arna would arrive with boxes of food she had prepared, wrapped, and frozen. When we tried to reimburse her for the cost of the groceries, she quickly changed the subject or dramatically understated the amount we knew she must have spent. And on hot days, she encouraged us to bring all three kids to her house to swim and relax. As Matthew and Taryn slid down the slide into the pool, I bounced Carly up and down in the shallow end, the water seeming to wash away her anxiety, bringing a smile to her face. Tammy could relax and watch the family; a seemingly normal summer afternoon.

Though she pushed through the year of treatment with incredible grace, Tammy would constantly test the boundaries of her mortality with her oncologist. Our children were young: the girls two and Matthew seven. "Will I survive to see Matthew bar mitzvahed at age twelve?" she once asked.

"Yes, likely," her oncologist, Dr. Reitman, answered matter-of-factly.

"How about their weddings?" Tammy pressed on.

"I'm not so sure," again delivered with a cool evenness.

"How do most lymphoma patients die?" Tammy asked, her voice rasping. I looked down at my lap. Some questions, I think, should not be asked.

"Pneumonia," the doctor replied, and uncrossed her legs to stand. The appointment was clearly over, as we had reached a subject she was not prepared to embrace.

Although I compartmentalized Tammy's cancer like I do everything else, there were times it could not be pushed to the corner. One night she was reading in bed and had dozed off. The bandana she wore at night to keep her head warm had slipped off and lay on the pillow next to her. Tammy's skin was slightly gray from the previous day's round of chemo. I had to face the fact that my wife was very sick. I slipped into our bathroom and shut the door, feeling a wave of panic creeping over me.

"What the hell are we going to do?" I murmured to myself. "What if I'm alone?"

My hands shook as I splashed my face with water. At thirty-five, this was not a question I ever dreamt I would ask myself. Although I seldom allowed myself time to ponder a life without Tammy, I was paralyzed momentarily at the prospect. Our focus as a team was always on solving problems and fixing what was wrong. Cancer was merely a thing to be fixed and moved beyond. A stumbling block, but not a final destination. But the image of Tammy looking like a shadow of herself jolted me off track. I stole one of her Ativans and crept back into bed.

❦

Excerpt from Northland Educational Centre, June 1997:

Sandra Welsman, Registered Physiotherapist

Carly is a sweet 2½ year old girl with global developmental delay, possibly P.D.D. and ASD on the severe end of the spectrum. She started at Northland in March 1997 in the Junior room and has made steady progress in all areas . . . she has recently acquired the skill of walking a few steps with one hand held. Our goal for Carly is independent standing and walking. She is following the MEDEK program of exercises. Carly is resistant to being handled and will try to fight out of exercises . . . It is recommended that Cary continue physiotherapy over the summer . . .

Excerpt from Northland Educational Centre, June 1997:

B. Nash-Fenton, B.Sc., D.S.P., C.C.C., reg. CASLPO
Speech-Language Pathologist

Carly is beginning to understand language at the single word level when the content is very concrete . . . parents should attempt to model simple labels for objects, actions, prepositions, etc. Keep utterances short.

Carly demonstrated ability to make a choice between two actual foods, she was introduced to pictures . . . establishing eye contact during the exchange is ongoing goal. Carly's feeding skills are also being monitored by myself and an Occupational Therapist. She currently is attempting to drink from a cup, although requires assistance to remember to close her lips after drinking to keep liquid in her mouth . . .

Excerpt from Northland Educational Centre, June 1997:

T. Ruben, Occupational Therapist

Carly continues to make progress as presently reassessed on the Insite Development Profile . . . She removes her Velcroed shoes, socks, pants and shirt independently as long as they are loose. She pulls off sleeves herself, a skill we struggled with, and pulls shirt over her head. Carly is able to assist in putting on her clothes. Carly is able to jump with two feet off the ground . . . now mounts riding toys unassisted and can push herself forward. We have started teaching steering with the bike on the Miller Boards so that her fear of falling off will provoke her to solve the problem and "turn" her wheel . . . Carly is an affectionate and fun child. Her self-stim behaviors of rocking and eyes to the ceiling are still prevalent, however, when she is engaged these diminish. This is why a one-to-one shadow staff is crucial in Carly's early years . . .

During her treatment, Tammy was encouraged to practice yoga and take a course in visualization. One day I came home to find her with a small Ziploc bag, filling it with dried lentils and pinning it to the bulletin board that hung over her computer. Tammy spent many hours online researching both lymphoma and autism, the two forces that controlled our life. Every time she looked up, she would see the bag of lentils. "They represent teeny tiny lymph nodes—the size they should be if I were healthy," she said. Tammy put an identical Ziploc under her pillow. Occasionally, under her breath, Tammy would sing a song she had made up, invoking her lymph glands to shrink and the cancer to leave her body. All this from a woman who claimed cancer was *not* a battle.

The months of Tammy's treatment went well. As summer gave

way to fall, the cancer retreated, leaving us in a new permanent state of limbo. Tammy's is a wait-and-see form of cancer.

Throughout the year, our house had been oddly peaceful. Matthew, who had never been a particularly calm boy, adopted a mature and helpful nature. He took on the role of big brother with enthusiasm. He would sit on the floor with both girls next to him reading from one of his picture books. Taryn would look up at him hanging on his every word; Carly stared off at images only she could see. Although he probably was deprived of the type of attention a seven-year-old wants, Matthew never acted out.

"It's just one more way we're messing up our kids," I joked to Tammy. "They'll get over it."

We had spoken to him about Tammy's cancer in the way we were advised. Mom is sick. The medicine she's taking will make her lose her hair and may make her tired. But the doctors are making her well. That was the mantra we repeated, perhaps as much to calm our fears as to calm his.

Our son was growing out of his short-temperedness and tantrums and turning into a sweet boy. Tammy called him her Bo-Bo Head; his still-small body a life support system to his robust cranium. Matthew's childish chubby cheeks were beginning to thin, but when he smiled they still rose into pinchable wedges at either side of his mouth. Somehow this horrible disease brought out a kindness that would become a permanent characteristic in our son.

The girls, just months past their second birthday, were too young to feel the shifting sands beneath them. Could Carly even grasp the situation? Her medical reports continued to describe her as cognitively and developmentally delayed. Though we tried to maintain similar schedules and activities for the girls, their differences were marked. Taryn walked and chattered with a permanent smile on her face. Her short dark hair clung to her head like a swimming cap. Carly, on the other hand, seldom laughed—unless being tickled, bounced, or bathed.

I have a black-and-white photo I took of the three kids that summer. Taryn is standing, grasping the side of a chaise lounge on our patio. She looks directly at the camera with a grin so wide her eyes nearly squeeze shut. Carly sits on the ground beside her, her legs splayed out for balance. Both of them wearing summer dresses of crinkly cotton. Carly's dress poufs out about her like a dollop of whipped cream. She looks toward the sky, her mouth turned down in a pensive frown, but her eyes wide as if contemplating the firmament. Matthew, the big brother, stands arm crossed, leaning on the chair looking protectively down at his little sisters. This picture aptly summed them up. A son feeling the need to guard. One daughter growing into a fun-loving, playful ham, and another drifting skyward, away from us.

As the months passed after Tammy's last treatment in August of 1997, we didn't see her remission as the closing of a book. In the years to come, the constant monitoring would remind us that every day free of cancer meant no more than that. One more day that it hadn't resurfaced. Now every night-sweat, unusual bruise, persistent cough, or swollen gland sent Tammy into a fearful spin, only calming slightly with the reassurance of her doctor that she was still in remission. Milestone dates were looked at not as accomplishments, but as sand trickling through the hourglass. The form of lymphoma Tammy had, we were reminded, was treatable, not curable.

Nevertheless, with chemo behind her, Tammy began clearing out the artifacts of that surreal year. The wigs and books on cancer survival were donated. Supplements and pill bottles were thrown away. She kept the card with a quote from Zora Neale Hurston,

"There are years that ask questions and years that answer." I'm not sure which this one was, but as long as the two sides cancel out in the end, we're doing fine. Lastly, Tammy unpinned the little bag of lentils hanging on her bulletin board. But rather than throwing them away, she placed them in her desk drawer.

3

≈§≈

Climbing the Well-Greased Ladder

When Carly was three and a half, we were waiting in a clinical ward at the Hospital for Sick Children. Carly was a part of a drug trial for secretin, a hormone that researchers briefly thought might be beneficial to children afflicted by autism. Tammy struck up a conversation with a mother whose six-year-old son was sitting on the edge of the hospital bed, playing with his Game Boy. There was a fairly typical cadence to conversations among parents with children living with autism.

"Is your son . . . ?" Tammy started.

"Yeah. Autism. Your daughter?" the woman responded with a tired smile.

"Same."

"Who's your doctor?"

"Stephensen. Yours?" asked Tammy.

"Constantarios."

"What are you doing for him?"

"Gluten- and casein-free diet. Occupational therapy. Behavioral therapy. Communication therapy. How about you?"

"Same. Diet thing doesn't seem to do much, though. We're starting to explore medications like risperidone. How do you pay for everything?" There is an unspoken code among autism families that makes all topics of conversation fair game.

"Debt. My husband's family kicks in somewhat. How do you guys cope?"

"Bourbon," joked Tammy. And then, "Kidding," just in case.

Carly was to have a sleep-deprived MRI as part of the secretin study. The boy was in for an appointment with the doctor running the study. But Tammy and I were startled.

"Your son *really* has autism?" Tammy asked, now focusing on the child. The boy sat quietly playing with his Game Boy while his mother chatted with us. He made no odd noises, did not spontaneously get up and jump around flapping his hands. On occasion he'd look up at his mother and then go back to his game. If there is such a thing as normal, this boy portrayed it.

Diagnosed with autism at the age of two, the woman told us, her son had been undergoing a form of behavior therapy called applied behavior analysis, or ABA. He had made such incredible progress that his behaviors were largely under control. So much so, in fact, that she kept his diagnosis from family members and even her son's second-grade teacher so that he wouldn't be labeled. I was struck by the fact that this family had the option of keeping their son's autism to themselves. I was not embarrassed by my daughter's diagnosis, but there was no hiding her unusual characteristics. Tammy had once filmed a video to show the doctors how Carly behaved at home. The small cassette was euphemistically labeled "Kooky Carly." It shows Carly tearing around the house like an overwound toy, unable to stop. Chaos swirled around her like dust around Pig-Pen from the

Peanuts cartoons as she darted from room to room, jumping up and down, flinging herself on furniture and the floor while bleating and whining. Discretion was not an option for us.

We had read about ABA and seen a news piece the previous year, but between the doctors' appointments, getting Carly enrolled in Northland, and Tammy's cancer, we just hadn't pursued it. The woman went on to tell us the name of her son's therapist, something we would later learn was an immense act of charity. Canada has no national program of support for children with autism and nothing akin to the IDEA act in the U.S. It was up to the parent to scrounge for resources and pay out-of-pocket for therapy. But with the rising rate of autism, ABA therapists were in short supply and high demand. Any hours of therapy you could secure for your child were precious.

The little boy was attentive, sweet, and calm. He seemed happy. He was everything we wanted Carly to be. That afternoon, we became converts to the religion of ABA.

The next day, Tammy contacted the therapist, Elizabeth Benedetto. ABA, with all of its imposing procedures, tasks, and trials, spread through our life like a virus. The annual fees would amount to $50,000 to $60,000 a year; we had no idea how we were going to survive financially. Carly had been attending Northland for about two years, and while her progress was not apparent to the untrained eye, the school gave us the perception of stability.

Carly had evolved from sitting on the floor rocking and crying to being able to subtly fend for herself. Now four years old, Carly would scamper to the kitchen, grab a chair, and pull it over to the cupboard above the microwave where she knew we kept crackers and Fruit Roll-Ups—snacks parents hate to admit they buy. Though this skill in itself was an accomplishment, the destruction she would wreak negated any pleasure in her progress. Carly would hurl the contents of the cabinet to the floor, rip open the packages, and dump their contents—all quicker than a tired adult could run to stop her.

The tuition at Northland was over $20,000 and only through financial aid were we able to get by. In order to receive a fee reduction, we had to go through an annual review with the school's financial director. It felt like a humiliating medical procedure with our private parts exposed in the chilled air of the examination room as he pored over our tax returns and reviewed the expenses of raising Carly and her two siblings.

Tammy and I concluded that if we depleted our savings and extended our mortgage, we could afford one year of the intensive intervention while keeping Carly at Northland. Everything we had read made us believe that it was now or never. A child's development was most easily influenced before they were six, we were told by autism service agencies. The combination of integrated services at school and one-on-one ABA in the afternoons and weekends was our best hope of snatching our daughter back from the thick murk that enveloped her.

If our life had been invaded by outsiders prior to starting ABA, once Elizabeth, her second-in-command, Kevin, and their troupe of young, energetic therapists entered our house, any sheath of privacy was stripped away. Our home became a laboratory of social science. What makes ABA's approach different from other forms of autism education is that it is scientific, not subjective. The psychologist and therapy teams develop plans on current behavior, and set goals for the student. Data is taken to track performance and remove the personal bias of the individual therapist. In this way, a child's progress is driven by her ability, not by the whim of the instructor. At first, every task is broken down to its core and repeated with mind-numbing frequency. With each repetition, the therapist tracks and graphs the child's success and failure rates and occurrences of specific behaviors and actions. Positive outcomes are encouraged through the use of *reinforcers*—a few minutes of play with a fiddle toy or a treat to entrench the positive behavior. In Carly's case, we learned that she would dance on the moon for Lay's potato chips.

Our basement became filled with the telltale signs of the ABA therapists. Bins and Ziploc bags filled with assorted plastic pieces, blocks, toy animals, and rings—all debased from their intended source of childhood merriment to become scientific equipment. Sitting at a small brightly colored picnic table in our basement rec room, Carly would spend the recommended forty hours every week sorting, stacking, and constructing while the therapists encouraged, cajoled, timed, and charted her results. While I didn't fully understand the approach, the image of the boy at the hospital with his Game Boy, so typical, so normal, propelled us both forward.

In addition to mornings at school and afternoons and weekends of ABA, we drew Barb, Carly's speech-language pathologist, tighter into the ever-expanding team recruited to prop, push, and drag Carly out of her depths. While ABA suppliers and therapists would come and go over the next decade, Barb Nash-Fenton would become a steady fixture in the three-ring circus of our life with Carly. Barb was unwavering in her belief and commitment. She and Carly worked together several days a week at school, and later we would engage her to work with our daughter at home in the afternoons.

Barb was part mother, part teacher, and part magician. A petite woman, then in her early forties, she had a quiet, confident demeanor. Her weekly reports and recommendations read like marching orders. As lost soldiers, we were all too happy to cede control. After years of seeing doctors who offered little practical help, it was a relief to have Barb's calm direction. Her presence alone brought the tension down. With daily contact at Northland, Barb witnessed a side of Carly that the rest of us did not.

"There is something there," she would say. "She knows how to get herself out of situations she doesn't want to be in. She problem solves, and that takes intelligence," she encouraged us. After years of people diagnosing Carly and itemizing her deficiencies, Barb was the first person to chronicle Carly's strengths and look for ways to exploit them.

Barb worked alongside the ABA therapy team. While they focused on skill mastery and behavior control, Barb explored ways to help Carly communicate. We reasoned that Carly's frustration and outbursts must at least be in part due to her inability to make her wishes known.

Barb had started with PROMPT, a form of speech therapy where the therapist manipulates the student's jaw and mouth into position. Words were broken down into single sounds, and then strung together. "We got the *c* sound out of Carly today!" one of her post-session summaries observed enthusiastically. PROMPT seemed to work a bit, for a while. Carly could make sounds like *ooce* for juice, *cackah* for cracker, and even say *mama*. But over time, even these simple words disappeared. I was thoroughly disheartened when meaningful sounds were mastered one week, then lost the next. There were periods where Carly would make a step forward, being able to say Matthew's name ("Ma-ah-foo"), for instance, only to have the skill evaporate. For months they would work on a single consonant. At this rate, we'd all be old before Carly could say her name.

The ABA therapists would then be instructed on how to continue to prompt Carly to use this sound as much as possible through the week. Maybe she'd be able to do it again next week. Maybe not.

Barb added sign language and then picture exchange techniques—endlessly looking for ways to help Carly communicate. This last approach, known as PECS, was decidedly low-tech but effective. Carly had stacks of cards containing photographs of things she might want and she would merely have to point to make a request. Although cumbersome, it beat screaming in frustration. Carly quickly got the hang of selecting cards for what she wanted most. Images of juice, cookies, storybooks, and swimming were used with frequency. Broccoli and carrots much less so. She never pointed to "I love you."

Barb believed that Carly's inability to communicate fueled her anguish and tantrums. At the end of each weekly home session, Barb painstakingly drafted clinical notes summarizing the appointment and providing us with instructions that read like a how-to manual. She wanted us to use multiple forms of communication, the theory being that one skill builds on the other.

Carly had mastered a hard *g* sound after months of laboring. It's one of the harder consonants to teach because of the pulled-back position of the tongue, Barb told us. When Carly found she could no longer replicate it, Barb was crushed. I came home once to find Barb, Mari, and Tammy in our family room, Carly lying on the couch with her head hanging back off the edge. As Tammy steadied Carly's body, Barb supported her head and attempted to use gravity to drop Carly's mouth into position to make the elusive sound, but to no avail. Barb shot me a look, a rapid raising of both eyebrows, as if to say, "Well, we tried." Barb was a cross between educator and the Army's Corps of Engineers; she never showed her frustration.

When Carly was four—just as she was entering the world of ABA— we began to witness her exile from the community of her "neuro-typical" peers. Taryn attended a neighborhood nursery school and we became friends with a family up the street. They, too, had twin girls, and despite Carly's obvious lack of ability to connect, the Millses always included Carly in any plans they made with Taryn and their daughters, Sydney and Katherine. Carly seemed to have a connection with the girls' father in particular. A family doctor, Tony was calm and matter-of-fact. He seemed to look right past Carly's oddness and see something much deeper. In return, he was one of the only people other than Tammy, Mari, or me who could hold Carly without making her cry. She loved his unruly beard and metal-framed glasses.

After school, the three girls often went back to Lauren and Tony's, and Tammy would bring Carly over to join them. Their neighbor, Kathy, had a daughter who also attended the preschool, and was another fixture of these chaotic play groups. The mothers all got along well and it created a welcome community for Tammy, who spent so much of her time pulled into the vortex of Carly's doctors' appointments. But one morning, nearly a year after this ritual began, we were reminded that Carly was seen more as a visitor than as a member of the community. Kathy was planning a birthday party for her daughter. The invitation arrived addressed to Taryn. Not Carly *and* Taryn, just Taryn. Who invites just one twin to a party? At first Tammy tried to rationalize that maybe it was a space thing. But given the size of the family's home and the fact that it was to be an outdoor party, she quickly faced the truth.

The family's niece had been living with them while she finished a college course and often babysat for Carly; we were sure they were keenly aware of the challenges we lived with. A line was being drawn, one we would see over and over in the years to come. Our "normal" four-year-old would be included, and our disabled four-year-old would not. This little piggy gets roast beef, and this little piggy gets none. Uncharacteristically, Tammy bit her lip and sent Taryn to the party.

Slights were not uncommon. Sometime later that summer, another mutual friend of Lauren's and Tammy's was planning a party for *her* daughter. The Weavers lived several streets away and Mari's sister worked as a nanny for their children. In fact, Mari would often walk Carly and Taryn over in their strollers so the girls could play together. When the invitation for their daughter's party arrived, again without Carly's name on it, it stung like a hard slap on a cold cheek. Tammy, not prone to tears, phoned Lauren and sobbed.

Ten minutes after Tammy got off the phone with Lauren, the mother phoned to apologize and include Carly. Lauren had clearly set her straight. In the end, Carly attended (with help from Mari), and she did great. I generally noticed that the kids were more accepting of Carly's uniqueness than the parents.

Had Carly and Taryn not been twins, the double standard of their treatment by friends and members of our community would have been less obvious. But as it was, we had a constant reminder of the normal childhood Carly was missing out on. We were forever attempting to integrate Carly into Taryn's world; the one with mainstream schools and activities, friends and parties, dance, swimming and art classes. Carly's world was one of doctors and therapists. That was not a place for Taryn.

So when it came time to invite Taryn's school friends to her birthday parties (wasn't it *their* birthday parties?), were we to put Carly's name on the invitation? We decided that the only way for people to see the girls as equals was to treat them as such. While they may not share a social network, they did share a birthday. They both deserved the same respect. It worked in some cases; thoughtful moms sent a card and gift to a girl they'd never met just because she was Taryn's sister. Others, clueless of the hurt they would cause, chose to ignore Carly's existence.

We couldn't tell whether Carly felt the strangling loneliness that came from being left out. With her lack of telltale emotions, it was easy to assume she didn't know the difference between being included and not. There was some relief in the delusion that she didn't understand the sights and sounds swirling around her. But Tammy and I always felt as if we were being shunned by a clique. Getting Carly to blend in and be accepted would be impossible. Winning a popularity contest was never the goal; merely having a friend would be a relief. Carly's being shunned was a painful reminder of our child's difference. If she was not included in a five-year-old's birthday party, would she ever be accepted anywhere?

Excerpt from Northland Educational Centre, June 1999:

CLASSROOM REPORT

Carly is beginning to show an interest in symbolic play, particularly in the Daily Living Center . . . Carly is able to identify five body parts and she enjoys the shape sorter and puzzles when encouraged to do so. We continue to work on increasing Carly's attention span.

Carly continues to use a combination of communication systems in order to have her needs met. These include sign, gestures, sounds and photos. A recent addition to her verbal approximations is the "s" sound, which she has used to request "chips" and, in a different context, "swing." She has been observed to combine "words" by signing "more" and saying "s" to request "more chips."

Carly enjoys gross motor play such as running, jumping and climbing on playground equipment. She is propelling herself well on a riding toy and now able to turn corners . . . she has been practicing throwing and catching games. Carly has also been working on "turning" activities and has shown good wrist movement when turning objects such as jar lids.

Matching, sorting and copying are all important goals for Carly. She is now able to sort two colors, match identical objects as well as pictures to objects she is motivated by.

Carly has learned to independently remove her shoes and socks and shirt if they are loose. She is working on independently putting on her socks. She drinks from a cup with no spillage. Next year we will introduce such fasteners as zippers, snaps and buttons . . .

After two years at Northland, just past Carly's fourth birthday, she began to outgrow the services that the school provided. And even the reduced fees outgrew our credit line. We moved on to the public school system's watered-down services for special-needs education. There were suitable placements for a child with more common disabilities. However, for a child like Carly with a mixed bag of behavioral and what we presumed were intellectual deficits, there was no perfect fit. The philosophy of the public education system in our area was to offer "good enough" for as many as possible. It's what our friend and lawyer Martha Ellison once called "equality with a vengeance." Provide a bit to everyone, but not enough for anyone.

Even though we were prepared to send our ABA therapists into the classroom at our expense, the rules of the school board forbade outside staff from working in the classroom. In one of the neighborhood schools, however, the principal was prepared to be flexible and admit a worker with Carly. Then, partway through the year, we were called to a meeting. The teacher stood in front of us with a written statement.

"Your daughter does not seem to like me or the environment of our classroom," she read from her script. Her hand shook slightly as she spoke, and she avoided our stunned gaze. She was a fastidious woman who kept her classroom tidy and efficient, and Carly's needs were anything but efficient. The principal and school board administrators looked on in sycophantic sympathy.

"Doesn't *like* you?" I interrupted, incredulously. "She's *autistic*, for God's sake. She doesn't 'like' anyone."

"I just don't think I can do this," the teacher responded.

As far as we could tell, the teacher had made no effort to learn about autism or our daughter's needs. Nor was she required to actually teach Carly, since we had provided a trained ABA therapist to run all programming for the half-day sessions. In fact, Carly wasn't even *in* the classroom very much because her therapist withdrew her to a private work space in the hall when she needed quiet and greater focus. But it was clear the battle was already lost. Carly was asked to leave the school by the end of winter break.

We were told that there were more appropriate schools for Carly to attend, though a tour with the director of special education made it clear that there weren't. There were specialized schools for the deaf, the blind, the medically fragile. There were schools for the developmentally handicapped. The administrators stonewalled and bullied Tammy to visit a school nearly an hour east of Toronto that they promised "is perfect for Carly."

"It is *not* perfect," Tammy said. "Carly cannot sit on a bus for two hours a day. What if she has to go to the bathroom? She can't tell anyone. What happens in the winter when at the slightest dusting of snow the bus service is canceled? Who will come to the house to help us? We moved into this neighborhood so that Carly could put on her knapsack and walk to school like all the other kids."

Tammy was resolute. Just because we were made an offer did not mean we had to accept it. While the school board would attempt to make us feel grateful for their largesse, we, too, could dig in our heels. Through our sheer stubbornness borne from a lack of reasonable options, Carly remained in the local public school for the next few years. However, when a new principal arrived, it became all too clear that the improvised program we were running was no longer acceptable. Either Carly would have to be assigned to another school with a developmentally handicapped classroom or we would have to make our own arrangements to educate her.

❧

Excerpt from psychological assessment, February 2000:

Dr. Susan Marcotte, PhD, C. Psych
Registered Psychologist
Carly attends school in the morning and therapy in the afternoon. Carly is a child who needs a lot of direct one-on-one care. She can be extremely destructive and dangerous to herself, both at home and at school, unless she is well supervised. Carly spends a great deal of time out of focus and also rocking on a chair. Her communication skills are limited . . . Carly has recently begun an Applied Behavior Analysis Program.

ASSESSMENT RESULTS

It is evident from this profile that Carly continues to demonstrate global developmental delay and functions within the Developmentally Disabled range. Carly presents as a child whose presentation in all three domains, stereotypic behaviors, communications skills and social interaction skills, falls within the spectrum of Autism/Pervasive Developmental Disorder. Carly is a child who avoids establishing eye contact, will often spend her time spinning items and rocking back and forth. She makes sounds repeatedly and used to flap her hands. In group settings, Carly tends to stay to herself. She does not use toys appropriately and will often respond to requests with negativity.

Carly is not an easy child to look after and she is a child that requires a great deal of direction in order to assure that she is using her time productively. Developmentally, Carly functions between an 18-month and 2-year level. Carly's social and communication skills are her weakest areas of development. Cognitively, Carly functions between a 2- and 3-year-old level. Carly appears to have benefitted from Applied Behavior Analysis intervention in the short time period in which she has begun. It would benefit her to continue receiving this type of approach to her learning. Carly's parents may wish to consider a year in which Carly receives ABA half days and some half days with an opportunity for inclusion in a regular Senior Kindergarten classroom with a shadow . . .

Tammy's friend Beverly, who was a grade-school teacher, suggested we visit a small elementary school about fifteen minutes from our house. Crestwood Heights was a community school nestled into a tree-lined neighborhood of curved roads and straight hedges. Walking through the front door, we felt like we were stepping back in time, in a peaceful, nostalgic way. The school had a special-needs classroom, and while most of the children would be younger than Carly, who was around six years old, the small class size and the offer of allowing us to bring in an educational assistant trained in ABA was about as good as it could get. We would never know why this school had never been presented to us as an option in the past. The only task remaining was to find a worker who would meet our requirements—someone patient, energetic, and willing to be trained in ABA and work full-time with Carly. Furthermore, she would have to be an appropriate teaching assistant in the eyes of the school board.

Several years earlier, Beverly had introduced us to a young woman named Dana Dalal, who had been a teacher's assistant in Beverly's classroom. "You have to meet her," Beverly had told us on a number of occasions. "She works with a little girl like Carly who also goes to Northland part-time and is in my classroom in the afternoons. Dana is amazing."

When Tammy finally called to inquire if Dana would be willing to work with Carly for a few hours on the weekends, we learned that she also worked part-time for Liz, our ABA provider. Autism, it turns out, is not only a closed world, it's a small one, too. After meeting her, we called Liz to request that Dana pick up some after-school ABA shifts with Carly.

Dana was calm and professional and, most important, not rattled by Carly's outbursts, tantrums, and the constant humming noises she made, like a teakettle wailing endlessly for attention. She peered through dark-rimmed glasses with an intensity and wisdom uncommon in any twenty-three-year-olds I knew. The fit with Carly was important, but as Dana was at our house twenty hours a week and occasionally came to synagogue with us on Saturday mornings to help us with Carly, the fit with *us* was equally critical. Carly's therapists held a position in the family somewhere between friend and family member. They are often present at mealtimes, family celebrations, and the inevitable arguments that break out between stressed-out spouses.

When it came time to find the educational assistant to help Carly at Crestwood Heights, we asked Dana if she had a clone or knew anyone like her who might be interested. Parents of kids with autism covet one another's prized therapists the way some people covet their neighbors' houses or cars. "Well, actually my brother is looking for work. He's just finishing his early education certification."

Carly had had only female therapists and helpers in the past. Part of their task was to help her bathe, dress, and use the bathroom. Neither Tammy nor I was too sure how we felt about a young man taking on such a personal role. But we agreed to meet Howard, because he would be working in the classroom with a female teacher.

Though they lack a physical resemblance, Dana and her brother shared a similar wiring. Their mother had made a career of early childhood education and owned a nonprofit group of day-care centers. In fact, she was a close friend of the executive director of Northland. It was evident that this was a family dynasty of talented people who loved working with children—especially those with exceptionalities. Howard had the perfect educational background and, as an avid summer camp counselor, we knew he had the required physical stamina and creativity.

I don't know yet whether I believe in divine intervention. For the most part, I think we get whatever we get and it's up to us to make a go of it. But like Mary Poppins, Howard dropped into our life at precisely the moment we needed him the most: August 6, 2001. Once Howard arrived, it was like he had always been there.

Although quiet, Howard exuded confidence with Carly. He had access to Carly's ABA team for training, but his intuition proved stronger than any textbook education we could have given him. While some might have been put off by his take-charge approach and the fact that he lived by the principle of asking for forgiveness, not permission, we welcomed his leadership. I came home from work one evening to find latches drilled into our kitchen cabinets to halt Carly's invasions and a swinging chair from IKEA hanging from our basement ceiling. I was impressed with Howard's initiative and tenacity but could never have imagined how much we'd come to rely on him.

The first year at Crestwood Heights, Howard developed Carly's curriculum using the supplies and tools in the classroom, the principles of Carly's ABA program, and his own imagination. The teacher had returned after taking some time away from teaching and seemed enthusiastic to have Howard run the show. Tammy and I appreciated that she spoke of Carly warmly and glowingly, but it quickly became clear to us that she had little intention of rolling up her sleeves to learn the tough lessons of educating a youngster with autism. She let Howard tackle the tricky task of keeping Carly focused on her work.

Carly's ever-expanding team resembled a Rube Goldberg

device—a series of interconnected parts, each serving individual functions, tenuously connected to one another. Howard became the lynchpin as he spent the greatest amount of time with Carly. At first Howard spent the school days at Crestwood with Carly, but within months, he was working with her after school as well. Although he was respectful of the ABA team leader and other therapists, it was clear within a matter of weeks that his bond was far tighter with Barb than with any of the other specialists. Where ABA followed rules and protocols, Barb and Howard followed Carly. They seemed to notice details about her that others missed.

"She's smart," Howard told us.

"Uh-huh," I responded, not wanting to dampen his enthusiasm.

We had seen the progress reports from school. Carly was beginning to point to letters on a letter board to spell words like *cat* or *dog*. She was completing 100-piece jigsaw puzzles faster than an adult. But the overall impression she gave—with her hyperactivity, table slapping, and wailing—made it hard to see our daughter as intelligent.

"No, really," he protested, sensing my skepticism, before recounting a story that had happened earlier in the week.

"Just watch Carly for a second," he had said to the teacher. "I'll be in the hallway."

The small bag of potato chips Howard had been using to reward Carly for completing a sorting exercise lay folded shut on the classroom table.

"I'd put those on your desk," he suggested to the teacher as he walked out the door.

"Howard, I've been teaching school for twenty-five years. I think I can keep Carly out of the chips for a minute," the woman replied.

When Howard left the room, closing the split door behind him, Carly grabbed for the crumpled yellow bag. One step ahead of her, the teacher snatched them away and put them on her desk at the front of the room. Having missed her chance, Carly sidled up to the desk, giving the woman what seemed to be a nuzzling.

"Oh, sweetie," she said, assuming Carly's act was one of affection.

Quickly, Carly attempted to reach around the teacher for the bounty, but her teacher was one step ahead of her again and moved the remaining chips out of Carly's reach.

Thwarted, Carly picked up the teacher's reading glasses and flung them to the center of the class. As the woman bolted to catch them, Carly snapped up the bag and dumped the remaining chips on the desk before taking handfuls and shoving them in her mouth with a satisfied "mmmmmm."

Excerpt from developmental pediatrician's assessment, February 10, 2002:

Dr. Nancy Robards, MD, FRCP
Developmental Pediatrician/Director
Child Development Centre
Carly has been experiencing behavioral problems for some time, however, this has been increasing over the last 3–6 months. This has been manifested by increasingly restless behavior, impulsivity and frenetic-like activity. She has developed some compulsions including touching things and tapping people on the head. She is unable to sit still and is in constant motion. She has an increase in stereotypic and repetitive behavior including grinding her teeth, increased sensitivity to noise, increased self-injurious behavior including head-banging . . . she has also experienced some emotional liability manifested by crying for thirty minutes to one hour at a time. There is more restlessness and she has developed significant foraging behavior. She will often rummage through the kitchen looking for food or if

food is out anywhere, she will go through the boxes looking for different items. She does eat some of this food, but really it is more the looking around for food that is problematic as opposed to overeating.

FORMULATION

We had a long discussion with Carly's parents regarding which were the most important target symptoms at the moment. We agreed that her repetitive behaviors and increased restlessness and activity were the most concerning . . . we have recommended the decrease in the dose of Luvox . . . we discussed the use of two other medications . . .

From Carly's eighth to tenth years, her education once again became a frayed patchwork of in-class and homeschooling. Howard needed time off during the day to complete additional college courses and was only able to work with Carly in the afternoons and weekends. A fight ensued with the school board over who would take over his job with Carly at Crestwood Heights. Our position was that a suitably trained ABA therapist was critical; ideally, someone that we selected and trained. The board's position was based on union seniority, and they thought that a thirty-five-year-old male accounting clerk who worked in the school system and wanted to work in the classroom was an appropriate choice. The winds that had blown favorably for the previous two years had clearly changed direction.

Tammy called to complain that Carly required ABA to learn and that putting her in a classroom for developmentally handicapped children with an untrained worker was negligent, if not criminal. "We have written reports from Carly's psychologist and developmental pediatrician stating that she requires ABA to learn new skills," she told the school superintendent. He resisted, claiming that ABA was the "flavor of the month" in treatment of autism and that Tammy had no right to interfere with the implementation of special education in the Toronto District School Board. "You do not get to determine how we teach children," he said, and hung up.

A series of pointless emails of escalating anger followed. As we sunk deeper into the bureaucratic quicksand, I decided to call the board directly and set up a face-to-face meeting. We agreed that Tammy wouldn't attend and that we'd try a good-cop/bad-cop approach. Tammy had already declared which one she was and carried a grudge as a form of exercise. I could at least fake tolerance.

I was led to a small conference room in the sprawling maze of cubicles and offices at the board of education. I gathered my thoughts and channeled calmness as I prepared to explain that their staffing plan was a misguided idea and would not be in Carly's best interests.

The superintendent did not attend, instead sending one of his direct reports. A woman in her late forties entered.

After a few pleasantries, I came right to the point. "Carly has been making real progress," I said, hoping that a positive start would ease the conversation. Keep it all about the student, I reasoned. "I'm sure we all want what's best for her. Tammy, our doctors, and I just don't think it's best for her to have someone without the right training. Kids with autism need the stability of routine, and her ABA program is her routine," I pointed out.

"Union rules are unequivocal," she told me. "We must give priority to union members with seniority and cannot let one of your therapists jump the queue."

"I don't understand how a man who was an accounting clerk last week is suitable to work with a girl with autism this week," I said, hoping my sarcasm underscored how ludicrous the board's plan appeared.

"I'm sure we will provide the candidate with appropriate training to support the teacher," she parried.

"Is he trained as an ABA therapist?" I asked rhetorically. "Will he come to our house for team meetings and to understand how to work with Carly?"

"All of our teachers take a seminar on ABA and autism now," she replied, referring to a two-hour lecture on the definition of applied behavior analysis provided to special ed teachers.

"Come on, Deborah." I exhaled. "You know that's not what I mean. We are willing to provide hours of training every week and the supervision of a Board Certified Behavior Analyst as well as a registered psychologist. And we're not even asking the board to pay for it!"

But I had my suspicions about what this was really about. The school board had caught wind of us bringing ABA into the classroom—a policy no-no. Furthermore, by bringing Howard into the school, even though he was officially an employee of the school board, we had compromised the seniority policies of the union. This seemed to be all about keeping the union happy.

Deborah continued to sit impassively. At the moment, she had all the power and she knew it. In its black-and-white operating system, public education was blind to the odd color of autism.

"So . . . you're telling me that to ensure my daughter's right to a proper education, I need a lawyer to discuss this further?" I asked. Her calm manner taunted me.

"There's really little else I can offer."

"So, you're telling me I need a lawyer to ensure my daughter can return to the classroom?" I repeated, the burn rising inside me. I needed to hear her invite me to battle.

She rose and held the door for me, making it clear the conversation was at an end.

I had my answer.

On the way home, I phoned Tammy. "I'm calling Martha," she said, referring to our friend Martha Ellison, one of Canada's most respected civil rights litigators. Within hours, she successfully petitioned the court for an interim injunction to allow Carly to stay in school with an appropriate assistant—one that Howard helped us find. The judge agreed the school board was required to provide Carly with the appropriate level of support and was running the risk of irreparable harm to Carly if it did not. Carly was back in school with an ABA therapist, and we learned the cynical lesson that it sometimes takes a lawyer to get an education.

By the following year, Carly no longer fit the profile for the classes offered at Crestwood Heights, even with a therapist present. She could not join "typical" classes for kids her age, and she was getting too advanced intellectually for the developmentally handicapped classroom she was in. Looking for a suitable classroom, we once again returned to the neighborhood public school she had attended several years before, armed with our injunction to ensure access. Howard had completed his studies and returned to Carly's side as her one-on-one classroom aide. We experimented with a first-grade classroom, since Carly lacked the academic skills to join an age-appropriate fifth-grade class. While she couldn't read or write, we reasoned that she would at least absorb some of the material.

Some days Carly was reasonably calm and seemed happy to be with typical kids. Other days her behavior was out of control. It was a tennis game of success and failure—one day sitting quietly able to do the schoolwork of her peers, others so disruptive Howard would withdraw Carly from class and bring her home.

Howard was a one-man school system; there was no substitute teacher were he to get sick or need a day off. We lived in fear of anything that would prevent him from arriving at our door in the morning—a personal appointment, a snowstorm, even a cold.

"Howard, I forbid you to get sick," Tammy once half-joked with him when the flu was ripping through our community. But it was no joke, because without Howard, we were adrift in an ocean of

Carly's mayhem. Whether out of good luck or his sheer determination, Howard has never missed a day of work without devising an alternative plan for Carly.

After six months, it was clear that Carly was not ready for a mainstream classroom, with its twenty-eight children and need for quiet and discipline. In the middle of class she would stand up and repeatedly slap the table and yelp, startling the students. This time, we didn't need the principal or school board to push us out. We knew it was time to go.

As an alternative to the public school, Howard attempted a partnership with a small Montessori school. Here he would take direction from the director and teacher and try to create structure in Carly's day in the less restricted environment. The school had hoped that if it worked with Carly, they would start a program for other children with autism the following year.

The venture withered after the first year, however, due to high costs and lack of resources. To provide the level of specialized education required would have cost parents nearly $60,000 per year. There weren't many takers.

We were exhausting all options. After six years of ABA, Carly had mastered a number of self-help skills, but her hyperactivity and verbal tics made her an educational pariah. While my career was gaining momentum, our credit line was maxed out, making attendance at one of the few private autism schools out of reach.

I could feel Tammy lying awake at night, her brain whirring through the meager options. "It would be so much easier if Carly were *more* disabled," she lamented. "If she were a little more blobby, at least we could contain her." What could I say in response? It was true. We had met families with children living with a full spectrum of challenges and, ironically, the ones with physically depleting disabilities had a place in the system. We were rejected like a transplanted organ.

A kid's 'tween years should be filled with excitement and discovery. Taryn was experimenting with dance and drama, soccer and overnight camp. But Carly's childhood felt like a slog through mud. It was hard to rejoice in her newfound abilities to sort letters and spell a few simple words or to take turns playing a game of checkers when minutes later she would spontaneously fling herself to the floor and bang her head or compulsively dump plates of food and glasses of juice.

With no public school options, we improvised our own school. Our basement family room, which had long served as both Tammy's office and space for Carly's ABA, became a one-room schoolhouse. Howard, Barb, and whichever ABA provider we were using at the time strung together hours of activities and programming to keep Carly busy. She wasn't getting a diet of academics, but her mind would have to wait for her body to catch up. To our list of responsibilities—parent, manager, advocate, therapist, and prison warden—we could now add schoolmaster. As Carly got bigger, it seemed our world got smaller.

4

⋙⋘

Sleeplessness

Even now, with the worst of it behind us, I have a sense of foreboding at bedtime. Through most of her childhood, Carly's constant movement and inability to settle tormented her sleep and ours. She would struggle to fall asleep at a reasonable hour and to stay asleep for more than four. All parents go through sleepless nights with their infants, but by forty I had hoped to be past this phase of my life.

One night, around eleven, when Carly was little, Tammy and I were in bed, as usual. Tammy can only fall asleep with the television on, so we'd watch Jon Stewart ridicule George Bush, or a news show on CNN—a group of guys I call the Screamers because they yell over one another to the point of childishness. Tammy, however, is a news junkie and follows the commentators and the politicians that they rip apart like most guys follow sports. But to me they look like old gray men raging against the system, and I can't understand how it relaxes her.

When I finally drifted off, I did so with one ear open as always, because I knew my night was just beginning. Sure enough, just after two in the morning Carly burst from her room and jolted me back into a hazy reality. She ran—Carly never walks, never moves peacefully—into the hall and bounded into our room. Each step was a heavy stomp, her hands slapping at her sides. But her fiery energy packed a mean punch. She didn't cry so much as bleat, a sound that immediately raised my blood pressure. What few words she had been able to form at three or four years old were long gone, replaced only with gestures and guttural noises. Perhaps forming words was more effort than it was worth, since gesturing, grabbing, and whining often produced quicker results. We despaired of ever actually hearing Carly's voice. The effort required for her to utter even the simple nouns she once learned far outweighed the benefit to her; it was quicker and easier to point to what she wanted or use the binders filled with picture symbols of things other people's mouths could prattle off without thought. Or perhaps as she developed, pathways in her brain—the complex network of neurons that told her mouth what to say—crisscrossed into a tangled mess, leaving her speechless.

She stood in the darkened room at the foot of our bed, stripped naked, and jumped up and down. She made the yelling and howling sounds that were her only form of verbal communication. I pulled myself heavily from my bed. "I guess it's my turn," I said sarcastically to my wife. She had learned that if she stayed in bed long enough, I would be the first to get up. This tactic left me with a double dose of resentment. I am not kind when I'm tired and aggravated. The sense of humor I often use to defuse a situation deserts me and is replaced with petulance. "It's *always* my turn," I throw in under my breath.

I shepherded Carly from our room and back to the sea of destruction that faced me in hers. Compelled by some unstoppable, inexplicable force, Carly had pulled the sheets, pillows, and blankets from her bed and emptied all the contents of her dresser onto the floor. She was now on her bare mattress jumping and flopping about as if possessed. "Oh, Carly," I said. I felt the creep of desperation in my stomach. This was not a new scene for me; it was one that played out over and over—almost every night. Carly's behavior was inexplicable, and without language, a mystery.

I put the sheets and quilt back on her bed and plumped up the pillows. It looked inviting to me, anyway. "Carly, get back in bed," I told her, a bit roughly. Although she complied, I knew this was the beginning of the day, not the end of a momentary disruption of the night. She flopped around on the bed as I sat on the edge trying to soothe her. "Shhhh," I said, or was it a command at this point? I lay next to her, hoping to project an infectious calm.

"Think of something peaceful," I suggested. "The ocean, for example. A walk on the beach." For me, visualization has always been a powerful ally. It's hard to know if Carly understood this technique. I tried not to talk down to her. An attempt at soothing her to sleep felt futile; hadn't I tried every trick I knew a hundred times before?

As the fit subsided, I viewed the carnage of clothing strewn around the room. "You must make her clean up all of her messes," the therapists had told us. "It's the only way to discourage her from doing it." I think they called it an "aversive"—a kind word for "negative reinforcement." In this case, cleaning up was designed to be a consequence of her action, to discourage her from making a mess next time. But making Carly do anything she doesn't want to do is a major struggle. For whom is the task really an "aversive," then?

"Piss off," I said to no one in particular; it seemed like the right sentiment. I was woozy with exhaustion. Not just a physical tiredness, but the type that comes from tedium, frustration, and anger. I usually can move beyond anger with some sort of catharsis, like provoking an argument or slamming a door, but this seemed like an inextinguishable fury. The only force keeping me moving forward was inertia—what choice did I have?—and a desire for normalcy. Though my life often felt like I was bailing water from a foundering vessel with a teacup, I believed that if I was determined enough, consistent enough, patient enough—I could bring order to chaos.

I lay next to Carly as she drifted off only to be startled back to wakefulness with a twitching spasm. So we lay this way as the rest of the household slept. We had purchased a clock radio that played a series of Zen-like nature sounds. I stared up at the ceiling, and listened to the track trying to determine when one cycle of chirping birds and bullfrogs ended and the next one began. It was like counting stars. Something mindless I could do at two-thirty in the morning when I should be sleeping. Carly was finally quiet, though not sleeping, so I headed back to my own bed.

On a good night, I might have fallen back to sleep and cobbled together something that resembled a sufficient amount of rest to function the next day. But this night was not a good night. I was jolted again by a crash in the kitchen. I ran downstairs to find Carly standing on a chair in front of a food cupboard. Boxes of crackers and pasta, cans of soup and stewed tomatoes lay around her on the floor.

"God damn it, Carly." The rush of emotion electrified my body. "Stop it. Just fucking stop it. I'm exhausted. If you want to live in this house, you need to get control of yourself," I snapped. I had slipped into the bleak place exhaustion and frustration sent me. But I didn't feel better after making these hurtful threats; I felt worse and worried that one day the threats may not be empty. This was not a sustainable existence, every night and every day, chasing Carly around the house, putting our things back together just in time for her to rip them apart again.

Several months before, Carly had snuck upstairs and filled the bath. We were unaware of what she was up to until we heard the flood of water pouring through the ceiling lights on the floor above. Another time, she smeared peanut butter on the den walls and furniture. While we cleaned up after her attack on the den, she grabbed a full container of baby powder and dumped it over the second-floor railing onto the carpeted stairs below. By the time Carly was seven, her uncontrollable movements and urges had taken on an untamed, destructive quality. Carly's actions were not mischief that we would laugh about when she was older, such as the time Taryn gave one side of her head a haircut. It was like living with a raccoon in the house, and there were no signs of her growing out of it.

At three in the morning, I was in no mood for cleaning up. I left the debris on the floor and took Carly back upstairs, put her on the toilet, and cleaned her up. Back in her room, I remade the bed for the third or fourth time that night and got her back under the covers. This time I knew I wouldn't be going back to my own room. Not tonight. I lay down next to her again, pinning her in with the blankets and the weight of my arms and legs across her. She sometimes likes the sensation of swaddling, but by this point, I mostly did it to hold her in place. I knew I wouldn't sleep, but at least I wouldn't be moving. Carly arched her back, screaming and flailing; the tight hospital corners my mother had taught me to make gave way as Carly sprang from the bed again. She jumped around the room yelping.

I considered getting Tammy up to give me some relief. This would have been a double-edged sword. Tammy wears her frustration much closer to the surface than I do. If she started yelling at Carly, I would feel worse than if I just dealt with this myself. Mothers are supposed to have limitless patience, but I know too well that this isn't true. Tammy was drained. Her daytimes were not so different from my nights. She spent thankless afternoons shadowing Carly and navigating the mostly unchartered waters of caring for a child severely afflicted with autism. Hers was a relentless struggle to seek assistance from government agencies—help for battle-scarred families like ours to cope with what no family should have to cope with alone.

Then there was the matter of Tammy's health. After years of struggling with cancer and colitis, she felt like an old woman although she was only forty. When I looked at her, I'd see a sadness that was not there when we first married. She often complained of an overwhelming sense of hopelessness. "I don't see a way out of this," she would say. But every day she persevered in her attempts to fix our daughter. "There really is little choice," I told friends who sympathetically inquired about our situation. "What else can we do?"

And so I tried to manage these nighttime battles on my own as best I could. If there was an alternative to this hell, I couldn't find it. On nights like this I found myself reflecting on the desperate case of a young mother, Dr. Killinger-Johnson, who had lived nearby. On a sticky morning during the summer of 2000, she awoke early, took her six-month-old baby, and jumped in front of a subway car as it entered the local station. I had driven by the house owned by Dr. Killinger-Johnson many times before the tragedy. The house was, and still remains, beautifully landscaped and pristine. At night, I used to like to peek in the window as I passed because the interior looked so elegant and peaceful. I liked to believe that the house's appearance reflected the lives of the people inside. Her death, and that of her child, was a sad and shocking story made worse by the fact that the she was a psychiatrist and the daughter of a psychologist who counseled those with depression. It seems that even experts in desperation are not immune to it.

Many were horrified by the story, but my wife often spoke empathetically about Dr. Killinger-Johnson. Not too publicly, mostly to me, she would say, "I can imagine what she was feeling. If not for Taryn and Matthew . . ." Then, eerily, her voice would drift off, ending with "I could never leave them motherless." She would take a deep breath and steel herself up for the next challenge. She clearly empathized with the dark hole inside the perfect-looking life of our neighbor. We, too, had a house and life that looked tidy on the outside but was a hurricane on the inside.

When Tammy would speak this way, a wave of nausea would flood over me. Not because she sounded irrational; in fact, it was just the opposite. Week after week of sleeplessness and exhaustion left me with little argumentative response. Because of Tammy's resolve, her tenacity, and her stalwart rescue missions for our daughter, I never considered her dark fantasy to be a legitimate risk. In reality, when things got too awful, Tammy would just get in her car and drive around until she calmed down. It didn't matter what time of night it was. And I just tried to breathe through it, not exactly praying, but repeating to myself, "Just let me get through one more night." We had become masters of surviving Carly.

Eventually morning ended the seemingly endless night; one that had never really begun. Light crept through the shades. Carly's room filled with the happy tweets of the birds that nested near the small portal window of her room. I sat on the edge of her bed. It was close to five-thirty, and she was finally calming down, though still far from placid. Her room looked like a tornado had hit it. But by afternoon, Mari would have done her magic; everything would be back in its place, creating a temporary sense of order. Carly's room would once again be a pretty one with custom-made pink and white drapes and a coordinated coverlet; an antique armoire and dresser with little lamps, picture frames, and figurines resting in the corners. It should, I thought, have been a room filled with giggles and "sleep tight, don't let the bedbugs bite," not chaos and turmoil.

I rested my head on my hands. My face felt numb and rubbery, the way your lip feels after a shot of Novocain. I looked at my sweet, tormented little girl, her thick wavy hair erupting from her head, the big green eyes with long eyelashes, and her broad cheekbones. "So beautiful," I whispered out loud. Inside I longed for something more. A father can give and give, but he wants something back. Just a hug. Or a silly malapropism. "Oh, Daddy! Look at the slobber!" Taryn had once said, referring to the neighbor's inflatable lobster floating in their pool. A smile and a sweet memory would be fair payment for all this.

I looked at her again; Carly was finally sleeping. Her breathing was calm and regular, her forehead damp with perspiration. I lay down gently next to her so as not to wake her, still longing for some sense of connection. I could feel my anger dissipate. There was so much I wanted for her, simple things, impossible things. "Carly, I want you to be calm and happy," I whispered. "I want you to speak. I want you to play and have friends and go to school. I want you to accomplish something you will feel proud of. I want you to sit at the dinner table and share in the conversation. I want you to have a first boyfriend whom I will regard with skepticism, and then a husband whom I'll welcome with open arms. I want you to have a life. I want you to know peace. I want . . ." I cuddled her closer. She was still just a little girl, soft and warm. She smelled sweet, like bath gel and shampoo.

I drifted off to sleep.

5

✦

Away from Home

Excerpt from pharmacology consult clinic, September 15, 2002:

Anne Murphy, MD, FRCPC
Peggy Fitzpatric, MD, FRCPC
Carly was sent to us on consult from Dr. Nancy Robards . . .
during the interview Carly was quite agitated and demonstrated
a number of repetitive sensory activities. She continues to lick
her hands and tap the bottom of her chin . . . some time was
spent with mom discussing the importance of respite care and it
is good that she has a contact at Kerry's Place. The number for
the clinical social worker was given to arrange for respite care.
The importance of sleep was stressed and it was suggested that
Carly's melatonin be increased to 9 mg at nighttime. In addition, we suggested an increase in the Risperdal . . .

At what point do people realize they've reached rock bottom? For addicts, I suppose it's when they've lost everything. No house. No job. No friends or family left willing to enable their death spiral. But I was getting the sense that for us there was no bottom. It seemed like there was always potential for a little more bad news, a few more challenges. Even though Carly was still a child, Tammy and I felt like we had already lived a lifetime of child-rearing. Although Carly was making some academic gains and we continued to battle for her place in the school system, her behaviors continued to confound and exhaust us. Nights were still an endless routine of making ruined beds and corralling Carly into her room. The incessant tantrumlike behaviors made Tammy's heart race and pushed me to the limits of forgiveness. The plaintive bleating and head banging became so routine that neither of us could feel sympathy—only frustration and anger.

As the days dragged into weeks and months, we realized this was not a life but a slow demise. It was either Carly or us. Years before, one of the staff at Northland, the special-needs school Carly attended as a toddler, introduced us to the idea of respite care. Respite is the chance for families raising disabled children to have a break. In principle, these little breaks were supposed to give the families a chance to regain their strength and perspective.

Run by various agencies, respite programs take place in either residential houses that have been converted to group homes or large institutional facilities. Pick your poison. The woman at Carly's school suggested we contact Caring Friends, an organization that ran six or seven residential homes for teens with autism who were too challenging to raise at home. The families of several of Carly's classmates made use of their services. The homes were located in diverse suburbs where larger houses were affordable and neighbors kept their distance. Clients, as they were known, might live in a residence on a part-time or full-time basis. In addition to these more permanent arrangements, families could plan occasional respite weekends. The executive director of the facilities suggested that this might be appropriate for us. Although Carly would be younger than the other residents, she explained, she would have her own room and sufficient staff to care for her.

On a parched summer afternoon when Carly was around five, Tammy and I drove out to visit a home that had space available for a weekend every month or two. It was a typical suburban Toronto home located in the labyrinth of a planned community about forty-five minutes east of our house. As we pulled up, the only distinguishing feature I noted was the large, somewhat battered transport van parked in the driveway. Over time, I was to learn that such a vehicle was the hallmark of group homes.

We walked up the path to the front door and the façade of normalcy began to fade. I noticed the cracked garage light, skeletal plants gasping in the dried flowerbed, and the sprung spring on the screen door, small signs I would learn are symptoms of houses that are not homes, inhabited by residents who have bigger things to tackle than aesthetics.

Andrea, the facility's manager, welcomed us in. She was a woman in her forties, casually dressed in jeans and a T-shirt. Like many of the other managers of residential homes we would meet over the years, she had a calm professionalism, almost a detachment from the noisy chaos of the house. As we chatted briefly, I was struck by the matter-of-factness in the details of handing one's child over to strangers. There was no judgment, no probing of *why* we were doing what we were doing. Andrea was more interested in Carly's issues, her condition, what she needed. It was a relief that guilt was not a required payment for the services provided.

"We can get more of the details later," said Andrea. "Why don't I show you around the house and introduce you to some of the staff."

From the front hall, I looked around the house hoping for some measure of cheer. I could feel Tammy's anxiety rising. Her eyes darted around the open-space living and dining rooms; I think I heard her sigh. The furnishings, likely donated by well-meaning families, were sparse and well-tormented: a cracked leather sofa, and someone's uncle's La-Z-Boy that never had seen better days. An overhead light shone, its mismatched bulbs casting urine-colored light. The whitewashed walls were no match for the larger residents whose outbursts left them dented, scuffed, and pockmarked like a war zone. The kitchen extended into a family room where four or five boys sat around watching TV. The staff, a few young women, was making lunch. I saw the same multitasking we engaged in at home; trying to prepare sandwiches with one hand and blocking one of their charges from pillaging the refrigerator with the other.

Although I saw nothing overtly disturbing, there was little to comfort, either. The house had all the basics for survival. Unbreakable dishes and cups, clunky furniture, a table at which to eat. This was a place for strangers who lived together, but in the summer heat I felt no warmth.

I tried to maintain an upbeat air as I watched these gangly teenagers barking, flapping their arms, and shaking their heads. How could I leave my daughter, a girl no more than four feet tall, in this land of giants? My stomach churned.

"Are there any girls or smaller children who live here?" I asked Andrea.

"There is a girl, who is twelve. She lives here Monday to Friday. Her mother passed away earlier this year, and her father finds it difficult to manage," she explained. I could not meet Tammy's downward gaze. Only a few years past her first bout of lymphoma and chemo, I could see the film running in her mind—*will that be us?* But she was silent.

"And there is a little boy, about eight, who will be here some of the weekends," Andrea continued.

We would learn over and over that autism was primarily a world of boys. For every female diagnosed with the disorder, there are four males. Many grew to be large, loud near-men with stamping-mad tendencies. Their behaviors are vocal and physical and sometimes aggressive. Carly, on the other hand, had more feral traits—smearing gobs of cream cheese on the furniture, tearing into packages of food, or repetitively flinging the clothes from her dresser and cupboard. But she was not aggressive—never hit or bit others, shrieked, or grew violent. Carly was not like most kids with autism. Even in her oddness, Carly was odd.

"Do you do activities with the kids?" asked Tammy. "Carly doesn't sit still. She doesn't watch TV. She needs exercise."

"Depending on staff, we go out for walks or to the mall," the woman said hopefully.

The thought of Carly spending a weekend inside on a warm sunny day made my soul sink. I grew up in a time and place where days were spent outdoors—roaming and finding adventure. I knew that left to her own devices, Carly would sit and rock, twisting and breaking whatever small items she could get her tiny hands on.

"Respite is for you, not Carly," a friend would tell us as we lamented our decision over dinner out one night. I repeated this over and over in my head like a mantra. At home, we would try to make Carly's life as disciplined and perfect as we could. For two days every month, good enough would have to be good enough. I wanted to feel relief in the permission to let go, but all I felt was profound sadness. Looking over at Tammy, I saw blankness in her eyes. It was a look she wore most days now. In a glance I could see she felt a desperation so thick she was suffocating.

Andrea took us to the second floor, where we poked our heads into the bedrooms and bathrooms. The rooms were bland, with a few personal effects of their residents strewn on the bed or dresser. Some rooms were reminiscent of a college dorm; the clutter was typical of teenage boys, a canister of Axe Body Spray and a few post-ers of rock heroes or voluptuous movie stars. But all the rock post-ers and cans of body spray in the world will never make this home. Only home is home.

We finished the tour and sat in a small room used as the admin-istrative office. Andrea explained the schedule, handed us the ream of forms we would need to complete, and reviewed the qualifica-tions of the staff that worked in the house. We had no doubts that the program was well managed. It had come highly recommended by people we respected. But this did little to improve our spirits. Rather than seeing this as a gift, we saw this as the first stumble onto the slippery slope of resignation. Today it was the occasional resting point, but one day, we feared, it would be the final destination.

We drove home in silence. Neither of us strong enough to broach the subject. But it was understood: We would give this a try.

Several weeks later, we packed Carly's little overnight bag for her first respite weekend. "Pack some of Carly's favorite things," Andrea had suggested. A toy. A blanket. A pillow. But Carly had formed no attachments save for potato chips. She did not take comfort in pos-sessions or people, from what we could tell. But we packed the blan-ket and stuffed animals that we tucked Carly into bed with every night. And a few of the stim toys—objects that she liked to fiddle with to relax herself—such as the octagon of colorful wooden tubes and bells strung together with elastic thread that she could stretch and rattle. Optimistically, we included some of the picture books I read to her every night.

Tammy and I tried to explain to her siblings why Carly was going away for a weekend. "It's like a sleepover," I lied. I can't remem-ber what we explained to Carly. We clung to the belief that she didn't fully comprehend her surroundings. There were never tear-ful good-byes when we dropped her off at day programs or school like other normal kids. Perhaps parting from her family carried no fear or anxiety for her. I wish I could say the same for me.

I have limited recollection of the first few times Carly stayed at Caring Friends. I cannot recall what we did in those first weekends of freedom. Did we laugh? Run errands? Go out with friends? Probably we slept. Fitfully.

I do, however, remember the last. Tammy and I had quickly learned that the key to survival was to take turns with thankless tasks. Both the dropping off and the picking up duties had to be shared, as neither of us could handle that much emotional stress in one weekend. Leaving Carly filled me with a sense of loss and guilt, followed by the giddiness of knowing I could slow down if only for two days, followed by the guilt over feeling giddiness. The pick-up on Sunday brought relief that Carly seemed no worse for wear from her weekend. It also brought the dread of facing the next week back in the hole in which we started.

It was my turn to drive pick-up duty on what would be Carly's final stay at Caring Friends. That weekend, we had done what the social worker at the agency that funded our respite program suggested: We acted like a regular family. On Saturday, Tammy and I took Matthew and Taryn to see a movie and out for dinner, and on Sunday, we relaxed with *The New York Times* over extended cups of coffee.

When I got to the house on Sunday evening, I found her on the sofa in the den, rocking back and forth, her hands over her ears. This did not surprise me, as it was the only state of rest she knew, other than sleep. She was wearing a soiled T-shirt and the elastic-waisted jeans she had been wearing when she arrived on Friday. And she reeked. At five Carly was still not consistently toilet trained.

After cleaning her up the best I could and disposing of the soiled diaper, I sought out the shift manager. "What the hell?" I asked her. "Why is Carly in the same clothes from Friday? And she's filthy!"

"I'm not sure," she said. "The worker that was with her this afternoon is gone for the day," as if this were a logical explanation. Then, "And we've been a little short-staffed this weekend."

For a brief moment I actually empathized. I knew what it was like to herd cats with one hand. As I gathered up Carly, so small and shabby, my open-mindedness dissipated. Over the past months, Carly had come home clean and healthy. Sometimes she would bring a small craft she had done. Not knowing all the details of how Carly's time had been spent while away made it easier to accept that everything was fine. Or if not fine, then acceptable. But seeing Carly in a state of seeming neglect and the staff's unapologetic nature led me to wonder whether this was not a thoroughly unusual circumstance.

The shift manager took out a clipboard as we were leaving. "Shall I put you down for the same weekend next month?" she asked.

"No, I don't think so," I said. Then, just in case, I added, "We'll call you during the week," as I led Carly out the door into the chilled dusk.

Exhaustion had given us the permission to place Carly in respite. The sleeplessness, the inability to spend time with Taryn and Matthew, or even to take a shower without worrying about what hell Carly was causing, was unsustainable. Handing our child to others to care for—was that not a final act of desperation? I realized, as I fastened Carly into her booster seat and closed the car door, that even this extreme act failed to stop our free fall. Placing Carly in the hands of others, even for a few days, left a hollow feeling in my gut. I could not relax despite the quiet in the house. Looking at my soiled daughter rocking in her car seat, my conscience jeered, "I told you so."

As the dizzying fall continued, I lamented as I knew we had not yet reached rock bottom.

6

It Takes a Village

"Susan," I said, "what can we expect?" We had come back in for another consult with the psychologist who had been following Carly's development since our daughter was four years old. I had reread her latest evaluation over and over, each time feeling more lost.

Tammy sat in the chair next to mine as Dr. Marcotte reviewed the findings in the latest of what would become biannual evaluations. She hedged. "You two are doing everything you can for her. More than most. Keep in her face. Keep pushing her."

"What will her future look like?" I try again, hoping for some measure of specificity. I like things in neat steps and stages.

"It's very hard to tell how far a child like Carly may progress."

We sit in silence, Tammy looking worn, drained. Having now survived nearly a decade of Hurricane Carly, we had hoped for some measure of promise. Some tiny piece of stony land that wouldn't sink under our step.

"But what *might* her future look like? As an adult?" I press on, undeterred.

"Carly may be able to function somewhat independently. Maybe even a vocational job."

My family is a family of professionals. Each generation encouraged to stretch farther than the previous. Mopping the floors at McDonald's was not ever a part of the plan. Today I snort at my arrogance and small-mindedness. Tammy and I had had high expectations for all of our children. To be happy and independent, for sure, but to do something important and worldly. We had clung to some hope that Carly would emerge from this as a child emerges from a *phase*.

"I see," I lie. "And our living situation?" It's all I can manage to articulate. I don't like choking up in public, and I see Tammy is now fighting hard not to cry. She squeezed her hands tightly in her lap and looked out the window.

"You can only do your best, for as long as possible," the doctor continued. "There are group facilities you can explore when the time comes . . ." she said vaguely.

"I see," I said again. But I still didn't.

I battled the deflating loss of hope that Carly would ever catch up to her siblings. Along with the grief came a crushing *boredom*. I had hoped that by the time Taryn and Carly were well into their primary school years that life would be busy with family activities. Although I don't consider myself the super dad, the type that coaches soccer, plays football with his kids, and volunteers at the school, I did look forward to spending time with my children. Matthew and I had taken up karate when he was about nine. Two or three times a week we trained at a dojo nearby and it became a routine we continued until we both earned our black belts around the time he finished high school.

Taryn and I played games, or I would take her to swimming, soccer, and hockey practice and watch her outpace boys twice her size. She had earned the nickname "Minnie" for her diminutive stature—all skinniness and smiles. Carly, however, was impossible to engage. Despite the fact that she never stopped moving, she didn't *do* anything. Unless being guided through an activity by one of the therapists, Carly would lapse into one of two modes: sit and rock or run and destroy.

We met other families in the autism community. Many seemed to embrace their child's disorder as if their uniqueness was as benign as left-handedness or freckles. "I think they're in denial," Tammy once said.

I sensed their admiration of their child's unusual behavior to be genuine, and I was jealous. I saw no beauty in this condition. Autism was a thief. The opportunities it stole from Carly were obvious: the chance to participate, to play, to learn, to fit in. It stole a sister from Matthew and Taryn. It stole energy and money and patience. It was stealing our daughter, bit by bit. I saw no beauty, only evil. What force of good attempts to rob a parent of the love of a child? I was greedy; while I had two children with whom I could speak, play, and be a father, I wanted all three.

Some parents that we met through our autism network and from programs Carly attended were capable of filling the role of therapist. In fact, a main tenet of ABA is to include parents in the training so they can provide consistent direction. Tammy and I marveled at their patience, sitting on the floor and supervising their youngsters as they put colored pegs in holes for a reward. The mere thought of it made me yawn. I found that the style of communicating with my child in the manner of a therapist turned me from a parent into an instructor, further distancing me from my daughter rather than bringing me closer.

"I feel like I should spend time learning Carly's programs," I told

Tammy. "At least I'd have something to do with her." Lowering my voice out of embarrassment, I added, "But I hate doing those repetitive tasks. It's so freakin' dull."

"We're good at getting stuff done for Carly," Tammy reminded me. "But we are *not* therapists."

During the whirly years of her childhood, the only time Carly was calm was on long walks to the park. When she was constrained by her stroller or a swing, I had a sense of peace; it was as close to a normal father-daughter experience as I could get. Taryn preferred to run all the way to the park. Carly, on the other hand, would melt down into a tantrum if we didn't use the stroller. We began calling her the Countess von Carly because she wanted to be pushed in her carriage, even when she was six years old. Eventually, we bought an oversized stroller for children with physical disabilities rather than fight.

Flying through the air, snugly squeezed into a safety swing designed for children half her age, Carly seemed to find a serenity she couldn't find on the ground. The motion and the wind in her face seemed to provide a sensory relief we could not replicate elsewhere. She could swing for hours, her eyes closed, hands over her ears, and making a humming sound through her closed lips. *Brrrr, brrrr, brrrrr. Mmm. Mmm.* As I watched the other kids play, my mind drifted. What if I could just take a gram of Taryn and inject it into Carly? I dreamt of what it might be like to have twins who were both normal. Maybe Carly was dreaming the same thing.

While Carly swung, Taryn ran off to the jungle gym, her long brown hair swinging from side to side. Other parents chased their kids, saying "I'm coming to get you! I'm coming to get you!" before grabbing their giggling children and swinging them into the air. Taryn loved it when I did that. When the three of us were together, however, I stood grounded behind Carly's swing and could only watch Taryn play while I endlessly pushed Carly. There seemed to be no limits on how Carly's Carlyness could drain resources away from her twin. I looked at Taryn, feeling as if my guilt were apparent to all. I would have loved to have the time and energy to run after her and play. Or to read with her or play a game after dinner without dozing off from lack of sleep. As I looked across the playground, I gritted my teeth. "It's just so unfair," I whispered to the wind caused by Carly's swing. Taryn never seemed to mind, though, and was quick to strike up a friendship with the other kids scampering up the tubular yellow play structure.

Sometimes Taryn would go off on errands or do activities with Tammy and I would take Carly to the park by herself, another form of divide and conquer. Whether in a stroller, a swing, or through the bumpy road of her development, it seemed that pushing Carly was the only thing I did for the first ten years of her life.

Though Carly would never look up at me or acknowledge my existence, I spoke endlessly to her. I asked her questions I knew she could not answer, imagining how lonely it must feel to be among people and yet ignored. "How was your day, Carly? Should we go swimming this weekend, Carly? Would you like to go to the zoo, Science Center, the moon?" It didn't really matter, I just couldn't stand the silence. *Brrrr. Brrrrr. Brrrrr. MMMMMM.* The only thing worse than a one-way conversation is no conversation at all.

Like the wind, water lulled Carly to a temporary calm, making the bath an important daily ritual. Sometimes she would take several a day. Until Taryn was old enough to prefer showering, the two girls would share the oversized bathtub. Mari would supervise, helping Carly wash, and the sisters would giggle and splash one another. Taryn would swim to Carly and wrap her arms around her sister's middle, making her laugh. We have a picture of Carly in the bath with Taryn at about three, looking like any other kid. But Taryn started losing interest in co-bathing when Carly started having accidents in the tub. "She's making poo-berries in the bath,"

Taryn said once, referring to the pellet-sized stools. With autism, even something as basic as evacuation can't be typical.

As one year of ABA therapy faded into the next, Carly was undeniably making progress, as Dr. Marcotte's report noted. Perhaps not at the rate or to the degree of miraculous transformation we had hoped for, but enough to know there was no going back. Sliding into debt, we girded ourselves for an uncertain timeline and an even more uncertain outcome. I had resigned myself to an expensive life. Raising Carly was like renovating a home: an endless money drain for things that are as essential as good plumbing and wiring, but of little aesthetic or pleasurable value. Carly was still a long way from fluidly living a life like other children, and her development was not remarkable. She could neither speak nor dress herself properly, nor display any real skills that would make her independent.

We had celebrated the girls' birthday one year with an arts-and-crafts party. Tammy continued to seek a commonality between the twins and strove to satisfy the needs of two very differently abled kids with one event. Sitting at the activities table with a few other children, Carly spontaneously grabbed a large bead and strung it on a cord. "Wow! That's amazing," said one of our friends, truly excited to see Carly engage in the activities.

"That's a two-hundred-fifty-thousand-dollar bead," Tammy quipped dryly, referring to the amount of therapy required to get her this far. We were trying to celebrate the progress while keeping our more palpable sense of disappointment at bay. Our persistence was not so much out of enthusiasm as desperation: We really had no other options. Carly was mastering some basic academic skills— identifying objects by pointing with a closed fist when asked, correctly pointing to words or answers to simple math equations printed on flash cards when prompted by the teacher. Yet she was filled with a static electricity that kept her buzzing and moving in a noisy commotion that made a typical school classroom an impossibility.

As it became clear that Carly understood the concept of selecting items that she wanted, Howard and Barb moved on to an activity schedule. Barb wanted to give Carly the ability to express more complete thoughts and her ABA therapists wanted to be able to show her a visual schedule of events for the day and week. To help them, I needed to print out hundreds of comic strip–like illustrations— times of the day represented by a line-drawn clock, activities, toys, or food. When the guy at the Kinko's down the street got to know me by name, I realized it was time to purchase my own laminating machine.

Every few weeks, I sat on the playroom floor in the basement— Carly's in-home classroom. I printed and laminated dozens of little individual cards, each representing individual actions and themes that could be arranged in a sequence of events by the ABA therapists. I attached small pieces of Velcro to the back of each of the hundreds of squares. I created extra sets, as they seemed to get lost or damaged as quickly as I could assemble them.

In her room was a large board with a strip of Velcro on it. Howard could arrange the activities in order to show her what she needed to do. Get up. Use the toilet. Brush teeth. Take off pajamas. Pick out clothes. Put on underwear. Put on T-shirt. Put on sweatshirt. Put on pants. Put on socks. It's a long list when you break down every part of your daily routine in nanoseconds.

We did this for every activity Carly needed to engage in—at home and in school. We taught Carly that as she completed one task, she was to remove the little card from the Velcro strip and put it in a box. When she completed a series of actions, she received a reward to reinforce positive behavior. Some families have little lines drawn on the backs of closet doors, marking the heights of their children as they grow. Many parents refuse to paint over the symbolic forward march of time. In our house, we still have a strip of Velcro on the back of the coat closet door with the sequence: *breakfast, brush teeth, put on coat, wait for bus, free time.* The last item seemed like a non sequitur, but I don't question it. Nor do I question why after a decade, the cards are still stuck to the back of the door long after we've stopped using this system. It's our version of nostalgia, I guess.

Carly became adroit at using this method, so I was constantly redoing cards and pages with increasingly sophisticated items. My job was to sort the little Velcroed cards into categories and put them in Ziploc bags for Howard, Barb, and the ABA therapists to work their magic. I got pretty good at it, but I never got promoted. I'm not even sure my boss appreciated me.

While I was just the line worker, Tammy processed the paperwork for the government so we could be reimbursed for some of the costs of running the full-scale production that was Carly's life. Tammy also managed the HR component of hiring, shift scheduling, and procurement. We called this business of running Carly's life *Carly Inc.* "The pay is lousy, but the benefits suck," Tammy would say ironically.

Over her desk in the basement office, which she called "the dungeon," hung a bumper sticker emblazoned with the quote "Well-behaved women seldom make history," by Laurel Thatcher Ulrich (who herself looks remarkably well behaved). This humble office space, no more than a desk and a few basket-style filing drawers, was Carly Inc.'s official headquarters. An African proverb claims that "it takes a village to raise a child." But we've found that it takes something far more entrepreneurial.

Tammy's work space was the central nervous system of the doctors' reports, schedules, invoices, forms, and paperwork required to keep Carly up and moving in the right direction. Although Tammy had the educational background, the smarts, and the drive to run a private company, her struggles with depression and the overwhelming chaos of Carly kept her at home. Here she was the manager of Carly's world—a complex tangle of bureaucracy, dead ends, and uncharted territory in need of charting. And beyond helping Carly, Tammy—along with several other families who had become close friends—was successfully waging a battle to get the government to fund autism services in our province.

Some days I couldn't see the value in all the menial work we did to keep Carly afloat. I understood the logic of it all, but from my experience, she didn't use these tools to do much more than request juice or the bathroom. But I wasn't with her all day and so I never really got to see what she was capable of. One evening I got home a bit early from work. It was already dark and cold, sometime leading up to winter break when Carly was about nine. She had been working hard with Howard all afternoon following a day in school, and she was knackered. Howard had planned on working her program through the dinner routine—requesting items on the table, rewarding her for proper behavior and communication. Carly, on the other hand, had different ideas.

Darting to the front hall, Carly pulled Howard's leather jacket from the closet and dragged it to him. Tugging at his arm, she pulled him down to her and kissed his cheek and pushed him toward the front door. The three of us laughed.

"You want me to leave?" Howard asked in mock offense.

Carly went back to the closet and pulled out her dress coat, a long faux shearling that Tammy had bought for those times we brought Carly to nicer events like dinners out or synagogue. It still looked new from its infrequent use. Carly brought Tammy her purse and car keys and opened her communication book. Grasping Tammy's arm with her left hand, she pointed to the icon for McDonald's with her right, showing us she really was a kid like all others. Never before had I felt so enthusiastic about fast food.

◆

As Carly began mastering the skill of pointing to pictures of items she wanted—a toy, a snack, a drink—Barb and Howard brought in a string of communication devices for her to try. A local agency supported by government funding had a program that leased equipment at a discount to parents. However, getting the equipment was no easy task, requiring evaluations, paperwork, and appointments that could never be scheduled at our convenience. Nevertheless, over the years, we did make use of the service happily. One such piece of equipment, called a DynaVox, was a small plastic unit with a touchscreen that produced page after page of programmable images.

"Carly picks it up very quickly." Barb showed us the device. "She's got *I want orange juice* and *I want chips* down pretty well." She laughed. Barb and Howard never seemed to question whether Carly was capable—merely how to make the impossible possible. The device was temperamental and slow, but compared to sorting stacks of cards, it was rocket science.

In their early months together, Barb had taken on the role of teacher, Howard the student. Over time, Howard gained confidence and began developing programming ideas of his own. He had devised a communication bracelet to help Carly get what she needed when she was among those who didn't know her well. Like a charm bracelet, but rather than mementos, Carly's wrist was festooned with little metal tags engraved with words such as *washroom*, *juice*, or *I need my communication book*. (She had quickly learned to use the *I want a break* tag to escape from engaging in the demanding tasks she loathed.) Unlike some of the ABA therapists who spoke to Carly in artificially exuberant, childlike tones, Barb talked to her as if she were an equal—something Howard had picked up on immediately. As Carly matured, they engaged her in the process of learning. "What should we work on today, Carly?" Barb would ask as they began a session. It seemed Barb never doubted Carly's determination and ability to grow. Tammy and I seldom got to experience Carly's moments of growth. She saved these for school or sessions with Howard. We had to satisfy ourselves with the secondhand reports of Carly's accomplishments as if watching it all through murky glass.

We would hold team meetings every few months to review Carly's progress and adjust her program accordingly. The ten or twelve people required to keep Carly moving forward would crowd around our dining room table to debate what was working. Pressed shoulder to shoulder, we pored over the large blue binders of charts and lists documenting what tasks Carly was working on and debated her progress at mastering these skills. The process of taking and reviewing data was a fundamental component to ABA's approach of helping our daughter become more socialized. Yet the scientific and clinical nature was at the same time dehumanizing.

The team sessions were long and exhausting. Words like *antecedent, way-points, reinforcers*, and *data points* flew around the room. I would lose track of the details, relying on the team leader to ensure they were documented and incorporated into Carly's program. While I sometimes could not follow the minutiae of Carly's ABA program, I could always count on Barb and Howard to come up with practical solutions of their own.

One afternoon after Barb's session with Carly, Tammy commented that it was getting harder and harder to get Carly to eat without throwing a fit.

"Well, I know she can't always have a choice at mealtime, but we need to find opportunities to let her make a decision about things. Take two pictures from the picture deck, like one of hamburgers and the other of spaghetti, and have her point to the one she prefers. Let her know there are only two options. You need to give her a chance to speak up."

While at times it turned us into short-order cooks, giving Carly a say in matters—something she never had before—ended one of many battles waged every day.

Howard dutifully balanced the repetitive style of ABA with Barb's more creative and intuitive approach. Carly formed a bond with Howard unlike any she had had with prior therapists. One night I came home a bit late from work to find Taryn, Carly, and Howard watching a movie and sharing a bowl of popcorn. Carly was slumped against Howard's shoulder like his adoring sister.

While not exactly compliant with Howard, Carly seemed to listen. Though she seldom met anyone's gaze head-on, Carly would turn her long-lashed doe eyes to Howard plaintively at times, and we felt she was trying to project her muted thoughts directly into his mind. Perhaps Carly responded to Howard differently because he was a guy, someone with a different approach or style. Or maybe it was because he was willing to brainstorm new approaches and not merely follow the ABA rules. Howard had an endless repertoire of activities to keep Carly physically active and engaged. Carly sensed in Howard someone who would never give up on her; someone who saw past the toileting accidents and outbursts, the screaming and destruction. Howard demanded more from Carly than anyone else. One afternoon I found him leading Carly down the sidewalk wearing in-line skates, a skill I never would have thought to teach my daughter. Carly's sticklike legs were rigidly shuffling along the pavement as she grasped Howard's arm with both hands. She looked determined, if not amused.

The years approaching adolescence were formative for all of us. At times, our household felt like some grand social experiment more than it did a family. Space and time were filled with therapists, clipboards, charts, and paraphernalia. Taryn took it all in stride, seeming not to notice. She was figuring out who she was through her hobbies, school, and activities. She was easy to please, upbeat, and bubbly. As long as she had her friends around her and an activity to engage in, she beamed. Somehow in the shadow of autism, Taryn continued to bloom. Matthew was eager to help, sometimes going overboard with a label gun, making our house look like a giant tag sale. He looked up to Howard like a big brother, and I'd often find him helping Howard with tasks or emulating the clipped style in which therapists gave Carly direction. I could see the devotion to his sister, even when he was a young child.

After three or four years of ABA, it was evident that we would not have the same outcome as the family who had introduced us to it in the first place. The rewards were meager, and yet there were rewards. We persevered, propelled by Howard and Barb's devotion and the data provided by therapists indicating small improvements. I came to think of us as a slow-grinding train. I couldn't fathom our destination, but took solace in the belief that we were at least moving forward.

7

A Sinking Feeling

Although Carly was learning, her insomnia and hyperactivity were worsening. She had taken to grabbing forks, knives, or other utensils and sharply hitting the edges of the marble counters in our kitchen. Even after we had them repaired, years later they still look as if they've been gnawed by gerbils. Stillness defied Carly's personal law of nature. We had not reentered the terrifying waters of respite care since she was five, but with our nerves frayed, we were ready to jump overboard again. That we hadn't killed one another in the ensuing months after our last respite experience was testament to the endurance of the human spirit.

Carly was now toilet trained, attending a public school program with an aide, and receiving intensive ABA therapy every afternoon and on weekends. But getting her to this point—the logistics and planning, the cajoling of school boards and staff, and struggling to finance Carly's complex life—sucked all our spirit. With my work schedule, I was of little assistance except at night and on weekends, so most of the role of managing Carly's life fell to Tammy.

We had no breaks from the mayhem that ruled our house other than occasional weekend day programs, our nanny, or an iron-willed babysitter. One evening Tammy and I went to a farewell party for a colleague at a small restaurant downtown. A friend of Tammy's who lived down the street had a teenage daughter named Samantha who was more grown-up than most of the adults we knew, so when she offered to babysit for a few hours, we took her up on it. We had gotten Carly ready for bed and hoped all Samantha would have to do was read to her and tuck her in. Taryn and Matthew could help out—or at least take care of themselves.

At about 9:30 that night I glanced at my cell and noticed I had missed six phone calls from the house and one from a number I didn't recognize. The party had been so noisy that I hadn't heard the ringer. When I finally picked up, it was Samantha's mother—and she didn't sound very happy. It seemed that Carly had been out of control and Samantha had been trying to reach us for over an hour. When she didn't get through, she had called her mother in for backup. Carly had pooped in her bed, and the teen wasn't sure what to do. I guess the other kids she babysat for didn't use their beds as toilets. That was the last time she offered to babysit.

Our resolve had worn thin. Nights were still sleepless. Days chaotic. Even something as simple as an evening out was becoming impossible. Maintaining a cadre of well-trained, capable staff for weekend support was a full-time job and an enormous expense. Despite the unsettling experience with Caring Friends, we began exploring respite options again.

Through a friend of Tammy's, we met a young woman who worked for an organization called Riverside Autism Services. Riverside focused mainly on the needs of adults with autism, but they also dabbled in some youth support. Zoe was one of their regional managers and despite her bulging caseload, she agreed to meet with us at our house one evening. We discussed how we needed a break from Carly, but our breaks had often backfired, causing more heartache than comfort. I was humbled by Zoe's willingness to voluntarily tangle with the autism monster. At 8:00 p.m., her day was going on twelve hours and she still had a forty-five-minute commute home after our meeting.

"It's fine," she reassured me when I apologized a second time for the late hour. "I meet with most of my families at night." I saw no weariness in her explanation, only optimism and fortitude.

We explained our trepidation of any type of group facility. "Carly really needs one-on-one supervision," we told Zoe. "She's a flight risk. And if she's not engaged, she will either sit and rock, or get into trouble."

"There *are* options," she reassured us. "It's true, most of the clients we support are older. But I'm sure we can come up with a solution."

Several weeks later, Zoe phoned to say she had found a suitable respite program for Carly. One of the residential facilities Riverside ran was a home about twenty minutes from ours. It was inhabited during the week by a young man. His workers had discovered how much he enjoyed being in the country and, in particular, on a farm. They had arranged for him to spend several weekends a month north of Toronto, and thus the three-bedroom house he lived in in the city would be empty.

"This will be perfect for Carly," Zoe told us. At most, there might be one other child in the home when Carly was there, but she'd have her own room and plenty of supervision. On some weekends, she would be the only one. It would be lonely, we thought, but at least there would be no chance of her being overlooked.

"And because it's part of a bigger regional program," Zoe

continued, "they will include Carly in their outings and activities with other kids and young adults. We have a van."

Of course they did.

We girded ourselves for another exploration and headed out on a weekend morning to visit the home. Although only several miles west of us, it was a different world. The house was located in a once working-class neighborhood that now was home to the unworking class. The area did not strike me as dangerous-looking, but it had a fatigue I had come to associate with autism. The treeless lot was fenced in, and while there were a few other houses just like it up and down the street, high-rise apartments elbowed their way onto every block.

The man who regularly inhabited the home had autism and was blind. He lived unaware of the darkness; the worn, mismatched furniture; the ceiling light over the laminated kitchen table in the dining room hanging askance, one glass bulb-cover missing. Carly, on the other hand, could see, and it saddened me to think of her being sent to such a dreary place.

The day we visited, there was a teenage girl at the house for the weekend. "Her name is Carla," said Victoria, the woman managing the house. Tammy and I looked at each other, our eyes like saucers at the coincidence.

When we went to see the bedroom where Carly would stay, Carla was sitting on her bed rocking. She did not look up when we entered, made no acknowledgment of our arrival in her personal space. Tammy gasped slightly. Although maybe sixteen years old, Carla had the same lost look in her eyes that Carly wore so often. She was dressed in clean, simple clothing selected more for the convenience of caregivers than for fashion. Her light brown hair pulled back in a ponytail looked much the same as Carly's. Too much like Carly's.

For a moment I felt as if I were peering through a portal to the future, and a cloud of nausea passed over me. I looked at the young woman, trying to connect with her. "Hi," I said hopefully. "I have a daughter named Carly who may come to stay here once in a while."

Carla did not respond. She continued to stare at some other place, her eyes offering no sign she'd heard me. I wondered if she had already given up trying to escape her body and was resigned to this existence. She looked neither sad nor happy, just vacant, the way I've seen gorillas look at the zoo. Her room was a nondescript bedroom—a room with no signs that it actually belonged to any-one. Bare and soulless as a cheap motel room. Maybe rock posters and body spray would have been a nice touch. What hope was she being offered anyway? I wondered.

I asked Victoria about the girl's wrists. They were oddly wrapped in gauze and elastic. "She chews at them. We have to keep her wrists bandaged to protect them," she said with her strong, kind voice. There was no evidence of judgment or pity. It was a statement. It was what this girl does. She rocks and chews.

Tammy stepped into the hall. She was crying now, soft sobs, her chin on her chest. I looked away. This *cannot* be Carly. Not ever. I bit down on the inside of my lip. If she descended this far, could we ever reach her?

Back downstairs, Victoria took Tammy's arm with a compassion I found calming. Victoria spoke with a strong Jamaican accent that lilted. "I know," she said, looking directly into Tammy's eyes, as if answering an unasked question. "It's gonna be awright."

I had come to despise the residential facility workers who seemed *too* sweet. I didn't trust them. I couldn't help but feel they were putting on an act for us, desperate parents, and that a darker side would emerge once our backs were turned. I despised even more the cranky ones who no longer even bothered to hide their disdain for the people they were hired to care for. Victoria, however, had a sincerity that warmed even the shabbiness of the house and I caught my breath again.

Standing in the living room, preparing to leave, I noted the quiet of the house. A bit melancholy, but peaceful, unlike the other facilities we had visited. Those places were filled with the sounds of autism, as uncontrolled and startling as the birdcage at the zoo. Though worn, this house was calm.

We drove home in silence, as we always did after the disturbing experiences that life with Carly brought. Both of us were too gouged and raw to talk. I was haunted by the images of Carla lost somewhere inside herself. She looked as empty as a discarded vessel. But what if she were full of thoughts and dreams, or worse, anger? Not a something, but a someone.

Carly, please forgive me for asking you to stay here. Please don't hate me forever. Please don't feel abandoned and lose hope and start chewing your hands raw until they need to be taped up.

My sense of desperation gave way to a new emotion: fear. Hands-gone-cold, short-shallow-breath fear. Like claustrophobia, I felt boxed in unlike ever before.

But I could not say a word to Tammy. She looked out the window of the passenger seat, silent. Matthew and Taryn were kids, and Carly was Carly, and Tammy was sinking, and I had to be strong. In this moment, I had no words. And small talk would be as distasteful as dancing at a funeral.

As I drove, I tried to force Carla from my mind, instead filling it with thoughts about my evening routine with Carly. Dinner, then a bath, then into bed to read. After toweling off, Carly would insist on applying a cloyingly sweet-scented skin cream, so she could breathe in the fragrance. One dab on the front of each hand and then the back. On each forearm and then just above the knee. Always in that order, or the disruption to the routine would send her into a frenzy and we'd have to start again.

Then into her bed with its heavy quilt, as if the weight could stop her restlessness. What will we read tonight, Carly? *The Gypsy Princess, Ramona the Pest, Harriet the Spy*? She sat up, hands over her ears. *Brrr. Brrrr. Brrrr. Mmmmm.* Did she listen? She didn't run away, so I believed she did. I would stop reading for a moment and scoop her in my arms in a bear hug, just to feel her as my child. She was small and thin for her age. Her eyes slightly down-turned but beautiful. Her skin fair and soft. As I held her I imagined we were having a silent conversation. Sometimes I would whisper to her, "I know you're in there, Carly. I know you understand." Though I knew no such thing.

I tried to block out the images of respite care and dreary houses and strangers watching over my daughter. And mostly to not think about the sadness I felt when I saw Carla. I cannot bear to think these two girls shared a similar fate. If I lathered on enough body lotion, held her tightly enough, read loud enough often enough, could I stop Carly's descent?

I gripped the steering wheel, whitening my knuckles, staring straight ahead. I didn't say a word. My muscles tight, I sat rigidly. If you saw me like this, you would not be able to tell what I was thinking, if I was thinking.

As I escaped into my silence, I wondered if Carly and I were really so very different.

8

Uncommon

Experts tell us that those afflicted with autism live in their own spheres. Their universe looks odd to us, and ours is overwhelming for them. But the families with autism also live in a netherworld. We are not a part of the autistic child's domain, nor are we fully a part of society. I noted that friends could pack up the kids and take off, coming home relaxed and recharged. That would never be us. We lived life as one giant special provision, and it felt like a force field was holding us back from joining in.

I just wanted to be normal. Nonexceptional. Not requiring a précis, an introduction, or an explanation. It felt like we always needed an excuse for why we preferred the secluded booth at the back of the restaurant where Carly's noises would go unnoticed. Or an apology for why I was cranky or sleepy in the middle of the day. Or a reason why we couldn't attend an event at someone's house for fear of Carly blowing through the house like Hurricane Rita. Our friends were always welcoming of us, but they needn't have worried about our accepting an invitation with Carly. There was nothing restful about a dinner party where Tammy or I were on duty to keep Carly corralled—away from anything that could be stained, broken, or mangled.

This sense of self-imposed isolation was often a topic of conversation between Tammy and me. Once at a large family event in Boston, I looked around the room surveying all the other guests with their children. The adults mingled, laughed, and danced. The kids jumped around to the music and ran in and out of the crowd. We had left Carly at home with her babysitter, as family trips without help weren't even imaginable. Matthew, who was twelve at the time, had left the noisy party to wait outside. He found large crowds and loud environments overwhelming. Taryn, who *lived* for parties, was having a blast playing with her cousins and dancing. Only one out of all five of us seemed able to jump in. Tammy and I stood at the edge of the crowd, and looked on. We did not belong. It seemed like everything about us was just weird. Our Portuguese water dog hated to get wet, our cat was on antidepressants for "inappropriate urination," and attending family events was *work*, not pleasure. I began to wonder if there was anything *not* odd about us.

We fought the slippery slope that could lead to isolation. We tried to do what other families did. What people on TV shows and movies did. What we did ourselves, in the years BC, Before Carly.

One summer when the girls were still small, we took the entire family on vacation to Vermont. Another summer it was a cottage by a lake in upstate New York. We kept to ourselves for the most part. Carly would take short walks and swim. While Carly was still a toddler, she could fit in a bike trailer and happily doze and watch the world whiz past. But the risk of meltdowns or food flinging kept us on guard and on the move.

In 1999, we packed up the van and drove to Lake Placid. We

stayed in a small cluster of cabins that had the reassuring smell of pine paneling and dampness. The screened-in porch faced a lush green yard that sloped down to a lake. We had become accustomed to searching for venues with gradual water entries so Carly could slowly wade in. The weather that summer was unseasonably cold, but it didn't stop the kids from splashing in the water and scrunching their toes through the puttylike silt on the water's edge. We explored the Olympic Village where Tammy, Matthew, and Taryn rode the bobsled track that had been turned into a cart ride. Carly dozed in her oversized stroller, so I waited at the bottom. In the evenings, we sometimes stopped at Mountain Mist, a soft ice cream stand near town. The hand-painted signs, screened service windows, yellow bug lights, and white-uniformed, fresh-faced girls serving the swirls of ice cream on Styrofoam-like cones hadn't changed in half a century. I felt like my father, taking my family on a 1960s road trip.

I only recall one reality jolt during that week: a full-plate-toss freak-out at lunch in a small-town luncheonette. The impetus for the outburst is of little consequence—it seldom is. The result, however, required a hasty retreat, an apology with gazes averted, and a large tip for the unfortunate waiter who was left with the mess.

On our way home, we drove through Vermont. My wife had heard about the Shelburne Museum and thought it would keep our mismatched clan's attention for a few hours. We were encouraged by everyone's good spirits and so attempted one of the exhibits, the large period home belonging to the museum's founder. With the requisite warning to Taryn and Matthew not to touch anything, we pushed Carly up the ramp in her oversized stroller. "You can't bring the stroller in," a security guard as old as the house said.

"It's kind of like a wheelchair for her," I explained. "My daughter has a disability."

I had gotten used to trying to give context to those for whom

Carly was a mystery. Her legs, arms, and hands work, maybe too well. She's *hyper*-mobile. "I think it's better for everyone if my daughter stays in her stroller," I said. For a moment his rheumy eyes squinted slightly as he looked at Carly. I was hopeful he would concede as Tammy and the other two started to walk past him.

"Sorry," he repeated, standing blocking the entrance.

"You don't allow disabled people in?" I asked. A hint of sarcasm.

"Strollers have to stay out," he stonewalled.

"It's the only way she can get around without getting into trouble," hoping his sense of empathy for the collectibles on display would eclipse his commitment to following the rule book.

"We don't allow strollers into the house," he concluded.

I left to take a walk while the other three wandered in. There are battles worth escalating and others worth just swearing about later.

As Carly got older, family holidays became more daunting. As we were now no longer able to constrain her, it meant that someone had to constantly be holding her hand. And since sending her off to play with her siblings was not an option, it meant we all had to keep moving, like nomads. Staying home where we had a team of people to help us seemed like a more restful option.

One summer we went with our friends the Shepherds to the mountains north of Montreal called the Laurentians. Their two eldest children were close in age with our kids and often played together. Their youngest was around two, and we reasoned that we'd have similar needs, since both families had one kid that would require extra care. "We can ask Mari if she'd be willing to come," Tammy suggested. "She can watch over Sam and Carly if we want to go out with the other kids for a little while. At least we'll be able to eat dinner without chasing Carly."

We knew some families traveled with their nannies, but it was something I rolled my eyes at. It struck me as bourgeois and a little affected. However, when we were presented with the alternative of not taking a summer vacation, or worse, taking one by ourselves without the help, it seemed like a brilliant solution.

While not a completely relaxing week, the experience opened our eyes to the possibility of entourage vacations. Having extra hands made getting through the day easier. Carly's lack of sleep meant, in fairness, we had to choose between either giving Mari extra time off during the day to nap because she had stayed up with Carly at night or staying up with Carly ourselves. But it was a trade-off that for us no longer seemed odd or onerous. The reward was that I had a few beautiful photographs of Carly sitting by the lake, gazing dreamily at the sunrise, we have memories that we still talk about, and we got to behave like we imagined others did, if even for just a week.

The pursuit of normal means compromise. You get a vacation, but not without help. You can sleep at night, but not relax during the day—or relax during the day but be up at night. You can take two kids go-karting, but not the third. Almost normal.

As we had survived the two-week break and even enjoyed ourselves, we attempted it again the following year. This time, Howard joined us as Carly's one-on one camp counselor. He took her on paddleboats, horseback riding, and go-karting. His job was to keep her in constant motion while we relaxed. At twenty-three years old, he didn't seem to mind.

On one of the first afternoons, as the adults were hanging out by the lake and the other kids were building cities out of sand, Howard and Carly jogged down the lawn toward us, with Carly in her swimsuit. We had not known Carly to be much of an athlete, but Howard had been taking her to community swim, and she seemed to enjoy it. I watched in horror as Carly darted down the dock several hundred yards *ahead* of Howard. Before anyone could move, Carly ran off the end of the dock and jumped into the cold lake.

Tammy and I jumped to our feet with a gasp as Howard calmly walked down the dock. I looked on in utter amazement as Carly crudely dog-paddled alongside the dock back toward land.

"What the hell?" I asked Howard.

"Carly loves the water," he said matter-of-factly. "She's been swimming like that for a few months now."

I began to realize that Howard knew Carly far better than I did. As she reached the shore and stripped off her wet bathing suit, Howard answered before I could ask: "She hates wet clothes," he explained, as if introducing me to a stranger. I wondered how many parents need a twenty-three-year-old kid to help them make sense of their child.

For a few years, taking a trip with Howard to support Carly seemed to work. But when Howard got married, traveling with us became more challenging. And as Carly headed into adolescence, her behavior became more erratic and chaotic. Vacations together were anything but time off. We had started to meet other families through the autism advocacy work Tammy did who were clawing their way through a similar path. "You and the other kids still deserve a life," one said to us. "Just go away without Carly. You have a nanny and therapists."

The first time we did, I noticed Carly seemed agitated when she saw our suitcases in the hall. "Do you think she cares that we're leaving her behind?" I asked.

"Please don't ask that," Tammy answered.

The winter holiday period seemed to be the worst for us. The change in schedule, high expectations of joy, and lack of support staff due to the statutory holiday all conspired to make the Yuletide gray. But clearly we were not alone in the struggle to maintain a semblance of a normal family life. One year, a friend's twenty-year-old autistic son had what she termed a *freak-out*. Maybe it was the color of Aunt Rose's sweater or the parsley in the stuffing. It never really matters what sets off a person with autism. Whatever it was resulted in six police officers escorting the young man—who can become violent, much to his own remorse—to the local emergency room in handcuffs, where he had to be sedated. She later sardonically posted on her Facebook status, "So *this* is Christmas."

Like our autism brethren, we learned to spend time with our other kids, together in twos and fours though seldom as five because if it were five, then it would be six—Carly always had a helper in tow.

Tammy and I did our best to institute date night, even if it was just going out to a movie to sit in the dark quietly and not move.

And as Carly grew from toddler to child to adolescent, we formed our own odd reality. It was a place of good enough. Not perfect for her, certainly not perfect for us. But compromises are the staff of life. I stopped thinking of us as a traveling sideshow. While not typical, for us, this was about as normal as it would get.

Another Dream

The same dream I have at least once a month. Just a different situation. Carly is perseverating, stuck in a spin cycle of some repetitive behavior. The socks all have to be out of the drawer, or the plates all have to be off the table, or she has to wash her hands five more times, soap on the front, soap on the back, then repeat. Classic OCD. This is part of the dream, but it is real life, too.

I am roiling with frustration. In my dream this has been going on all day and I'm at my busting-open point. Probably because it has also been going on all day for real. I yell, "Stop. E-nough," and slap her just hard enough to hurt me. "This is not fair," I plead.

"No, it's not fair," Carly cries. Then, "Mom. MOM. Dad slapped me."

We look at each other in utter disbelief at the words from the broken machinery of her mouth.

I hug her in tears that will not stop. Now I am the one perseverating. We run to tell Tammy of how a slap cured Carly.

I'm beginning to dread sleep, but wonder if it will be the only place I will ever hear my little girl's voice.

Part II

❧

A Voice Inside

And after the fire a still small voice.
—*1 Kings 19:12*

9

Breaking the Silence

Q: @CarlysVoice: Carly, do you think what you are able to do is a miracle?
A: No, it took me a long time and a lot of hard work. Even before i spelled I communicated with picture symbols and had a lot of therapy. It did not happen over night and i worked so hard to get to this point.

"Carly's been writing all day," Howard said excitedly into the phone.

"She's been doing what?!" I yelled back.

I was swerving down Route 64 from the south rim of the Grand Canyon toward Flagstaff. It was March 10, 2005—spring vacation—and Tammy and I had decided to take Taryn and Matthew away for a break in the routine. Years before, Tammy and I had fallen in love with the isolating openness of the Arizona and New Mexican desert. Somehow the ocean of multicolored sand interrupted by sun-toasted red clay mesas and grandfatherly Saguaro cacti brought us peace. We had made several trips to the Southwest in the years before autism framed our life. Now that Carly was ten years old, we needed solitude more than ever.

As we descended the mountains and drove south watching the outdoor thermometer in the rental car rise from just above freezing to nearly 80 degrees, my cell phone rang. The reception was frustratingly broken. As best I could make out, and what I repeated to my wife and children, was that Barb and Howard had been working with Carly all afternoon, and she had been typing out words and short phrases on her voice output device. To date, they had been using the electronic unit as a sophisticated picture book with a voice. Carly would touch the picture of the items or activities and the digitized voice would approximate a conversation. It was primitive, but less so than Carly's frustrated wails, finger pointing, and grabbing.

We lost the phone connection. I sat silently, absorbing the news, when the phone rang again moments later, and I put it on speaker so we all could hear Howard.

He told us that he had spent the afternoon clearing items from the voice output device to free up memory in anticipation of Barb arriving for her appointment with Carly. "I was going to delete the alphabet function," he said. "She isn't using it for much. We need more space for additional pictures and symbols." Had he deleted that, what happened that afternoon might never have happened. Or at least not for many months.

He reported that Carly was restless and cranky that day; whining, running around the room, unwilling to complete her tasks. "What do you want?" Barb asked, her voice edged with exasperation. "Sit down and help us understand what you need." Barb corralled Carly back to her chair at their worktable. To their astonishment, Carly reached across to grab the device and touched the alphabet screen, slowly tapping out the letters *"H-E-L-P T-E-E-T-H H-U-R-T"* with her right index finger.

Barb and Howard were stunned. In the past few months, with

the help of therapists, Carly had learned to identify images and colors, and even developed basic math and vocabulary skills. In addition, they had worked with her on fine motor skills like cutting, pasting, and drawing—all the things that should come naturally to a small child but were seemingly impossible tasks for our autistic ten-year-old.

But she had never spontaneously expressed herself or communicated feelings of any kind. Nothing that had happened in previous days would have prepared them for what they just witnessed.

At first speechless, Barb and Howard hovered over Carly as if she were waking from a decade-long coma. Howard ran upstairs in search of Tylenol, thrilled to comply with her plea for help. Carly ran behind the couch and vomited.

Howard bounded back down the stairs. They cleaned Carly up, hugged her, and cheered, tears in their eyes.

After years of isolation, the miraculous breakthrough had them floored with joy.

And now Howard was trying to recount this to us through a bad wireless connection. Feeling somewhat confused by the news, we said good-bye, agreeing to phone when we reached the hotel later that afternoon.

"Well?" I turned to Tammy as we continued driving. The other kids were silent in the backseat. Anyone who knew Carly as we did would be incredulous. Spelling independently? Words with meaning? Not Carly. How could she? She was a girl who still had toileting accidents. A child whose only words were garbled sounds, and whose tantrums and destructive acts were her strongest skills. This is not a child who writes, we thought. This is not even a child who understands. Carly is "cognitively impaired." Isn't that what all the doctors had been telling us for ten years?

"Do you think it's possible?" Tammy asked, one eyebrow cocked and a dubious smile on her face.

"I know how badly Barb and Howard want it to be," I said, feeling both eyebrows rise. "It's possible they're exaggerating. Or that they helped her." I bit my lip and tried to digest what I had just heard myself say. I've heard that denial is a way of coping with grief. But I also think it works when we are confronted with something that violently disrupts our worldview. It wasn't that I doubted Barb and Howard's veracity, but what they were telling me was as incomprehensible as learning that a relative believed to be dead was in fact alive. My heart and head raced as I played the scene out in my mind over and over.

We drove in an electrified silence. Matthew and Taryn had stopped baiting each other in the backseat of the rental car. They recognized that this was not a trivial moment and were temporarily shocked into uncharacteristic muteness.

"There must be some sort of syndrome that affects, you know, people who work closely with disabled people. Sort of a Stockholm syndrome," I finally offered. Tammy and I trusted Barb and Howard completely, but we weren't sure if we could imagine that Carly was writing exactly as they were telling us.

"They wouldn't do that," Tammy said. Or was she asking?

We drove on in a pensive quiet for a while longer. "What exactly did he say again?" Tammy asked, as if the event was slowly seeping into her consciousness. I repeated the story over and over as we picked at it like investigators exploring a mystery.

"Figures," I finally concluded. "We're three thousand miles away and Carly finally has a breakthrough." But I was smiling as I thought of Carly; possibly for the first time in a long, long time.

Tammy and I had supported the therapists' efforts to find some means of helping Carly communicate, but neither of us had much hope of Carly ever becoming proficient at any of these skills. She remained trapped in a noisy and chaotic muteness. As we watched our other children mature into their 'tween and teen years, Carly was still a mystery to us; the child we didn't really know. One of her psychological-education reports noted that Carly seemed to have receptive understanding of about fifty words by the time she was six or seven. If that trend continued, she should have understood only about one hundred to two hundred at the point she spelled for Barb—approximately the number of words in a well-versed two-year-old's vocabulary. We really had no idea, though, what she did and did not understand.

When we returned home from our trip, we quickly realized that this small portal into Carly's world would be one that opened and closed, randomly and capriciously. Days would pass and she wouldn't type a single word with Barb or Howard. And never with Tammy, her siblings, or me. In fact, it would be months before I would actually see Carly type at all, further fueling my skepticism. In my head, I knew what Howard and Barb told me was true, but who could blame me for asking why, if she could type, did she consistently refuse to do so? The following months left me in a hopeful limbo.

At Barb's suggestion, we labeled everything in the house to help Carly learn how to spell. "We're going to take a whole new approach to teaching her," she said. "We need to move away from sign language, pictures, and symbols. This kid needs to type." Barb would now shift her meticulous, painstaking approach from matching words and pictures, and coaxing tiny syllables from Carly's mouth, to labeling her world with words and letters and forcing her to type them out. It all sounded so promising and deluded at the same time. But Barb, like Howard, has a way of proselytizing. They don't so much *suggest* as *tell*. Both share a calm intensity and patience that is required of those who work with the disabled. But, unlike any other team of therapists we had worked with, their creativity in coming up with new solutions and ideas suggested that they never stopped thinking about Carly, even when they were off the clock.

So through the summer of 2005, stickers began appearing all over our house. Mirrors, windows, doors, and cupboards were marked, making our house look like a bizarre 3-D how-to manual. To this day, I still come across random stickers on pieces of furniture, nooks, and crannies like archeological artifacts. Barb looked for ways to make Carly use letters and words, even when she wouldn't type. "Write out a list of choices on a piece of paper," she told us. "Make her point to what she wants." Over time, we realized Carly knew far more than we had imagined. Howard and Barb cooked up schemes to force Carly into the world of words. They handed her a juice box without a straw and made her point to the word *straw* before giving her one. Anything she wanted she would work for.

With Howard and Barb, Carly began to have occasional short conversations, tapping out one letter at a time with her right index finger. It could sometimes take an entire hour for Carly to complete a three-word sentence. But they were words. Words with meaning.

One afternoon while working Carly accidentally hit one of her therapists, Dina. When Howard explained that Dina was hurt, Carly spontaneously typed "*sorry*" with no help. We had been told that children with autism don't exhibit empathy. Over time we would start questioning many things we had been told about Carly.

Was it possible there was more to Carly's personality than we had thought? After all, Carly *was* autism. Autism, tantrums, and neediness. When you raise a severely disabled child, you begin to see the flaws above all else. There were momentary smiles; infrequent heartwarming acts of love, such as a snuggle and a giggle. But there was a wall that couldn't be breached, locking her in and us out. Bit by bit, now a few stones were beginning to crumble.

After Carly had been writing for about a year, we started to see more clarity and complexity in her writing. Startlingly, for the most part, her spelling was correct, her diction and grammar almost flawless.

When Barb showed up for her session one afternoon, Howard informed her that Carly had been writing in full thoughts all day. Barb gave him her inquisitive look, her head half-turned, a slight furrow in her brow. She didn't exactly doubt him, but she needed to see exactly what he meant with her own eyes.

So when Carly returned from the bathroom that afternoon, she took hold of her DynaWrite and tapped out, *"Look I will work for food."* I think Barb and Howard fell off their chairs. Rather than a few basic words, our daughter had full cogent thoughts. Even more, she had an attitude. A colleague of mine has an adult brother with autism. We used to joke that he and Carly probably sat in their rooms at night scheming and laughing at the rest of us. Although they didn't speak, perhaps they had full-blown dialogues going on in their heads. I paused to ponder this observation and realized we had probably not been far from the truth.

"Will you type for Taryn?" Barb asked her later that afternoon.

"No way," she wrote.

Barb smiled at Carly's use of typical 'tween slang. Barb and Howard pushed on, curious to see where this would go. After an explosive bout of whining and crying, Carly returned to her computer and painstakingly responded, *"you are mean. Ill stop spelling. Stop. I want to play."*

When Carly couldn't come up with anything specific to do, Barb suggested they go outside. *"Outside,"* Carly readily spelled.

"How about taking a drive to my house?" Barb asked.

The floodgate of words had been opened, and Barb wanted to see what else would flow forth. They climbed into Howard's car, thinking they could contain Carly in one place and get her to write more. *"I want to go Barb house for food,"* Carly offered. Her teachers were eager to comply. Once on the road, however, Carly flipped out. It started with a plaintive whine and sobbing and then escalated as Carly grabbed at Howard, who was in the driver's seat, while she was buckled in behind him. She flopped back in the seat of the car over and over, screaming and crying, throwing herself hard against the constraints of the safety belt.

"What's wrong? What's going on?" they asked over and over.

When they finally arrived at Barb's several minutes later and turned off the car, Carly calmed sufficiently to respond.

"You need a seat belt," Carly observed. Sheepishly, Howard acknowledged he hadn't fastened his when leaving our house.

Once at Barb's house, the duo couldn't help but push Carly further to see what else she might have to say. We had already learned that for Carly, food is a great motivator. Salty snacks are king. Popcorn, French fries, crackers, even pickles are her weakness. The Ruler Supreme of all motivators was Lay's potato chips. I think we could get her to walk across a fire pit of burning coals for a single chip.

"Carly, type five words and I'll give you the chips," promised Barb.

A small, sly smile seemed to cross Carly's face.

"Five words," she typed.

Barb and Howard burst out laughing, shaking their heads in disbelief.

"Okay, you win," said Barb, doling out five chips.

"Just give me the bloody chips okay," typed Carly.

"How did she learn *that* expression?" asked Howard in amused shock.

They moved to Barb's den to give Carly a well-deserved break. However, when Carly noticed Barb's husband, Barry, relaxing on the sofa with his newspaper and a bowl of popcorn, her impulsive nature took hold and she grabbed violently. "Stop," said Barb. "If you want something, you must ask for it." She pushed the DynaWrite in front of Carly. Carly flew into a rage and threw herself on the floor. The flopping, kicking, and crying were nothing new to Howard and Barb. But Barry, not having been calloused by firsthand experience with Carly over the years, quickly gave in to her demands and handed her the bowl of popcorn.

Having turned the game in her favor, Carly sat down at the table in the next room with the computer in front of her and coyly typed to Barb, *"I want nice man."*

As Howard and Barb shook their heads in satisfied amazement at Carly's quick mastery of emotional manipulation, Carly chided, *"I need salt."*

As years of noisy silence died, a prima donna was born.

Excerpt from psychological assessment, April 2006:

Dr. Susan Marcotte, PhD, C. Psych
Registered Pyschologist
Carly's parents have requested a full-psycho-educational assessment of Carly to provide an updated account of her cognitive and academic profile to determine her areas of strength and learning needs . . .

The consistency in school, classroom and educational assistant appears to have been helpful to Carly. Most notably, there was a period of time during the 2002/2003 school year that Carly did not receive ABA within the classroom, during which time she was seen to regress. Once her ABA therapy programs were reintroduced within the classroom, her behavior began to improve noticeably.

Carly seems to have progressed in nonverbal areas of the academic curriculum . . . she appears to have relatively stronger

problem solving skills. With her ABA therapist, she is demonstrating skills to type words and concepts. She will type her
responses consistently for familiar people.

DEVELOPMENTAL SKILLS

A variety of measures were utilized to examine developmental
skills . . . Previously, her skills were assessed to be within the
"Well Below Average" range (<1 percentile), consistent with a
1 year, 10 month level. The Wechsler Individual Achievement
Test and the Peabody Individual Achievement Test were used
to evaluate current levels of achievement in the areas of reading
comprehension, spelling, general mathematics, and math computational skills. (Only subtests that could be administered in
a multiple choice or written output format were administered
given Carly's verbal output and fine motor difficulties.) . . .
Carly generally demonstrated academic skills at approximately
Grade 3 level with the exception of her math computational
skills, which are weaker at a Grade 1 level. While Carly's academic skills may not be in the average range of functioning,
they do suggest continued academic progress.

In summary, Carly is an 11 year old girl who continues to
present with Autism in addition to a severe communication disorder. Previously, Carly's presentation was also indicative of a
Moderate Developmental Disability. However, during the current assessment Carly demonstrated considerable progress in
being able to learn and share her knowledge and she was able
to demonstrate perceptual reasoning skills within the Average
range.

10

ⁿᵉˢᵉ

From a Whisper to a Shout

I want to say to all the autism experts that keep on saying that I'm not really writing that you proved that you are not an autism expert.

—Carly

During the first months that Carly was typing, she used various pieces of equipment known as voice output devices. One, the DynaVox, was a red plastic box with a touchscreen face that could be programmed with picture symbols of things Carly may want. Different food items, activities, even emotions. Carly would carry the DynaVox around on a strap, slung like a purse over her shoulder. The device, however, had no printing option, leaving it as mute as Carly. Like a personal secretary, Barb would copy down word for word both sides of any conversation on her pad of yellow-lined paper and give it to us at the end of each session with a list of recommendations. Once we bought Carly a laptop, Barb would type the spoken dialogue in between Carly's writing, like a court reporter.

A few other therapists had witnessed Carly typing, but we hadn't seen it ourselves yet. And any time they took out a video camera to film Carly, she stopped typing. I'm sure they were worried that we didn't believe them, but for how long would anyone trust that Carly could type full, cogent thoughts without actually seeing it? Given her behavior for the past decade and everything we'd been told about her prognosis, I was more likely to believe our dog could speak.

"Are you ready to show Mom that you can spell?" Barb asked Carly. It was early fall of 2005 and Carly had recently had her second major breakthrough—typing in full sentences.

"she does not like me. She just likes my sister," Carly responded. Her words, in some ways, were all the more powerful because her face did not show any sense of emotion.

"Your mother loves you very much," Barb assured her. "What can she do to show that to you?"

Carly usually rebuffed hugs and kisses. Because we had so long assumed her cognition was far below that of her sister, our conversations with her were simple; seldom more than demands for compliance: "Carly, let's get dressed. Carly, let's go swimming. Carly, stay in your bed." We were constantly doing for Carly, but did she know how much we loved her? Did she know that seldom a moment of the day would pass without her creeping into our thoughts?

Barb and Howard were holding one of their after-school sessions at Barb's house. Carly led Barb into her living room and sat next to her on the sofa. With the voice output device on her lap, Carly was ready to open up and have a heart-to-heart with her confidante.

"I want Mom to spend time with me. With little me," Carly pouted. *"I want to go away with her like Taryn,"* she said, referring to a short trip Tammy had taken with Taryn a few months earlier. She went on to complain that we sent her away on weekends, referring to a weekly residential program she had begun to attend at a camp north of the city for children with autism.

Barb was winded. I'm not prepared for this, she thought. As a speech pathologist, she knew strategies to help kids communicate.

Now she felt she was being thrown into a much tougher role, that of a psychologist. In the eight years of working with Carly, she had never had a conversation with her, much less heard an emotional outpouring like this. She was terrified of wasting the moment, saying something wrong and losing Carly back down the dark tunnel of silence. I need a brilliant answer, she thought, and called to Howard, who was sitting just out of view in the hallway.

"You don't need to be a doctor," he said. "You have kids. Think like a mother."

Barb went on to reassure Carly of Tammy's commitment and love.

"This is something that your mother needs to hear, Carly. Can I tell your mother we discussed this?" Barb asked.

"Yes. But not that I spell," Carly replied, paying no attention to the impossibility of the task.

"How can I tell her if I don't tell her you spelled all this?" Barb pointed out.

"You will find a way," she said, cryptically.

"Carly, we are all so proud of you. You are making such great progress. You know, spelling is really going to help you out in the end. Just think, if you spell for people, you'll get the things you want. Do you think you can spell for your mom and dad?"

"No. Stop," she answered. Then, *"Maybe."*

Another glimmer of hope. Or was it? I'd like to say this revelation came with a watershed sense of relief. That would be a lie. Carly wouldn't type spontaneously. She would never sit down at a computer or use her voice output device and initiate conversation. If we attempted to place one in front of her, she would push it away as if it were Brussels sprouts. Getting her to write took coaxing and reinforcement, generally with potato chips. And she never spoke with Tammy, her siblings, or me unless Barb or Howard was at her side. Years later we would learn that what we thought was teen stubbornness was in fact OCD, obsessive-compulsive disorder. It wasn't that Carly didn't want to type with us; she was unable to force her body to do so unless the situation was exactly right for her. By right, it meant having Barb and Howard at her side.

Barb raced over to our house immediately after concluding her session with Carly. Tammy, Barb, and I sat on the back porch, a covered, open-air extension of our kitchen. It was a place Tammy and I would often escape to for an early-morning coffee or glass of wine in the evening. "Is it cocktail hour yet?" I would joke at nine in the morning after a particularly rough night. Even in the fall, though faded, the garden bloomed resiliently and the light was warm and golden.

Barb was tearful as she told us about the conversation. "She is so intelligent," she said. "She has an awareness, understanding, and feelings so much more sophisticated than any of us had imagined," she marveled. "She may look like she is not listening, or not understanding, but I think we know now that's probably not the case." The underlying knowledge of how hurt Carly felt for being treated like the ugly stepsister hung between the three of us as we silently sat sipping a drink.

"I don't know what to say," I lamely offered.

"I wish she would talk to us. Tell us how she feels," Tammy said.

"I wouldn't engage in a power struggle," Barb intuitively reasoned. "I would speak in front of her the same way you speak with Taryn. Don't say anything in her presence you wouldn't say to your other kids. Don't make her type just for practice or to please us; she knows how to spell. She'll type when it can be used to satisfy her own needs, not ours."

Carly's growing awareness was in *some* ways exciting; it meant she had intelligence far greater than we imagined. It also meant that the often-harsh language and brutal honesty that should have been reserved for moments behind closed doors had not been lost on her.

She was a silent witness to her life in our family. This realization left me with an overpowering sense of guilt. I was angry at myself and others who spoke hurtful words, mistakenly assuming they floated over Carly's head. I regretted every scolding and the callous comments I would make about Carly's behavior when speaking with others directly in front of her. Several years later she told us, *"You know how people talk behind people's back? With me, they talk in front of my back."*

Regret for our past, frustration in our present, and anxiety about our future created a vortex of emotion. Tammy looked thoughtful. She may have felt a sense of guilt in what Carly told Barb, but she did not let it show. My wife is a pragmatist and likely was already thinking ahead to what had to change in our life. We had to relearn how to be with our daughter. There were so many bad habits to break. While her outbursts and uncontrolled behavior would continue to limit the degree to which Carly would be able to participate in all aspects of our family life, we immediately ceased talking in front of her about events we believed were too challenging for her to handle.

We never did let on to Carly that Barb had spoken with us about feeling like a second-class citizen. Instead, we immediately made plans to experiment with a simple overnight vacation. Matthew was planning on spending a weekend with a friend and his family who had moved out of the city to what had been their country house. We told Carly we wanted to take her downtown to stay overnight in a hotel. "We can swim in the pool, go out for dinner, and watch TV in bed. Sound good?"

"Eh ess," she replied with what I imagined to be a gleeful smile.

"Should we invite Taryn?"

"Eh ess," she said a second time.

I was grateful that Carly's jealousy was not so deep-rooted that it would drive a wedge between the girls.

We began looking for little ways to include Carly in activities we had formerly thought would not interest her. As long as we had Howard at her side, we mustered the energy and confidence to venture back to restaurants, holiday dinners at friends', and even the occasional movie. Howard was able to cajole and convince Carly to behave in ways Tammy and I could not. And when Carly erupted into flailing tantrums, he had the patience to whisk her away and get her refocused. For both Tammy and me, the wailing set off internal chemical reactions that left us filled with despair. But Howard was firm and calm and seemingly unscathed by Carly's temperament.

I had so many questions to ask her. I still do. This awareness that Carly was so there but so unreachable made me despondent. I felt I was owed an explanation for what was going on inside her body that caused her outbursts or her compulsiveness. Yet on these points she was mute. Even when posed by her tireless pair of helpers, she would not answer questions that would offer any insight into her internal struggles. I would even have been satisfied with silly banter, the kind Taryn, Matthew, and I engaged in, about school, TV shows, or my annoying habit of speaking in imaginary foreign accents and making up tales of adventures in my fictional past. Carly, I'm sure, had an opinion about all of this. But she would not engage.

It was like having a buffet laid before me and then told not to partake. No manner of sly manipulation would break the stalemate. "What would you like for dessert, Carly?" I would ask. "Cake, cookies, or ice cream." We seldom even served dessert, but if it would get her typing, I'd gladly have served candy for breakfast. Carly would sit with her voice output device between us, rocking in her chair and humming. No dessert was served.

After she began typing, we cycled through various types of equipment hoping that Carly's recalcitrance could be assuaged. Each was met with a similar lack of enthusiasm. The energetic consultants at the agency that supplied the equipment would optimistically push a new version of the DynaWrite or some such device in front of Carly and inquire, "Do you like it?"

"No" Carly would choose from the words printed in front of her.

It would be several years before we understood why Carly refused to type on the light, quick, and convenient equipment. As she began telling us that she wanted to *"be normal, like my sister Taryn,"* it occurred to us that the devices that were intended to help her *join* our world instead made her feel more like one who does not belong. They made her feel like she was disabled; like she stood out from other kids her age. When I look back, I can only shake my head at the absurdity of the logic. The squawking, bleating, flopping, and flapping were much more obvious signs of her disability. But since these couldn't be controlled, Carly focused on the handful of things that could. She had no interest in a bright red plastic device with a strap worn over her shoulder that in effect said, "Disabled Kid Who Can't Speak."

Laptops were still expensive and relatively slow to start up compared to the devices offered to us, but we reasoned that it was a good alternative. No kid wants an "Augmentative Communication Device" emblazoned with a metal tag identifying it as leased from a government agency. But every kid wants their own computer. Thus began our love-hate relationship with technology. For the next three years we churned through numerous laptops as they were dropped, slammed shut, and choked to death with the detritus of potato chips and juice.

We began archiving our conversations with Carly. First, Carly typed only with Barb and Howard, the valiant magicians who pulled language out of her through her fingertip. Later, Carly began conversing with a few therapists, doctors, or workers that she bonded with—always with Howard by her side. Most of the time Carly worked either at our dining room or kitchen table, or at the round worktable set up in the basement. Her therapists would sit several feet away, one on either side, and they would pass the computer back and forth to Carly. Howard often sat to her right and kept a small bowl of chips in sight, but out of grasp. From the start, Barb and Howard were careful never to touch Carly as she typed. She was highly ritualistic because of her OCD, and they didn't want her to become dependent on physical encouragement. Their sessions sounded like a one-way conversation between adults. I could often hear the voices of Barb and Howard rise and fall, but I could never hear my daughter, or even the mechanical voice from her device or computer. Carly's written words would chronicle her childhood.

Bit by bit we were rewarded with glimpses of Carly's hidden personality. She was becoming like one of those cakes with the charms and coins baked in. I looked forward to coming home from work to find out if there was a little surprise. Had she unveiled anything of what was going on inside?

We once asked her why she kept dumping the contents of her dresser onto the floor or why she stripped her bed incessantly.

"I know I'm not supposed but I can't help myself. That's why I hit myself sometimes. I'm trying to stop my body from doing something it shouldn't."

In the long stretches when Carly would refuse to type in front of Tammy or me, Barb became a vocal advocate. She continuously reminded us to find ways to make Carly communicate with words. She developed a sheet of standard questions and laminated it, placing copies around the house and in a communication book. Rather than a binder of pictures and symbols alone, Carly now had pages of phrases, words, and concepts (*"I feel sad"*) that she could rifle through and point at to make herself understood. "I want her to feel like she's in control," Barb counseled us. "So much of her life is dictated to her, she needs to feel like the director now."

That Carly could begin expressing herself was a relief for all of us. It meant that over time, she would be assured of some measure of independence. Some of the walls isolating her from us could be breached. More amazing was the sense of self that was emerging. I felt like we were discovering the lost city of Angkor. As we hacked through the tangled vines and overgrowth that shrouded Carly from us, we were discovering a fully formed, intricate personality.

Keeping Carly busy was still one of our biggest goals. Because of her restlessness, there was no "just hanging out." Tammy found a winter holiday camp at a community center nearby that would keep her occupied while school was closed for the winter break. One of her therapists, Dina, agreed to supervise her, as the program was designed for nonchallenged kids. There were really very few programs for kids with autism, and what the hell, we thought, shouldn't she be around other kids whose behavior we wanted her to imitate? As long as those running the programs would have her, and the activities could be modified with her ABA therapist's assistance, we were game.

The camp week was successful. Interestingly, the other kids—all around nine or ten years old—warmly welcomed Carly. They were fascinated by her odd behavior, juxtaposed with her eagerness to be a part of the activity. I have always been heartened and amazed that kids welcome Carly far more than many adults do. I had anticipated a backlash or teasing, but over the years those have occurred infrequently. Somehow, even when she won't write, Carly has an ability to engage other children that I cannot explain. Perhaps it comes from her sudden smile and giggle: fleeting and surprising but infectious.

When Barb asked her the following week how she enjoyed the program, Carly was hesitant to write. Barb went on to ask her who was in her group.

"Boys," Carly answered.

Thinking she had opened the door, Barb went on asking questions but got no response. Finally, Barb hit on the idea of asking if she had flirted with the boys.

"*Yes*," Carly coolly answered.

Barb shot a look at Howard. "Do you think she knows what flirting is?" I'm not even sure Taryn understood the concept of flirting at the time. "What do you mean by 'flirting'?" Barb pressed her.

"*I gave them hugs and fliped my hair,*" Carly answered to the stunned silence of her teachers.

"Did you have a boyfriend there?"

"*Come on. I am too good looking,*" Carly concluded with an air of cockiness. She then signed "finished" by waving her hands, palm to chest, signaling she was done speaking for the day.

Tammy called Dina to tell her what Carly had written and see how she had been acting around the other kids.

"Oh my God," Dina replied, laughing. "I was wondering what she was doing. She kept hitting her hair."

By all accounts, our daughter should be devoid of self-confidence. She cannot speak, independently engage in activities, or even wash and care for herself. If we were to believe her words, however, she did not see herself as out of the game.

I give Tammy credit for nurturing Carly's self-esteem. "Why is it that they make these kids *look* so disabled?" she once asked me, referring to how teachers tied bandanas around the necks of kids who drooled or dressed them for the convenience of the caregivers in bibs and easy-fastening clothing. Tammy had always focused on making Carly look and feel as appropriate as her twin, by styling her hair and dressing her in the same types of jeans and shirts that her sister had. Carly was beautiful. At eleven, her awkward gangly body was filling out; her complexion was smooth and bright. In the years that would follow, we would learn that Carly saw herself as a typical kid locked in a body over which she had little control. I would like to think that by treating her similarly to her twin, we helped instill this sense of self.

As Carly's voice became stronger and steadier, we began to see a playfulness, coyness, and an ability to manipulate. Before she wrote, one schoolteacher noted that Carly was the only person she knew who didn't speak but could lie, referring to how Carly used her communication bracelet to request a bathroom break to avoid unpleasant tasks. But with words, Carly was proving that she could go head-to-head with the adults that controlled her world.

We had been trying to bribe Carly to type in longer sentences. When she typed two words, we gave her two chips.

"We want you to type lots of words. If you type an eight-word sentence, you'll get eight chips," Howard encouraged her.

"You don't need numbers. Just give me the bag," she demanded.

At that point, laughing, they gave her the bag. She had earned it for her wit as much as for her proficiency. Carly concluded the session by saying she wanted a hug from Howard, something she had never expressed before.

Not every session with Barb and Howard was as productive. Some days she refused to type and they would work on other communication methods like sorting words written on flash cards to help Carly learn vocabulary. We imagined that writing for Carly was like exercising a muscle. It was difficult and awkward. She typed painstakingly slowly with her right index finger. Attempts by her occupational therapist to engage other fingers in the effort failed. We felt that in time, however, she might become more fluent. This has not been the case, and it would be many months before she could reveal how hard it was for her to sit and focus on the task of spelling.

Despite these dry periods of writing, Barb and the team—at our urging—refused to use other forms of encouraging Carly to type, such as facilitated communication. FC had been around since the seventies as a technique of helping children with a variety of challenges that limited their oral or physical abilities to communicate. The facilitator helped by supporting the arm or wrist of the person as they expressed themselves using a keyboard or computer. However, there had been a number of studies discrediting the veracity of the writing by those using FC. We didn't want to get involved with anything that could be misconstrued as therapists influencing Carly's words or intent. We wanted to understand our daughter truthfully.

We had so many questions for her; we ached to have full conversations as spontaneously as we did with our other children. Though we tried, Carly would not sit and have a conversation with her family members. We only had witnessed her typing firsthand in the previous months because Carly finally allowed Howard to videotape some of their sessions so he could show us what she was capable of.

Still not understanding the controlling power of Carly's obsessive-compulsive disorder, we tried endlessly to convince Carly to write with us. Drawing on her years of experience working with other children with speech-language challenges, Barb told us that keeping kids engaged is the first step to teaching them to communicate. She continuously looked for ways to let Carly guide the conversations. "If she's motivated, she'll type," Barb said. One afternoon Barb pulled out one of her large photo albums filled with family pictures. "Let's look through it," she told Carly, "and you can ask me anything you want about the people you see."

Barb slowly turned the pages of plastic-covered images of family events and vacations, images that are generally more interesting to those familiar with the subjects in the picture. Carly, however, was intrigued and was able to settle, looking in the general direction of the album. She tapped at an old black-and-white picture at a family gathering.

"Is that woman your mother?" she typed.

Startled, Barb asked how she knew that.

"She looks like you," Carly replied.

"Who's that?" Carly asked pointing to a picture of a teenage boy shooting baskets in front of the house.

"My son, Brandon."

"He's hot."

Before Barb could ask whether Carly was referring to his appearance or his body temperature, Carly went on to ask, *"Does he have a girlfriend?"*

Howard, who is always quick to smile at Carly's antics, burst out laughing. "Oh Carly, where is this coming from?"

But this interest gave Barb an idea. Why not ask if Carly would like to have a weekly chat with Brandon, who lived away at college? Using the webcam and instant messaging, Brandon would be able to talk to Carly, and she could respond in writing. Clearly she was motivated by boys, and what better way to start getting her to communicate with the outside world.

The next week, Barb arranged for their first online conversation.

With Brandon sitting at his desk in his dorm room, Carly started the conversation by asking, *"Why do you have a grocery cart in your room?"*

Brandon turned to look behind him and laughed. "Oh, my roommates and I use it to haul groceries and stuff."

"Do you have a girlfriend?" Carly continued.

"Um, yeah," he replied.

"That's not good," she chided. *"Is she as cute as me?"*

They all laughed. "No," Brandon flattered her. "You're way cuter."

Carly seemed satisfied and signaled that she had had enough typing for the day.

"Did you like that, Carly?" Barb asked. "We can do it again."

"Esss," she replied, this time out of her mouth.

And by a stroke of luck, we discovered that the topic of boys could help us bridge the divide.

11

A Shaken Can of Coke

Q: *What's the one word you'd use to describe autism?*
A: That's a hard question. I don't think you can just pick one. I think I would say things don't always look like they appear. Just because in your eyes I might not look smart does not mean that's the case.

—From a conversation with a producer of ABC News

Like a wobbly foal exploring its freedom, Carly's voice started small and gained strength. As she opened up, she became more of a daughter and less of a charge. As long as Howard was present, Carly would hold court at the kitchen table with Tammy, Matthew, or Taryn looking over her shoulder and have short conversations after dinner. Howard would lean back like a grade-school student defying the teacher's plea, his lanky frame cantilevered in his chair propped up on its back legs. From this precarious position, he would guard the bowl of chips used as reinforcement for Carly completing a phrase or sentence. He had a patient way of looking Carly in the eye and speaking firmly but calmly, as if drilling words into her to initiate a conversation. Most of the time her siblings cheered her on with words of encouragement. As we learned that Carly had a sassy sense of humor and a greater vocabulary than we had imagined, Taryn couldn't resist testing her to see how far she would go.

"Do you know what *constipated* means?" Taryn asked her nonchalantly one evening after hearing us discuss Carly's lack of bowel movement that day. Taryn was not asking out of sisterly love; she had a mischievous twinkle in her eye.

"When you can't shit," Carly replied unfazed.

I don't know what makes me laugh more. Her flip answers or the lack of expression on her face when she's cracking jokes. Matthew walked into the room and asked Carly how she was.

"Dad?" she asked, ignoring Matthew's question.

"Yes, Carly?"

"Did you drop Matthew on his head as a baby?"

"No. No, Carly, we didn't."

She was becoming quite the troublemaker. But I wished her increasingly clever expressions matched an evolution in her behavior. Rather than becoming more calm and in control, as Carly ended her preteen years, her levels of agitation and explosive outbursts were becoming more frequent and ferocious. She had started violently slapping herself on the thighs, arms, and neck. If the fit escalated, Carly would throw herself to the floor and bang her head or slap her hands or feet onto the hard surface. Her pediatrician and clinicians could bring little understanding, and Carly was mute on the subject when asked. Perhaps it's puberty, reasoned one of her doctors.

The therapists' response was to intervene and get her to focus on something else, which they call *redirecting*. Containing Carly was like subduing a bucking bronco. Carly's lean, sturdy frame was strong from years of rocking and struggling with her support workers. Taryn and Matthew would scold her, telling her to stop while Howard or I would attempt to hold her and restrain her from hurting herself.

"I can't stand watching Carly do that to herself," Tammy cried despondently. "It makes me sick to my stomach every time she does that. What good is it if she's smart inside if she's such a mess on the outside?"

I suppose we realized how Carly must have been suffering. I know we were. There were days when the house felt like a pressure cooker. Carly's outbursts, after a long day of work, left me raw and short-tempered. Taryn and Matthew would withdraw to their rooms to hide from the chaos. But Tammy and I had nowhere to run. We wanted to believe it was some sort of behavior that Carly could control. Her doctors seemed unable to find any physiological reasons for her discomfort. They tested her ears, eyes, and stomach and shrugged their shoulders. While Carly seemed to have a growing vocabulary and understanding of her situation, on the topic of her outbursts she was unable to offer any clues to the cause or even articulate how she was feeling.

I came to dread the nights. Howard and Mari would be gone for the day. Carly would drift off to sleep fine, but by three in the morning be up jumping around her room bleating and braying like a cornered horse.

After months of unreturned phone calls and unsatisfying answers from our doctors, Tammy was determined to get action. We called the Cleveland Clinic because of its holistic approach. They agreed to look at all of Carly's charts and let us know if they felt they could help. "I don't care how much this costs," Tammy said. "She can't go on like this."

As we assembled the charts and files to send them, Carly's condition was deteriorating. It was so bad that Barb had discontinued her sessions. "There's no point in me trying to make her work while she's so behavioral," she said sympathetically. Tammy and Howard had on more than one occasion brought Carly to the emergency room hoping that if a doctor saw her in the midst of a meltdown, they would be sympathetic and admit her for more advanced tests. After waiting three hours one afternoon, they were sent home with no solutions, feeling more hopeless. Eventually, Tammy called our pediatrician and left a message that we wanted Carly admitted to the Hospital for Sick Children, Canada's preeminent pediatric hospital. And still we waited. Canada's healthcare system is socialized. This means that all citizens receive excellent care paid for by the government, but wait times and a sense of urgency are generally the cost of this privilege.

Enough.

One morning in September 2007, after six months of escalating behavior, Tammy decided to take matters into her own hands. While I was at work, she and Howard corralled Carly into the back of her SUV and drove to the hospital. "We're going to sit there until they admit her. Until this becomes the doctors' problem, we won't get any help."

Howard, Mari, Tammy, and I took turns staying at the hospital through the day and night over the next week. Tammy had to run between carpooling Taryn and Matthew, food shopping, and errands, and I had to keep ducking in and out to get to my office, which was only a few blocks away. We all practiced triage with the rest of our life while we snaked our way through the red tape of the diagnostic departments of the hospital. The problem we were experiencing was that each specialist only looked at Carly from his or her unique perspective. Psychologists looked at her behaviorally. Ear, nose, and throat (a practice my wife refers to as Ears, Nose, and Wallet) from an upper respiratory perspective. Neurologists looked at her brain scans and saw no abnormalities. MRIs of every inch of her body, in fact, showed nothing. On paper she was good to go. But her violent outbursts at night and lack of sleep worsened. Her body was so black-and-blue, the Children's Aid Society had been called in by one of the less experienced nurses without our knowledge. A primly dressed bureaucrat showed up to interview Tammy and me. Fortunately, when the woman from CAS arrived, our pediatrician was in the room and escorted her into the hall for a discussion. She did not return.

On the second or third night, around ten, as I tried to settle down on the small daybed with its hermetically sealed mattress, Carly flung herself from the hospital bed and began pounding herself. A nurse came in to check on the commotion, took one look at Carly beating her neck and legs as I tried to contain her, and burst into tears. She ran out, leaving us alone again.

The following afternoon Howard came by to visit. He brought a bag full of books and games that Carly enjoyed. I didn't really play with Carly so much as oversee her at this stage, so I was surprised to hear that she played Connect Four. Skeptical, actually.

"She's great at it. She beats me all the time," Howard said.

I looked at him dubiously. Connect Four requires the players to focus and strategize. It's like tic-tac-toe on steroids. This was not something I believed Carly could do readily. But after playing several games with her and losing, I felt like a fool for doubting Howard.

The week slowly progressed, and seldom more than one test was conducted each day, leaving hours of dead time. We pleaded with Carly to type and tell us what she was feeling inside and why she was slapping herself. She had taken to winding up her arm for leverage and smacking her neck just below her jaw with such impact it sounded like a paddle on a wet behind. You could hear the smack all the way down the hall. By then, however, she was as mute as she had been as a four-year-old.

By the eighth day, we finally felt like we were making progress. The team of doctors who had been coming and going, seemingly in no set pattern, finally met to confer on Carly's case. Although they could not come up with any diagnosis of a physical nature, they agreed to bring in a psychiatrist with a background in pharmacology and experience working with problem adolescents.

The next day we met Dr. Stein. She was woman in her early fifties with dark hair and an exotic look and manner that suggested a well-traveled and somewhat bohemian spirit. She was quiet, a listener in the manner of psychiatrists.

Carly was off to the side of the conference table in the doctor's small hospital office, alternating between sitting and splaying herself on the institutional blue pleather couch. I had become increasingly defensive in the presence of doctors who repeatedly asked about Carly's symptoms and then left us feeling like we were making it all up because they could not find any clinical explanation. At first, I was a little unsettled by the way Dr. Stein would stop talking and stare at Carly. I realized after the fact that she was merely watching and observing, since Carly was unable to answer any questions directly.

After a few minutes Dr. Stein spoke directly to Carly, something few specialists did. "I am not an expert in autism, Carly," she said, "but the doctors here thought I might be able to help by exploring some different medications."

She turned and said to us, "I'm usually brought in as a last stop with challenging cases. I'm wondering if Carly is attending to noises or voices inside of her," she pondered out loud.

"You think she has schizophrenia?" I asked, my eyes widening.

"No, but sometimes people with rapid mood cycles and forms of depression may hear and see things."

Typically, I wouldn't be too thrilled by a diagnosis of a mood disorder. My mother had suffered with depression her whole life, and I lived through the devastation it wreaks. In this case, however, I was happy for any concrete conclusion. So much of Carly's Carly-ness was indefinable.

Dr. Stein agreed to see Carly on a regular basis over the coming weeks and to try a course of medication called gabapentin. Originally developed for epilepsy, the drug was sometimes now used for severe nerve pain and headaches. As Carly had been pounding her body so fiercely, Dr. Stein wondered if it couldn't be some form of nonspecific neuralgia. Gabapentin had also been used successfully with some people who suffered from bipolar and mood disorders, so it kind of felt like a panacea in Carly's case.

Carly was discharged a day later, having completed every diagnostic test the team could imagine with the team finding nothing out of the ordinary.

"It could be related to the onset of puberty," our pediatrician reminded us. "Let's see how she does with Dr. Stein for the next few months."

Again, did we have a choice?

In the coming months, Carly was a closely monitored lab rat as the doctors titrated her medications up and down. Some had such adverse paradoxical effects—sedating medications that made her intensely hyperactive—that she was on and then off them within days.

Tammy took to emailing Dr. Stein in the midst of the turmoil because to wait until the next day would somehow blunt the pain and make us lose focus.

A few days later we'd be back for another consult with the psychiatrists. Blood tests were ordered to be sure the medications weren't causing some irreparable harm. Months of careful, calculated experimentation followed under the direction of the medical team. Add a white capsule and a red tablet to the orange horse pill. Let's see how we do with that. Better? Worse? The same?

A few weeks later Tammy sent another note reporting on Carly's progress. Some days she was unchanged. Others she seemed twitchy. Maybe her stomach hurt, but Carly wouldn't say. One evening after a rebalancing of her medication, she fell asleep around eleven, but no sooner had she dozed off than she sprang from her bed and started spinning in circles, her face looking possessed. Other nights she'd fling herself to the floor and flail, making push-up motions. Many nights she would awaken at 3:00 a.m. and never go back to sleep. She used the bathroom and then spent the next four hours banging around her room, stripping her bed, taking things off her shelves, jumping on her bed, and jumping on the floor.

Tammy pleaded for the doctor to see us immediately. "I don't know how much longer we can keep this up . . . I am willing to continue with this medication trial but would like your feedback on what I have described thus far. I am afraid this situation is going to break up our family . . ." she wrote in an email one night after the bedlam had subsided.

All we could do was cope. And wait. We had no other options, no further recommendations or offers of help. Dr. Stein was always responsive and made time to see us. But medication had to be adjusted slowly and carefully—one at a time. Over a period of several months, the demons that possessed Carly seemed to subside. Not entirely, but enough that we had moved through the crisis phase. Carly had become sufficiently calm and focused to begin working with Barb again. This in itself felt like a major breakthrough.

"Tell them to stop yelling at me," she told Barb several weeks after being discharged from the hospital.

"Who's yelling at you?"

"Mom and Dad. At night when I yell and jump around. It's not fun for me. My legs and arms tingle and I can't make them stop. I have to move or it gets worse. I am hitting to stop this feeling."

She had told us once before that she struck herself to stop her body from doing something it wasn't supposed to do. But this violent behavior, we knew, had to have another cause. Carly had finally opened a sealed envelope. Why had she not been able to articulate this months earlier? I wondered. Carly works on her own timetable and all we can do is wait. I pictured Carly's brain whirring and churning and reorganizing itself. Chaos to order, of sorts. This little glimmer of insight was the breaking of a padlock. Even small children can tell their parents when something is wrong. But with Carly we were always guessing. Something as simple as stomach pain or a headache had to be intuited. Happy? Sad? Anxious? Carly was never able to provide any insight into what drove her actions. Doctors would ask us if we thought she was in pain as if we had a telepathic connection—adding frustration to an already hopeless experience.

"I seriously doubt this is restless leg syndrome," Dr. Stein said to Tammy one afternoon when on a hunch we suggested that we try a drug we had heard about for this unusual syndrome. "But Requip won't have any interaction with Carly's other meds, so it can't hurt."

Within two weeks of starting Carly on the additional medication, the battle between Carly and her limbs subsided, proving once again how random and capricious finding solutions for Carly could be—and how diligent and assertive we had to be as parents in looking for treatments. Although still hyper and often sleepless, Carly no longer pounded her body black-and-blue. We began to learn how to orchestrate the complex combination of behavioral therapy and medication, love and patience, to bring Carly along. Having Carly begin to participate in her treatment plan opened new doors and brought new insight. For more than a decade it had been the blind leading the blind. But with Carly's strengthening voice, we were beginning to see. Just a little.

12

Person Farm

I wish people would be understanding and caring. But how can they
be when they just don't get it. I can explain it but no one will give me a
chance. I want people to understand that autistic people are people and
we all have an inner voice.

—Carly

By the time she was eleven years old, Carly had cycled through four
or five schools. The local public school where we sidestepped the
unions and brought in an ABA-trained therapist, at our expense.
The nice little not-so-local public school with the segregated DH
(developmentally handicapped) classroom. A small Montessori
school that was experimenting with an autism classroom came
next. That was a $25,000 attempt at progress. Back to the local pub-
lic school with Howard in tow for one very successful year followed
by a dismal failure the next.

Carly wanted to learn. She had the ability to learn. However,
there was no place that offered the one-on-one approach she needed
and the flexibility to accommodate her physical and vocal outbursts;
her need to stand up and jump around every few minutes, her head
banging and compulsiveness. She was picking up communication
skills and, although not reliably, many self-help skills like dressing

and brushing her teeth. She could follow basic instructions. But she was a spring-loaded peg that didn't fit anywhere. Tammy was continuously exploring options and there weren't many. It was a relief to have Taryn enrolled in parochial school that went to eighth grade and Matthew in a nonparochial school that went all the way through high school. At least they were "settled" and doing well. But Carly's education was an ever-changing kaleidoscope. "I just want a solution that will last more than one year and won't cost sixty thousand dollars," Tammy lamented.

In addition to the musical chairs of her education, home care was still a massive challenge. Even a successful school program could keep Carly engaged only Monday through Friday, 8:00 a.m. until 3:00 p.m. That left roughly ninety hours a week that Carly was awake, at home, and required one-to-one supervision. Howard, despite his Superman status at our house, could cover only so many hours. To supplement, we engaged what seemed like a revolving door of therapists and support workers—some covered by various government agencies, some covered by revolving credit.

Nights continued to be the black hole of desperation. While on occasion Carly might sleep peacefully for six or seven hours, we could pretty much rest assured that we could never rest assured. None of her doctors had found a solution to her insomnia and agitation. On average we were getting about three hours of uninterrupted sleep at a time. I'm still amazed that Tammy and I weren't perpetually sick.

Rebecca, a friend with twin teenage boys with autism, suggested we look into a more stable solution. One of her sons was on the more severe end of the spectrum. At over six feet tall and weighing 185 pounds with an occasionally aggressive temperament, he was too much for the family to cope with full-time. Rebecca had already moved past the phase of grief and mourning and come to accept the fact that her son must leave home. Now a young man, he lived at a residential program run by Cedarview Institute for part of the week, and came home the other days where he had a one-on-one worker who took him to a specialized school for autism. They also had a nanny and an extended family who stepped in to help both financially and, on occasion, physically.

At Rebecca's suggestion, Tammy and I drove up to visit Cedarview. The girls were away at their overnight summer camps—Carly at a camp for children with various physical and developmental challenges—Matthew, then fifteen, was doing whatever it is that teenage boys do. The residence was located in a small town off the provincial highway that leads to what Torontonians call "cottage country"—a general term for hundreds of miles of lakes and forests stretching from an hour north of Toronto up to the edges of Georgian Bay and the Niagara Escarpment.

"How do Edward and Rebecca do it?" I asked Tammy as we drove for what seemed an eternity. "Sending him up here . . ." I wasn't criticizing; I was asking for permission.

"What choice do they have?"

The social worker who was coordinating our services suggested that we explore a routine for Carly that would have her living at Cedarview from Thursday to Sunday and at home the rest of the week. They had staff on duty twenty-four hours a day, seven days a week, which suited Carly's perpetual motion. The plan sounded good on paper, anyway. We would send therapists to Cedarview, in shifts, for about ten hours a day to supplement the residential staff. In short, we were creating a school and behavior program that would help Carly get academics *and* learn to better manage in the nonautistic world. When at home, she would work with Howard, Barb, and our ABA team.

Friends and family tried to encourage us for taking constructive measures. Placing Carly at Cedarview was never intended as a permanent solution to the permanent question that was her life. But it was something that could be done for a period while we thought through her young adult years. And possibly, just possibly, she would mature into a calmness that would allow her to live at home?

I felt that creeping sense of loss as we drove along the two-lane highway that snaked through the flat farm country north of Toronto. The road narrowed and we passed through small villages with century-old churches, farmhouses, and disused cemeteries where the town's founders were laid at rest. For many Torontonians, this route was a gateway to happy family weekends at the cottage. For me it felt more like the Odyssey.

We drove silently as I turned off the highway onto the rural route leading to Cedarview. We saw the brick house rising up before us. My pulse quickened and my throat tightened. I focused on the pinging noise of the pebbles popping up under my car and the dust wafting across the road. I could still change my mind, I thought. And go back to, what? I parked near the front door and got out.

The way a prospective house buyer sizes up a piece of property as he enters, I did the 360 look before climbing the steps to the covered porch. There were fields stretching out behind the main house, a large well-tended barn, a few gardens drying in the summer sun. What did I expect to see, a warning sign telling me to turn back before it was too late?

We passed through the worn screen door into the foyer where we were met by the executive director and a senior staff member. I glanced around the entrance hall, lined with cubbies for the residents' jackets, shoes, and outerwear. Each person had a hook and a basket, but it was hodgepodge of miscellaneous items, and I thought about how Tammy and Mari worked so hard to keep each of our children's clothes neatly stored in their closets and drawers. It's odd, the details that stick in my mind. Things of such little consequence at times of such great ones.

The director was very cheerful and clearly proud of his facility.

We had been told by the government agency that was managing Carly's file that he had an excellent reputation and ran a squeaky-clean program. I'll be the judge, I thought. I am suspicious from the start, though cynicism is something I can ill afford.

The tour of the facility, however, was impressive. Although it was shabby by the standards of a private home, I could not deny the house looked well run. It was clean, spacious, and sufficiently appointed for the six or seven kids who lived there on either a full- or part-time basis. We were shown the room that Carly would use and were assured that although she would be staying in it only three nights a week, no one else would use it when she was not there. We were encouraged to bring our own furniture and decorations to make it feel homey. However, the house manager reminded us, we would need to use the plastic-covered mattress they provided and meet other standards of the safety codes they followed. It was a further reminder that this is not a home; it is an institution.

Our tour concluded with a walk through the barn and the gardens that surrounded the home. A young man was weeding in the garden. "That's Greg," the director told us. "He loves weeding and gardening, and he earns an allowance to do it. He's saving up to buy a little refrigerator for his room." Greg looked up and gave us a widemouthed smile as if to say, "Isn't that cool?"

There was one other girl who lived in the house; she was a few years older than Carly and also nonverbal. From the description of the other residents, I quickly surmised that none of them received the same degree of therapeutic intervention that Carly got. The kids were placed at Cedarview because of their need for one-on-one supervision and their families' diminished strength. This place was their only option for survival. We were no better or worse, but that was little comfort.

We went back into the house and sat at the large island in the well-appointed kitchen. Big wooden cupboards and long counters stacked with cookware lined the walls. An enormous industrial refrigerator hummed. All things considered, I liked the room because it was unlike the sterile kitchens I'd seen in other residential facilities. Two young women in shorts and oversized shirts were preparing lunch. "It's a bit quieter here on weekends in the summer," the director told us. "Some kids go to camp or are away with their families."

"When she's here, will she be lonely?" I braced myself so my voice wouldn't crack. Seclusion is one of the things I feared most for my daughter. She was already so isolated. Unable to speak, unable to connect.

"We keep the kids busy," one of the young women offered up. "We take them swimming or into town and out for walks."

I heard the buzzing of a fly and looked out the window across the gardens at the fields below. There were a few cows grazing alongside an ostrich. It was a bizarre sight, but I'm used to weird by now. I wonder if Carly can be happy here, in this strange and unfamiliar place. Maybe the best I could hope for was a lack of unhappiness, I thought.

Through the morning Tammy had been solid. She asked all the practical questions. Schedules, pedigree of staff, work space for Carly's ABA therapists, Internet access, quality of food. She wound up a little bit as she attempted to explain the peculiar temperament of our daughter, an excitability that had gotten worse over the years.

I glanced into the next room where an unusually tall young man of about seventeen sat at a large table used for crafts and games. He sat with a mountain of crayons, picking one up at a time and breaking it in half and throwing it back on the enormous pile. All the while he made squawking sounds that went from being jarring to annoying. Tammy had no need to worry that our daughter would be out of place here.

"How do you manage the meds?" Tammy asked, concerned about accurately dosing the increasingly complicated buffet of Carly's medication.

We were shown a large, locked cupboard on the sidewall of the kitchen. It was designed to house cans of tomato sauce and tuna, but was now a vault of mood stabilizers, antiseizure medications, and antidepressants that were often used for people living with autism. Each resident's prescriptions were labeled and stored in their own individual boxes. "The shift supervisor dispenses the medicine," we were told. Confusion and overdosing was a constant fear of ours when anyone other than Tammy or me administered Carly's pills.

The tour and grilling complete, we agreed to a trial period. The director was pleased—glowing, really. He tried to give us the sense that life at Cedarview was like life at a resort or on a cruise ship. Happy, happy, happy. Activities, great supervision, excellent food, and fresh air. What else could anyone want for their child? My hackles went up again.

We knew a few people whose kids stayed at Cedarview. It would provide nighttime supervision and accommodate the daytime ABA therapy. The building felt more like a home than most facilities. With this meager rationalization, I agreed to the plan.

Tammy and I drove back to Toronto, somewhat relieved. We had been looking for a solution to our pending crisis. Fall was coming, and with it would come the unanswerable question: What should we do with Carly for school and staff support? It was only July, and we had a plan in place, so we allowed ourselves a sigh of relief.

13

❦

Growing, Apart

I was once told that a block of wood is only a block of wood if you want it
to be. So make it something else.

—Carly

The house was peaceful and even-keeled for the four days a week
that Carly was at Cedarview. Life took on an eerie calm and flow.
Homework, lessons, outings, and friends stopping by. It all seemed
so sane.

Inevitably I would walk into Carly's room to put something
away, however, and the image of her empty bed, her possessions
neatly in place, even just the smell of her body lotion, would halt
me in my tracks. It reminded me of the shrine that parents of lost
children maintain years after their child's death.

Yet, for the next two and a half years, life entered a period of
relative stability. Tammy's cancer was in remission; Taryn and Matthew were doing well at school; john st., the ad agency my partners and I started in 2001, was gaining momentum; and Carly had
a routine. On Wednesday or Thursday afternoons Howard would
drive Carly up to Cedarview and on Sundays the staff would drive

her partway back to a rest stop on the highway where I would meet them. In all of the time she was there, I only went to Cedarview four or five times. By not actually making the drive up, I could imagine myself to be an accomplice but not a felon—and that felt a bit better.

There were now two other families we knew with children residing at Cedarview on a part-time basis, and the fathers would wait together to meet the kids at the end of the weekend. Seeing my friends Edward and Ryan was a measure of consolation. Edward is a world-renowned classical musician, and Ryan is a successful partner at one of Canada's largest law firms. I figured if guys of such standing could handle the outsourcing of their children, then I should be able to suck it up, too. The logic was desperately flawed, but I looked for any crevice to stick my toe into. On Sunday afternoons, as the sunlight faded, we'd stand in front of the Tim Hortons drinking coffee and waiting for the dusty van to pull up and dump its contents into our arms.

"How was the week, kids?" one of us would ask as their sons and my daughter tumbled out. None of them spoke or spoke much, so we never got an answer. We'd get a proper report by phone later from the staff.

It would have been nice to think the three of them were like peas in a pod, a little tribe of autistic kids living together. The stuff of Disney movies and kids' novels. One boy was nine, the other sixteen, and Carly in between. But from what I could tell, they barely acknowledged each other's existence.

I imagined that Carly was forlorn, scared, and angry about her living situation, though in the early months, she never commented to Barb or Howard about any of these feelings. This was triage, and neither Tammy nor I wanted to probe too deeply into how Carly might feel about this living arrangement, as there were no alternatives we could come up with.

We engaged Autism Resources, one of Ontario's top providers

of ABA therapy, to oversee Carly's program. Dr. Marion Walden and her staff managed her program both at Cedarview and at home in an effort to create some structure and continuity in targeting the areas of behavior that were most troublesome for Carly. Autism Resources recruited staff that lived near the facility, and a senior supervisor drove up from Toronto at least once a month for training and staff evaluation. Howard and other staff filled her time in Toronto with activities and academics. We liked the idea of having private staff with Carly for up to eight hours a day. I kind of thought of it as "blasting" Carly with ABA in an effort to see how much progress she could make. It also gave me some peace of mind that our therapists could keep an eye on Carly's living situation and tell us if they saw anything alarming.

I tried not to think about the windswept isolation of Cedarview, particularly as the fall closed in with its rainy, gunmetal days. Carly bonded quickly with Mel and Genna, two of the therapists assigned to her, and it was of some comfort that she had two young women whose company she enjoyed. Up to this point, Carly typed only with Barb and Howard, so it was a significant breakthrough to have her typing with her new companions.

Mel was the senior of the two and took on a role of big sister. We established a few protocols almost immediately. Although the Internet coverage at Cedarview was spotty, we asked Mel to replicate the activity Howard had begun: having Carly instant message me every day or two, whenever I was at my desk during her shift. In addition, we asked Mel to save the conversations and lessons she worked on with Carly, and type in her side of the dialogue as best as possible. It wasn't only Carly who had been starved of language for eleven years. We all had an insatiable hunger to see everything Carly wrote down, particularly in the early days of her self-expression.

Carly's first emails from Cedarview were terse. Her inability to sit for long periods of time without the need to get up and jump around combined with the painstaking pace of her typing meant she could do little more than make simple requests or comments, in simply structured messages. Nevertheless, I felt like I had hit a vein of gold and each email was like a new strike.

I had come to check my personal email almost as regularly as my professional ones on the off chance Carly would send me a note. That was always more reliable than instant messaging, since in my line of work, I don't sit still for very long. Any note where the "From" line was accompanied by "Carly Fleischmann" got my immediate attention.

"I want to go to a movie," I read in one such message on a Friday morning in late 2006. She had been working with Mel, and they instituted a practice of giving Carly time at the start of each session to just talk about whatever she wanted. *"Is Howie coming? I want to see Nanny McPhee,"* the note finished.

If Taryn or Matthew asked me to take them to a movie, I would think nothing of it. I was happy to oblige. However, when this simple request came from Carly, I felt like taking an ad out in the local paper.

I quickly replied, hoping to catch the two of them still working.

"Hi Carly. I would love to see *Nanny McPhee*, but only if we can have lots of popcorn. I will email Howard to come too, okay? Not sure if he is in town or not. See you in a few days. I love you. Xoxo"

An hour later as I was back at my desk, I noticed another message had come in from Carly's account.

"Can we go out for dinner too. How much popcorn can I have. I will be good at the movie but what if its too hard to sit. Will you walk with me in the hallway. How about if I shake my hand that means I need to go out for a walk. Ok? Can I have candy too. I want Howard to come. Taryn and mom and matthew can come too."

I fired off a response: "Hi Carly. It's Dad. I think that's a great idea to shake your hand when you need to go out at the movie. Maybe you will like the movie so much you will be able to sit for a long time. You can take little breaks though when you need it. We can get a large popcorn to share. Let's see about the candy. Too much junk food isn't healthy. You're doing a great job writing. I hope you will write like this when you are home with us too. It helps us understand what you want."

Just after lunch, I noticed she had replied yet again. This was the longest volley of emails I had ever had with either of my daughters. *"I want candy too,"* she said. *"I have not had a lot at cedarview. I have been working for tractor rides and [to watch] ellen. So my tummy is junk free. Ok?"*

I grabbed the phone and called Mel's cell. "Holy crap! Did she really write all of this?" Carly had full conversations with Howard and Barb, but with me she tended toward short phrases and one-word answers.

"Yeah, she was really focused," said Mel. "But when she was done, she started slapping the table and got up to jump around."

"Well, give her a big reward. That was amazing. Can you tell her we'll take her this week?"

"Carly," I heard Mel say. "Dad says you can go see a movie when you get home from respite." Then to me, "I think she smiled."

I called Tammy and Howard to share the experience. Later I printed out the email and showed it to some of my colleagues who were aware of the struggles we'd had with Carly over the years, as if I were showing them her Harvard diploma. In the psychological yo-yo of Carly living at Cedarview, this was one of the highs.

Carly, Tammy, Howard, Taryn, and I went to see a movie sometime the next week. I braced myself, not knowing what to expect. Howard bought a large bucket of popcorn and handed Carly one kernel at a time for the next hour and a half. With only one break out to the hallway to jump around and flap her arms, she made it through the entire movie with noises so controlled, no one around us seemed to notice.

At home, Howard encouraged Carly to keep up the dialogue. It may seem odd that Carly preferred to talk to me on IM when I wasn't present rather than speaking with me when we were together, but I was just happy to have her addressing me directly. I felt as if I had been granted an audience with the queen. Like many parents do, Tammy and I saved all Matthew and Taryn's schoolwork and art projects in a big bin. In Carly's case, we saved and catalogued all of our discussions and emails, creating a time capsule of conversations.

Each of Carly's notes was like a tiny piece of a puzzle. While I usually have no patience for jigsaws, over the two years that she lived part-time at Cedarview, part-time at home, I eagerly collected the tiny random shards that, like a mosaic, began to form a beautiful picture of my daughter.

From: Carly Fleischmann
To: Arthur Fleischmann
I am going shopping with Howard.
He said I can make dinner
I don't know what to make
Will you eat my dinner

From: Carly Fleischmann
To: Arthur Fleischmann
Hi dad
How are you
I am doingfine
Why arnt you on msn
I wantto talk to you

From: Carly Fleischmann
To: Arthur Fleischmann
I want you to take me swimming
I don't think colin will and Howard is mean
Can you take me.

From: Carly Fleischmann
To: Arthur Fleischmann
Hi dad
I got my hair cut
Colin made me look funny Howard said
I saw your website. It is funny

From: Carly Fleischmann
To: Arthur Fleischmann
Howard is so silly
He made me fill up my pot of water in the bathroom sink
I am making kraft mac and cheese
Do you want some

From: Carly Fleischmann
To: Arthur Fleischmann
Hi dad I am talking to you in my room
I won and got to take my computer to my bed
I like spelling on my bed
We have lots of snow here and cars get stuck
Its so funny the wheels spin and the car does not mve
I want to go on a snow mobile
Can we do it
Willyou go on one
I thnk it would be fun

From: Carly Fleischmann

To: Arthur Fleischmann

Hi dad what does sassy mean

Howard said I am sassy in my emails

Is that a good thing

Do you want to talk to me

Cheeky means your cheeks get all red

Like when matthew sees a girl

Just joiking

That was being cheeky, right

Im not that dumb

Even though people think I am

But I will show them

I want to beat matthew in connect four tonight

I will win.

From: Carly Fleischmann

To: Arthur Fleischmann

I don't know what to do when I come home

I looked at black creek pioneer village because I want to walk around

It looks like fun

I saw go karting too but you drive to slow and mom wont drive

I sent pop pop a letter.

I want him to drive

From: Carly Fleischmann

To: Arthur Fleischmann

Joanne said Julie [*Howard's wife*] is going to pop

Can we go see the baby on Sunday

Is Howard going to come with the baby to the house

From: Carly Fleischmann
To: Arthur Fleischmann
Why did Julie not have her baby yet
Joanne said she was going to have it
When is her baby coming

From: Carly Fleischmann
To: Arthur Fleischmann
Why hasn't Howards baby come
Does he know that he's late
Just kidding

From: Carly Fleischmann
To: Arthur Fleischmann
What are we doing on Sunday
Can we go to the science center
I want to go with you
Can we see Howards baby

From: Carly Fleischmann
To: Arthur Fleischmann
Hi dad
When do I get to see you
I miss you
Cant wait till you come home
Love
Carly

On and on they went. My daughter likes outings. I never really knew that. Carly has a sense of humor. A sense of irony. And a sense of self-esteem. What else would I learn about my daughter? I wondered.

Barb and Howard were encouraging us to converse using instant messaging. "I want Carly to have the opportunity to voice her opinion," Barb told Tammy and me. "I know it's so slow, but give her the chance whenever you can."

"Well, when I'm at work, Howard, you can just have Carly log on. We can IM whenever I'm at my desk." Her typing was sufficiently slow that I could multitask, often holding a meeting or a phone conversation at my desk while she methodically tapped out characters that became words, words that became revelations.

One day at work I received the following email. *"whats a interview?"* she asked. Carly would sometimes start a dialogue with a question, but there were times I often felt like I was being dropped into the middle of a foreign film—I could understand some of the random words but felt like I was grasping for comprehension of the greater context. She strove for efficiency in typing given the enormity of the effort. I logged into instant messaging to practice live conversation, as Barb had suggested.

(4:08:54 PM) dad says:
Hi Carly, are you there now?
i will tell you about an interview.

(4:12:56 PM) Carly says:
what is it

(4:13:43 PM) dad says:
hi. an interview is when you want to get into a school or get a job, you have a meeting with the person who is in charge. you tell them about yourself and why you believe you should be allowed to attend the school. where do you want to interview?

(4:15:40 PM) Carly says:
can i spell in the interview

(4:15:45 PM) dad says:
Yes. of course.

(4:17:58 PM) Carly says:
Howard said he can get mee in to work at a baggle [*bagel*] store

(4:18:09 PM) dad says:
oh. that's a great idea!
i think we should speak with Claire [*Carly's senior ABA program director*] about adding some cooking exercises into your daily programs. and at Cedarview too!

(4:20:06 PM) Carly says:
when the store is closed

(4:20:27 PM) dad says:
you mean to work there making bagels when the store is not open?

(4:22:06 PM) Carly says:
yes to try it

(4:24:19 PM) Carly says:
but i need to have a interview

(4:24:32 PM) dad says:
okay. well dont worry. they will ask you questions and you will need to answer them. they will ask you things like: why do you want to make bagels?

(4:27:04 PM) Carly says:
because it will be fun

(4:29:20 PM) dad says:
they may ask you what you would like to do at the bagel store?

(4:32:06 PM) Carly says:

make lots of baggles

(4:32:17 PM) dad says:

what kind of bagels are your favourite?

(4:34:26 PM) Carly says:

with black things on top

(4:35:58 PM) dad says:

those are called poppy seeds. they might ask you why you think you would be a good person to hire for the bagel store.

(4:37:51 PM) Carly says:

i like poppy seed

what do i say

(4:40:17 PM) dad says:

i think you would tell them that you are a hard worker. and you are very honest. and they should give you a chance to show how you would be a good employee!

(4:47:06 PM) Carly says:

Howard says ineed to work on alot of things

(4:47:31 PM) dad says:

well, that's true. you have to be able to stay focused. and follow directions. but if you really want to do this, i think you can learn. you are very smart, Carly.

(4:55:54 PM) Carly says:

Howard said Claire can give me a interview

(4:56:26 PM) dad says:

you mean she can help you learn how to do an interview?

(5:03:42 PM) Carly says:

yes

(5:04:01 PM) dad says:

that would be great! and you could start practicing working in the kitchen at home and at Cedarview. if you could cook for me, what would you make? bagels??

(5:12:29 PM) Carly says:

can we go to Great Wolf Lodge to swim

The pacing of our conversations was slow and clumsy, as if passing through an interpreter. I wasn't always sure I was keeping up with her, or her with me. I would just be getting into the rhythm, and Carly would veer in a new direction. In this case, we went down the path of discussing a family trip to an indoor water park and hotel that was popular with kids. Parents who were less keen to run through the tepid water appreciated the hospitality of the hotel, which served alcohol in the lounges overlooking the pools.

By the summer of 2007, Carly had been shuttling between home and Cedarview for about nine months. I relied on these sometimes-terse conversations to get to know Carly, despite our physical separation. Although I deeply appreciated the fledgling connection forming between us through words, I nevertheless found the abruptness of how conversations started and ended, how some of my queries would go unanswered, jarring. Midconversation, it was not unusual for Carly to type *"I am done,"* crisply ending the exchange. Manners were not something worth expending effort on.

(10:47:05 AM) Carly says:

you never come get me

(10:47:33 AM) dad says:

Hi Carly. i am working tomorrow. but mom isn't so she will come get you in the afternoon. think about what you want to do at home this weekend. maybe swim?

(10:48:30 AM) Carly says:

swim

(10:48:43 AM) dad says:

good. i think the weather will be nice. Howard wants to come by and see you at home tomorrow. is that okay?

(10:54:01 AM) Carly says:

i need a cheesie

(10:54:28 AM) dad says:

well, you're writing for me, so i think you deserve a cheesie. ask for one.

(10:54:52 AM) Carly says:

good
hoy
my sister

(10:56:58 AM) dad says:

Taryn? she is at camp still.

(10:57:34 AM) Carly says:

miss her

(10:57:43 AM) dad says:

you will see her next month. she is staying at camp for two months this year.

(10:59:24 AM) Carly says:
mel needs to give me s

r

chr

mel please

(11:02:26 AM) dad says:
what do you need?
i dont understand.

(11:02:53 AM) Carly says:
cheesie

(11:03:35 AM) dad says:
ask mel for cheesie.

(11:06:12 AM) Carly says:
today my sister starts camp

(11:06:28 AM) dad says:
your sister has been at camp all month. but today is what's called "visitors' day."
Mom went up to visit Taryn at camp today. then Mom will come get you tomorrow.

It was a midweek visitors' day this year and Tammy drove up with the mothers of several girls attending the camp, staying overnight at a lodge nearby. I never knew how much information to give Carly. Not because I questioned her comprehension. I now knew she heard and understood everything. But I was becoming acutely aware of how much she did know. Even broaching the subject of Taryn attending camp in Algonquin Park and spending time with her mother during visitors' day while Carly sat in an air-conditioned house working made me sick with guilt.

(11:07:58 AM) Carly says:

are you going

(11:08:14 AM) dad says:

No. I am working today, and then going to the airport to pick up Matthew. Matthew was away for a month also. he will be home this afternoon. he wants to see you tomorrow too.

If possible, I now felt worse having to remind Carly that Matthew was attending a summer school program in Europe. Talk about the haves and have-nots. Usually the two don't exist so closely in the same family.

(11:10:29 AM) Carly says:

he wont remember me

Was she being literal or ironic? Understanding nuance would be one of the toughest challenges of chatting with Carly. And it wasn't like I could quickly ask, "Are you kidding?" without adding suffering to her already laborious efforts of typing.

(11:10:46 AM) dad says:

what do you mean!! of course he remembers you. he loves you. he has asked about you while he was away!!

(11:13:10 AM) Carly says:

mel trys to get me to type

(11:13:24 AM) dad says:

yes. because the more you type, the better you will become at it. and then you can type all the time so we can understand you.

(11:14:04 AM) Carly says:

very hard

(11:14:07 AM) dad says:

i know. but i promise you, it will get easier. now, i am a very fast typist. but i did not used to be!

(11:15:25 AM) Carly says:

say md

no

(11:16:07 AM) dad says:

really. if you type every day, you will become very fast. and it will be like speaking with your voice.

(11:18:07 AM) Carly says:

say really mel really

(11:18:28 AM) dad says:

what do you mean? i didnt understand you. you want me to tell Mel something?

This was all getting too Fellini-esque for me.

(11:20:18 AM) Carly says:

mel needs to take me to you

(11:20:44 AM) dad says:

you miss me? i will see you tomorrow afternoon. today i need to work and then get Matthew. sorry Carly. but it wont be long until i see you. what else are you doing today?

I hated when she asked to come home. It made me feel like I had swallowed a bowling ball. I hoped she would go off on another tangent.

(11:21:43) dad says:

are you still there? do you want to talk anymore?

(11:23:56 AM) Carly says:

mel needs new cars

Whoosh. Next topic.

(11:24:09 AM) dad says:

really? is her car broken or just getting old?

(11:26:44 AM) Carly says:

mel yes she started today

(11:26:56 AM) dad says:

she started what? looking for a new car? or you mean the car started today?

(11:27:39 AM) Carly says:

working

because she missed me

(11:29:12 AM) dad says:

yes! while you were at camp last month, i'm sure she missed you.

(11:30:10 AM) Carly says:

i am happy

(11:30:29 AM) dad says:

i'm glad. You are more comfortable at Cedarview than at camp?

(11:32:32 AM) Carly says:

mel really needs a job

(11:32:44 AM) dad says:
you are so funny. Mel has a job! she works with you, doesnt she??

(11:33:22 AM) Carly says:
just kidding

(11:33:31 AM) dad says:
you make me laugh! you have a good sense of humour. i think you are happier now that you are not at camp. are you able to sleep better?

Carly had spent a few weeks at an overnight camp and had just returned to Cedarview. Camp Kennebec was an integrated setting with some kids struggling with a variety of disabilities and other "typical" campers living alongside them. It was an imbalanced justice, but we tried to give to Carly some semblance of what we offered Taryn and Matthew. In the past, she seemed to enjoy her experience there, but this summer she hit a wall and spent most days crying or resisting all efforts to get her engaged. I finally had to pick her up a week early and bring her back to Cedarview.

(11:34:40 AM) Carly says:
her car is ugly

(11:34:50 AM) dad says:
dont be mean! i'm sure Mel's car is fine! it only has to get her from one place to another.

(11:35:30 AM) Carly says:
pretty much

(11:35:51 AM) dad says:
you didnt answer me, are you able to sleep better? i hope you are able to sleep at home tomorrow. . . .

(11:36:12 AM) Carly says:

yes

really

(11:36:46 AM) dad says:

oh good. Carly, I need to go soon. I have a meeting for work in a few minutes.

but then when i get home with Matthew later, i will turn on my computer again.

Would you like to speak with Matthew today?

(11:38:12 AM) Carly says:

got mel real

upset

(11:39:01 AM) dad says:

why was she upset? because you made fun of her car? ha ha.

(11:39:16 AM) Carly says:

yes

never make fun

(11:41:11 AM) dad says:

thats right. you shouldn't make fun. did you apologize to her?

(11:42:09 AM) Carly says:

bye i love you

At least this farewell had more optimism than her typical "I'm done"; that had a fatalist quality that made me uneasy.

(11:42:14 AM) dad says:

bye carly. i love you too. and i will see you tomorrow.

Although the conversations had a loopy quality, I was grateful for the chance to get to know my daughter, albeit from afar. One of the most heartwarming emails read, *"hi dad. it's me carly. can we go for a walk just you and me. can we talk on msn [*instant messaging*]?"*

Yes, Carly. We can talk and talk and talk. As much as you want.

Finally.

14

~∾∾~

A Roar Is Not Just a Roar

Arthur started to circle her. Arthur's head turned to Hooowie the owl. His mouth opened and said, "You stupid owl. This is a puny little girl."

The girl moved her head slowly and said, "Who are you calling puny?"

Every one around her was in shock. See, as you know humans never—and I mean never—are able to understand what we say. And here is a human that can.

Arthur stared into her eyes. He turned to all of us not with a look of shock, like what we all had on our face, but with a look of satisfaction. He said in his deep voice, "The prophecy has come true."

We could not believe our ears. I could not take it any more. I stood up as tall as I could and said, "Just because a human can hear what we can say does not mean that she is the chosen one."

Arthur whipped his head around. His eyes opened as big as my body. His mane shone bright in the moonlight and then he said in only the voice a lion can use, "Carlito are you saying you think she is not the one?"

I tried to stand up taller but it's hard when your legs start to tremble and your heart beats so fast that the rest of your body starts to shake. But I managed to stand my ground and look at Arthur straight in his eyes and say, "Yes that is what I am implying."

I could not believe it. I, a gecko, one of the smallest creatures in the jungle just looked the king in his eye and told him off.

—*Excerpt from* The Elephant Princess

"Carly is becoming more human," Taryn said to Tammy, missing the irony that Carly lived at a *farm* half the week. There was no trace of cruelty in Taryn's observation; she was making a blunt observation. In fact, Taryn had always been uncannily perceptive. Several years earlier, when she was around nine years old, Taryn and Tammy were running errands at a shopping plaza frequented by the elderly Jewish population in the neighborhood. "A lot of those women are really educated, you know, Mom," Taryn commented upon seeing a young Filipino woman escorting an old woman with a walker. She commented pensively, "They come to this country to forge a better life for themselves and end up holding an old Jewish lady's hand."

Taryn's comment referred to the fact that Carly was becoming more expressive and engaged than she had been during the twins' first decade together. The conversations with Mel went from awkward and simplistic to colloquial and, at times, heartfelt. Their dialogue became a dominant topic of conversation in our household. Within a few months of meeting Mel, Carly's conversations became more mature and introspective.

In the late summer of 2007, we were planning a trip to New York City to see a neurologist about Carly's inability to speak. The doctor was noted for his work with kids with autism. Tammy and I were still convinced that there was a physiological glitch we might uncover, one that if cured could help Carly both speak and be less hyperactive.

Tammy, Carly, Taryn, and I were going to make a weekend out of it, and we asked Carly what she'd like to see in the city, not sure if she was even aware of the sights of Manhattan. Carly was home from respite, and after dinner, we sat at the kitchen table, Taryn lounging like Cleopatra on the cushions that padded the window seat of the bay window. "What do you want to do in New York?" I asked Carly.

"The lady with the torch," she replied.

"How do you know about the Statue of Liberty?"

"I know stuff. The Zoo. Will Matthew be in the cage?"

This was the beginning of what would become a long tradition of Carly ribbing her brother about being an ape. Generally it accompanied a jab about his smell, something I have never noticed, but a scent that Taryn described flatly as "boy."

"Anything else you want to see?"

"Ground Zero."

Now I was really stunned, but Taryn just smiled in sort of a knowing way, leaving me to wonder if she and her sister had some sort of unspoken connection.

"What is Ground Zero?" I asked.

"Plane crashed."

"How did the plane crash?"

"Bad men."

We were experiencing firsthand some of the knowledge shock that Mel saw routinely at Cedarview. Of course, the news items such as the 9/11 terrorist attacks were ubiquitous, but we couldn't conceive, given how Carly behaved, that she was aware and processing news events.

Carly went on to say, *"I want to go to the fire ellen is going to."*

"I don't know what that is," I responded, eager to see where she was heading.

"tomorrow she said she wanted to go to the fire," said Carly.

"She means Ellen DeGeneres," Howard clarified. "She was watching her show this afternoon."

"Hmmm. What fire did Ellen want to go to?" I asked. "Oh. Do you mean the big forest fire burning in California? We are not going to be near there."

"we are going to the US, rite?"

"Yes, we are. But it's a very big country. We are going to be on the East Coast and the fires are on the West Coast."

"but ellen going to the fire"

"Yes, Ellen lives in Los Angeles, which is in California."

"we should make a fire in NY."

Was she joking? Confused? I know I was. Conversations with Carly continued to be murky and I sometimes felt as if I were in a half dream state.

"No, you don't understand. The fire in California is burning down buildings, forests. It's a very BAD thing."

"then why is she going"

"She is probably going to try to help people there whose houses have burned down. She will go and try to raise money for them and to cheer them up."

"can i give them money"

"You are so sweet, Carly," I said. "We can see if there is a charity that is taking donations and we can make a donation. Would you like that?"

"yes."

I gave Carly a tight hug, an act we called "squeezie hugs"—more from the side than front, which was the only way she was willing to do so. I felt a rush of pride mixed with surprise at her empathy and generosity of spirit—a trait not found in teenagers in general and supposedly not in those with autism specifically. I imagined she learned altruism from her big brother. Matthew had been unusually charitable from a young age, and seeing how Carly had been absorbing her surroundings long before she could write, it wasn't a stretch to think she picked up on some of her sibling's good qualities. After Hurricane Mitch in 1998, Matthew held a fundraiser in his fourth-grade class. I think it was a bake sale. By the time he graduated high school, he had done a series of annual events for causes such as muscular dystrophy (which was slowly paralyzing his best friend), various natural disasters, and autism, earning him the Governor General's award for community service. Of course, as his parents, we were moved. But clearly at least one of his sisters was also paying attention.

In addition to Carly's earnestness, I began to see a refreshing, teenage vibe in her conversations. Along with their introspective chats, Carly and Mel struck up the same kinds of conversations friends routinely have.

"Today is your birthday, Mel," said Carly.

"Yes, I am 29. Do you think that's old?"

"Yes."

"Well, I don't feel any older than I did yesterday. What did you do in Toronto this weekend?"

"Went to the Science Center."

"Did you see anything cool?"

"Yes"

"What was your favorite part?"

"liked the static ball."

"Me too! Did you try it out or did you watch other people?"

"I tried it."

"Did your hair stand up?"

"Yes."

"What else would you like to talk about, Carly?"

"Your birthday."

"What do you want to know?"

"Are you going to have a party?"

"I wish! Maybe I'll go for dinner with my boyfriend somewhere. I'm not really sure. Do you think I should have party?"

"Yes."

"What kind of party?"

"Dress up."

"Like a costume party?

"yes."

"What should I dress up as?"

"A rabbit."

"Kinda like Elle Woods."

"Her outfit was awesome."

"You're right. It was pretty nice."

"What would you dress up as?"

"Wesley Snipes. Do you like my ring?" Mel continued.

"Yes"

"Do you know what it means?"

"It means your going to get married."

"Do you want to help me research wedding stuff on the Internet today?"

"Sure."

"What should we look up?"

"Wedding dresses."

The two sat, side by side, at the cluttered desk in a disused office on the ground floor of the house. The staff had put aside work space where Carly could leave her computer and academic materials, shielded from the maelstrom created by eight young adults living with autism under one roof.

Mel searched wedding dress sites and Carly glanced around the room, her eyes occasionally resting on the computer screen for an instant or two. Except for Carly's occasional squawks and table slaps, one could have mistaken the two for close friends or sisters sharing an intimate moment. On occasion Carly covered her ears and made Carly noises. *MMMMM. MMMMMM WAH.* In time, Carly would inform us that she was able to hear and listen, despite these irritating sounds.

"Which dress do you like best, Carly?"

"First."

" 'Cause it's the prettiest?"

"It's okay"

"Just okay? Is it too boring for you?"

"Yes"

"What do you like? Big fluffy dresses like a princess?"

"Yes"

"What do like you better, sparkles or lace?"

"Sparkles."

"Me, too! Hey, Carly, what's your favorite band?"

"Greenday," responded Carly.

I hadn't realized she took any interest in bands, much less had a preferred group.

"What is your favorite song?"

"Time of Your Life."

"What is something you are scared of?" Mel asked, changing gears again. Whenever she sensed a conversation stalling, she would pepper Carly with questions and push her to stretch.

"I am scared of being alone."

"I am scared of being alone, too, sometimes! I also sometimes am scared that people don't like me."

"I like you."

"Thank you, Carly. I like you, too. If you could go on vacation where would you go?"

"San Francisco Zoo"

"Remember when we went to the zoo together? What was your favorite animal there?"

"The orangutan"

I thought back to Dr. Stephensen telling us that Carly was climbing a ladder. How far up she would go was the great unknown. I hadn't seen the doctor in many years, since we had moved on to other specialists who focused on autism specifically. Carly was indeed climbing up that ladder. And rather than a step stool, it seemed to be of the extension variety.

But because of Carly's inconsistent willingness to write and inability to control her outbursts, it was often hard to measure where on that ladder she was standing. Her therapists would read magazines, textbooks, and newspapers to her. Or they might watch TV and listen to the radio, even for a few minutes at a time. Carly would rock, often hands over her ears—particularly right hand to right ear—making humming or mooing noises. The staff persevered, never sure what Carly was retaining or what she was thinking. When Mel got her chatting, however, we learned she had near-perfect recall of facts. In fact, her knowledge appeared to far exceed the materials they covered in their lessons.

"Mel you are boring," Carly complained.

"Why?"

"Cause you make me work."

"Okay, well, working is a good thing, right?"

"No"

"Why do you say that?"

"Are people content working?"

"I think some people like their jobs and some people don't. That's why it's important to figure out what you like to do."

"ok, but do you like your job?"

"I love my job. I really liked taking psychology in university, but sometimes, to get to where I wanted to be, I had to do things I didn't like, like math. I hate math. Is there anything you like about working?"

"I make a recipe."

"Anything else?"

"I like talking on MSN"

"What else?"

"I like reasoning"

"What don't you like?"

"I hate Thinking Basics," she said, referring to a textbook Autism Resources had her working on.

"Why?"

"it's too easy."

"I agree. I have harder Thinking Basics books at home. Should I bring them to try?"

"No"

"What about the sexuality program, do you like it or hate it?"

"Mel, I know about sex."

"I know you know about sex. I don't think you get it, though."

"I do"

"Then if you get it, let's do a pop quiz. Name three types of birth control."

"Pill. Condom. Diaphragm."

"How does the birth control pill work?"

"it tricks your body into thinking it's pregnant."

"Okay. Let's talk about a recipe to make next week," Mel said, sensing Carly's teenage discomfort. "You tell me the ingredients and method, and I'll bring the ingredients with me next Thursday and we'll cook in the kitchen."

"I want to make spaghetti"

"Carly's famous pasta."

"tomato sauce. Noodles of any kind. Mushrooms. Nice peppers. Garlic 1 large clove. Parmesan."

"Awesome. I'll bring the ingredients and we'll make it next Thursday for lunch. What should we do now, academics?"

"Academics."

"Okay," said Mel taking out the science textbooks they had been reviewing. Although not following a specific lesson plan, every day they studied from junior high–level material. "What is cell theory?" Mel asked.

"The cell theory states that the cell is the smallest unit of living material," Carly responded.

"What is serotonin?" Mel read from the text.

"It's a neurotransmitter."

"And what is dopamine linked to?" Mel asked her.

"Alzheimer's."

After receiving the latest installment of their weekly discussion, I called Mel. "Is this for real?" I asked. I seemed to ask that frequently where Carly was concerned. "She sounds more grown-up than Matthew!" I had an ear-to-ear grin.

"Yeah, she gets it," Mel said. "Problem is she won't do the work consistently, so it's hard to see where she's at."

Carly was showing us a stubborn side, refusing to do work she felt was too easy or beneath her and making it virtually impossible to determine a baseline on which to create a lesson plan. Lacking a clear trajectory, Mel and the team did their best to cobble together an eclectic range of topics to keep Carly attentive. This left me with the extreme ends of emotion: excited about her intelligence and frustrated by her inconsistencies.

"If you were going to university or college, what would you want to major in?" Mel wanted to know.

"Psychology," Carly answered. I mused at how she had grown from wanting a job in a bagel store several years before to the more challenging and sophisticated goal.

"Okay. What kind of stuff would you want to learn about in psychology? Do you even know what psychology is?" asked Mel.

"the study of human behavior," Carly seemed to say with an eye roll.

"How do you know all this stuff?" Mel asked, genuinely perplexed.

"Look Mel, I'm an academic genius," Carly responded.

We all laughed at the attitude that was emerging in Carly's voice. From within the chaos came a trickle of strength and self-confidence that had to be nurtured somehow. What might be chided as arrogance in an adult we welcomed gladly from our child.

"Ha ha," replied Mel. "I know—but seriously, you weren't born with all that info in your head. You had to learn it somewhere. How did you learn?"

"I read."

The truth was that Carly never read on her own. She lacked the fine motor skills to hold a book and turn the pages. Furthermore, she was more likely to stim or rip a book apart if left with it unsupervised, so it was unclear to me how she was obtaining this knowledge.

"How long does it take you to read a book?"

"A moment," Carly answered. Years later we would learn this was no overstatement. Carly had an uncanny ability to glance at a page and respond to questions of comprehension with 90 percent accuracy at times.

"How do you remember all the facts in the book?"

"I just do."

"Can I ask you, do you read a lot about autism?"

"Yes."

"You must have read about applied behavior analysis?"

"Mel i know ABA"

"Okay. You know that with your knowledge, you could become a psychologist working on autism research? How come you never told your parents or Howard or Barb any of this stuff you know? Do they know you know all this stuff?"

"They love me."

Carly often speaks in non sequiturs. Perhaps it is nothing more than the speed bumps caused by the slow pace of her typing; her mind already racing well ahead of her fingers. Or perhaps the logic in her mind, clear as an Arizona sky, looks befuddled to us. Yet another mystery I hoped to solve one day.

"Of course they love you, but do they know all this stuff?" Mel asked, confused.

"No."

"Why not?"

"They don't ask."

"I think Mom, Dad, Howard, and Barb would love to talk to you about this stuff. Maybe we can all work together to get a professor to teach you new things. Or how about having a philosophical conversation with Dad about something in history or something about psychology?"

"That would be awesome."

"Would you ever want to start a book club with your family and friends? You read a book and discuss the book over dinner and drinks?"

I smiled reading this, picturing Carly holding court, a martini in one hand.

"Yes," she replied.

As Carly continued to mature, a fog seemed to be lifting. We took every opportunity to ask her about what was happening inside of her; what motivated the outbursts and perpetual motion. It had been something she was either unwilling or unable to articulate, though we continually probed. Just maybe if she gave us a little more insight, we would find something we had missed in all the years of exploration.

In one of their conversations, when Barb inquired why children with autism don't look people in the eye and whether they should be encouraged to, Carly replied, *"No. We see different than everyone else.*

We take pictures in our heads like a camera. It's like filling a camera with too many pictures. It gets overwhelming."

At the end of each of their sessions—even before leaving our house—Barb took out her own laptop and summarized the conversations and progress they had made. I read her emails off my Black-Berry while stopped at red lights on the drive home. Today that's a ticketable offense, but one that's worth the fine. These notes were like an addictive mystery that I couldn't put down—even at the risk of a car accident.

One particularly intriguing session, we learned how it was that Carly processed information. Barb had been telling Carly about a problem she was having with one of her other young clients. She said the boy was a bright five-year-old with autism. He frequently made noises and repeated phrases or words over and over—words he had picked up from watching cartoons.

"I find it very difficult to work with him when he stims. Carly, do you have any ideas how to stop this?"

"That's not stimming," Carly corrected Barb. *"People mix that up with stims but it's not. Stims are when we focus on sensory output to block out sensory input."*

Typically, *stims* referred to the repetitive behavior people with autism exhibit—flapping hands, wriggling fingers, or fiddling with an object.

"Isn't that what he is doing—focusing on his own talking 'output' to block out my 'input,' if I am asking him to do something he finds hard?" Barb pursued. She was stunned by Carly's clarity and sophisticated insight, and intrigued to learn—the master from the pupil.

"Knowing myself—and again remember I don't talk, you can't just talk as a stim. It has to be more engaging."

"I don't understand. Can you explain?" asked Barb.

Howard interjected, "When you were making noises just now,

was that a stim?" Carly had been making a humming sound while chewing her potato chips.

"I was making noise and changing the sound with my finger in my ear to block out audio input from the crunching of the chip."

"So back to my client, what is he doing if it's not stimming, and what can I do to help him?"

"He is audio filtering."

Barb and Howard looked at Carly dumbstruck.

"What is he filtering, and what should I do about it?" Barb was genuinely intrigued, as if consulting with a famed doctor.

"We take in over a hundred sounds a minute. We have a hard time process-ing all the sounds at once so it comes out later as a broken record."

"That's so interesting!" exclaimed Barb. "Is he listening while doing this?"

Carly nodded yes.

"How do I get him to stop?"

"Something is setting it off. Smells. Hairstyle. clothes or sounds can be a trigger," responded Carly.

"But what can I do?" continued Barb.

"How can you help someone when you are to stubborn to listen?" teased Carly.

"That's not fair. I am here to listen. If I don't understand some-thing, it's not fair to say that." She couldn't see Carly's face as she was looking toward Howard, but he said she said this all with one of her mischievous smiles.

"It could [be] something you are saying or making him do that acts as trigger. It's the method that reverberates the sentence or words in his head and to filter the meaning he repeats it over and over," Carly replied somewhat cryptically. It seemed that Carly's thoughts raced ahead of her abil-ity to type, and some of the words in the sentence were missing. Her paragraph was like Swiss cheese—we grasped the gist of her mean-ing, but the holes left us wanting a bit more.

"If I can make out what he is saying, would it help if I explain what it means? Would it stop then?" Barb asked.

"He has to do it himself so he could learn how to filter," Carly responded, and then signed she was done speaking.

We were astonished by how articulate Carly was—using simple metaphors to help us *neurotypicals* understand her condition. "It's just brilliant," Barb remarked, with a sense of relief. The observation of how Carly was absorbing information—taking in thousands of sounds and images at once—explained how she was gathering so much information. Newspapers are always spread over our kitchen table; the television or radio often left on. While it may not look as if she were perusing the way most of us do, Carly was reading much the same way a photocopier snaps a picture of the text and then stores it for future processing. Sounds would pour into her head and be sorted and filed for meaning at some later date. Some months later she pointed out that information could sit in an unprocessed state for hours, days, or weeks before she finally understood it and could respond—like an enormous pile of papers sitting on a desk, waiting to be filed.

Carly's imagination and wit would become other cornerstones of her personal. Humor, we are told, requires intelligence, so we were both surprised and encouraged when she began peppering her conversations with little jokes, jabs, and sarcasm. To celebrate Matthew's eighteenth birthday, Carly wrote him the following note:

Dear Matthew,

I want to wish you a happy birthday. Every one tells me that you love me and care about me. So because I love you and don't want to see you without any friends or a girlfriend, I have to tell you something. You smell.

*But that's ok because I, your caring sister, have gotten you a
present that will fix that. Now maybe you wont need to have any
imaginary friends.*

Naaaaaa. It's you I'm talking about.

But you will smell better.

Your loving, caring and popular sister,
Carly

Carly had Howard take her to the store where she picked out
bottles of a popular brand of body spray, cologne, and hair products.
Matthew took it all in stride.

In addition to her sense of humor, Carly had a well-developed
imagination. Late in 2007, completely of her own volition, Carly
had started writing a piece of fiction called *The Elephant Princess*.
One afternoon with Howard, she told him, *"I want to work on a special project."* Without any further explanation, she launched into a
Disney-like tale about a girl, a gecko, and a cast of anthropomorphic
characters that resembled people in her life.

The inspiration for her creative explosion came from our nightly
ritual of reading fantasy fiction, such as Angie Sage's *Flyte* and *Magyk*.
Cuddling up in Carly's big bed with a book was our favorite time of
the day. I had asked her why she preferred these books over others in
the genre, such as the Harry Potter series.

"I like them because they're about a girl who's a princess. She's like me,"
Carly answered.

"Oh, you're a princess?" I teased. If she could have, she would
have shot me a chilling glance, I'm sure. Though as we got to know
Carly more, it was no surprise that she would identify with a young
heroine that had to rage against strong forces to succeed.

One evening, around the same time, I had been pondering with
Howard why it was that Carly was still having trouble sleeping.

"She takes enough medicine to knock out an elephant," I exclaimed. Howard shook his head in perplexed agreement. Carly was sitting in the den, well out of earshot. Or so I supposed.

The next day, while at work, Carly texted me, *Why did you call me an elephant?* I had no idea what she was talking about, as the question came out of context.

"What does she mean, Howard?" I typed back.

I could almost hear Howard laughing at the computer. "You said last night that she took enough medicine to knock out an elephant. She must have heard you."

In addition to Carly's hyper-visual acuity, we were coming to understand that she was gifted with what I termed *peripheral hearing*. She was able to pick up on conversations several rooms away, even when it appeared that she was not paying attention or was engaged in another activity.

Carly had put the two thoughts together, the elephant and the princess, and a few days later began her novella. Through the end of 2007 and into 2008, Carly worked on her story a few times a week. It didn't really matter if we encouraged her or not; she only did it on her terms. She would sit at the computer and entire pages would pour out over the course of an afternoon. She never needed to go back and change words or edit her thoughts. They were complete scenes and narrative, carefully plotted out. Her writing was imaginative and witty, though sometimes her sentence structure was so complex and lacking in punctuation that I had to reread passages a few times to fully grasp the idea.

> *I want you to close your eyes and imagine a girl all alone in the middle of the jungle.*
>
> *All she can hear are the sounds of the animals.*
>
> *But what she does not know is that the sounds aren't just random sounds.*

In fact the animals are talking to each other.

People think that a lion's roar is its way to scare you.

But let me tell you from experience that a roar is just not a ROAR.

Actually a roar can mean many things depending on the tone.

I think that humankind is just oblivious to things that have been around for many years.

I think humans are such silly creatures.

See us animals are much smarter because we understand what is going on around us.

But that's another story for another day. I'm sorry I am just rambling on.

Ok.

So I think I was telling you that she heard sounds all around her.

They kept on getting closer and closer. Little did the girl know all us animals were talking about her.

Sorry for interrupting again, but I think I should tell you that every thousand years us animals need to pick the ruler of the world. And you thought we sit and do nothing all day. Well ok sorry for barging in again.

As all the animals got closer we all saw the same thing. That silly old owl that was supposed to be so smart, brought a human to be the next ruler. Not just a human but a twelve year old girl.

"No no no this cant be," said a voice in the group.

We all knew who said it. Arthur was the oldest and most feared animal in the world.

His voice was so deep it could make mountains crumble to the ground. All the animals respected what he has to say.

The moon shined in a straight line on the girl's head like a flash light beam. She stood in between four drooping old trees. She saw all the animals getting closer and closer to her and she started to tremble. Arthur walked towards the frightened little girl.

We all knew she saw him when her trembling stopped. In fact every thing stopped.

Her chest stopped moving. it was like watching a wall. Well, Arthur started to circle her

Arthur's head turned to Hoowie the owl. His mouth opened and he said, "You stupid owl. This is a puny little girl."

The girl moved her head slowly and said, "Who are you calling puny?"

Every one around her was in shock. See as you know humans never, and I mean never, are able to understand what we say. And here is a human that can.

Arthur stared into her eyes. He turned to all of us not with a look of shock like what we all had on are face but with a look of satisfaction. He said in his deep voice, "The prophecy has come true.

We were to understand that the narrator, the gecko, was Carly, and the character of the princess was based on Taryn. Through the tale they are inextricably intertwined, helping and scolding one another just as sisters do. We all got parts in Carly's play. I am a lion, fierce king of the jungle. Blush. Howard is Hoowie the wise owl. Barb, an adoptive mother of the princess. Matthew received his Carly bashing, showing up as the princess's nemesis, an ugly troll. And Tammy is Tamma, the elephant mother of the human princess.

If it weren't so funny, Tammy would be deeply offended. When I asked Carly how her writing was going once, she said, *"good. Tamma dies by exploding cell phone. Just kidding."* Tammy *does* spend an inordinate amount of time on her cell, so there is some truth in the jest.

As the story unfolded, a journey "through the gauntlet" to prove the princess's merit, we saw creative writing as a possible outlet for a nonaudible mind. It was also another way for us to peek inside Carly, to learn by observation. Although fantasy, the tale was reflective of Carly's life, and I was curious to see how she would portray her world. But creative writing is challenging under the ideal situations, and Carly's pace of typing, and struggles with focus and sitting, still made the endeavor formidable.

One afternoon Matthew was online with Carly—her preferred way of speaking with him, too.

"Hi, Carly. Do you want to talk?" Matthew asked her.

"no working on story. mom wants lip stick on a pig," she responded.

"I'm glad you're working on your story again. What do you mean mom wants lipstick on a pig?"

"she wants me to finish my story too fast and it's not going to look good. like a pig with lipstick. Duh."

"Oh, sorry," Matthew replied, missing the joke.

"you should be," Carly retorted.

"someone's got attitude!"

"so put it away," Carly sassed.

"you're full of it today, aren't you? why don't you put it away?"

"full of what?" she teased.

"attitude," Matthew replied, naïvely.

"duh i know sarcasm."

We think we know our children—they are either easygoing or intense, pleasant or cranky, book-smart, street-smart, or not-so-smart. Carly, however, was a medley and constantly changing. It was unnerving. When she was a small child, I imagined that she was like a stranger in a strange land. Perhaps she had conversations in her head, but she lived in a world where those around her spoke an incomprehensible foreign tongue making her a perpetual tourist among us. But I was wrong. She had been listening, learning, thinking. The far-off stares were not signs she was lost. She was pondering and processing. Writing lines of copy for her book, perhaps. Coming up with jokes or clever observations. And thinking—always thinking.

While I was amazed to find that Carly was a clever, sassy kid, it was also confounding. Carly neither lived in the world of the profoundly disabled nor fit in our world. Her intelligence was opening the door for an exciting future; her behavior kept her tethered, unable to cross the threshold. I felt both grateful and resentful. I knew many other families coping with children with autism who had not had the simple, powerful gift of having a conversation with their child. But I knew far more families who lived traditional, calm lives with their children at home, progressing normally.

It was Pandora's box. The more she opened up, the more she yearned to be like everyone else.

"Why can't I talk like you," she asked Barb.

"Your muscles don't work properly, but you do a great job with your computer."

"but what's wrong with my voice."

"Nothing is wrong with your voice. Your voice works fine. It has to do with the muscles in your mouth and tongue."

"fix it. I want to talk like Taryn."

"I want to be honest with you, Carly. We can work on your sounds, but I don't think you will ever talk like Taryn," Barb confessed. I was appreciative that she was having this conversation with Carly. I already felt like I delivered enough of the bad news in her life.

"that sucks," Carly responded. *"whats the point if I can't be normal. I want to be normal. Help me."*

"What's normal?" asked Barb

"like every other kid my age."

With her growing vocabulary and self-perception came the recognition of how unlike her twin she was. Their intellect and humor may have been similar, but that was about the extent of what they had in common.

One Wednesday evening, the night before she was to return to the respite program for the balance of the week, Carly wrote, *"I want to make money."*

"Why do you need money?" I asked. Carly had never asked for anything material.

"I want to buy the house next door. Because I want to live beside you," she replied before running from the room, flinging herself to the floor in the front hallway.

I was not prepared for the answer. Taryn went quiet and looked down at the table. Howard and I turned away from each other so as not to see the mutual hurt. The more we got to know Carly, the more we realized how unfair her life was becoming.

"We are not sending you away as *punishment*," I told her the next morning. "The staff at Cedarview is trained to help you in a way we can't at home." But I had trouble convincing myself, and realized that Carly was too intelligent to be comforted by this rationalization, either.

With Carly more frequently expressing her unhappiness, it was clear we'd need to start thinking about other options. Over the course of the year, I had made some peace with the decision to place Carly at Cedarview. Her friendship with Mel, her academic progress, and her accomplishments in communication all felt like triumphs that were worth the emotional price of sending her away. These triumphs, however, did not make living together full-time a possibility. Carly still required around-the-clock supervision. Residential care was our survival plan.

I found myself somewhat jealous of parents with children of lesser cognitive ability, as if they were more justified in placing their child in residential care—a callousness of which I am now ashamed. But we were like itinerants, never able to set down roots, constantly on the move.

Everything in our family was lived on extremes. When Carly was home, her presence was enormous and all-consuming. When she was gone, I felt empty and hollow. Carly's intelligence far exceeded that of most kids, but her behavior was far below that of the mainstream. The polar extremes were exhausting. Our life was too black-and-white, and I yearned for some gray—some in-between. I hoped that when Carly was away, absence would make the heart grow blinder and in time I would ache less while she was away, and be more at peace when she was at home. For the time being we would have to live in a binary world—Carly here or gone—and that would have to be good enough. At least for a little while.

Part III

❧

Ascension

Sometimes when you are in a crowded room the
best way to be heard is to yell. But the best way
to be understood is to explain yourself.
—*Carly, June 2009*

15

⁓৯৶

Daughter of the Commandment

In a world of silence, communication is everywhere. You just have to
know how to look.

—Carly

It is a ritual in our religion, as it is in many others, to celebrate a
child's coming of age. For parents of someone who is remarkably
challenged, these milestones are bittersweet. We had long ago
put to rest any hope that Carly would have the enjoyment of passing through the evolving markings of life: a first date, high school
graduation, attending university, walking down the aisle. We had
to content ourselves with celebrating Carly's own triumphs, such as
toilet training and, on occasion, writing.

Pushed by Barb, however, we reflected on our girls' bat mitzvah, the Jewish custom of marking the move from childhood to
adulthood—a symbolic transition when a child takes responsibility for her own acts of good or evil, generosity or selfishness. Jaded
into still seeing Carly for what she could *not* do, we assumed this
celebration would be one-sided in favor of Taryn. So many aspects
of Taryn's daily life were defined by her sister's autism and disability,

and in this case we felt she deserved the same experience her friends had. But, as two of Carly's greatest advocates, Barb and Howard insisted that Carly play a meaningful role in the religious service and celebration that would follow.

So as the fall of 2007 approached, we encouraged Carly to write a short speech that we would read at the event scheduled for January 2008. She and I had been having short conversations over email and instant messenger. I was generally home too late from work or the gym to eat dinner with the kids. So, after her bath, Carly would sit at the table while I ate, and we would either play a game of Connect Four (a game she quickly learned to trounce me in) or talk. Carly would sit with the laptop in front of her, me with my plate in front of me. I would encourage her to ask me questions or tell me anything she wanted. Had we eaten dinner as a family, all sitting around a table cluttered with dishes, we would have been focused on helping Carly feed herself properly and conversation would have been impossible. Although unconventional, it was our way of bonding.

"what will I say?" she asked me, referring to the topic of her bat mitzvah speech.

"I think you should thank people for coming," I replied. To date, her conversations and emails had been short and simple. We knew at this point that she was witty and had a good vocabulary. But other than *The Elephant Princess*, Carly had never written anything longer than a few sentences, so the notion of a speech was daunting.

"Maybe tell them a little bit about what it's like to be you. People are curious to understand autism, and now that you can write, you have the chance." I was enjoying the new stage of our relationship. Carly and I were actually conversing. The first twelve years of her life had been a noisy silence devoid of language or meaningful answers. As painfully slow as it was, I relished these interchanges and the ability to offer advice. I could be more than a caregiver: I could actually be her father.

Though she had been writing for the past year, we still had limited insight into Carly's puzzling behaviors, explosive outbursts, and odd noises. Carly was anything but calm, which made typing an onerous task. Her emails or instant messenger conversations over the past twelve months generally consisted of short requests. She also told us, several years later, that in the beginning she didn't like the sensation of touching the computer keys. Autism can affect senses in ways we can't even imagine. What feels like nothing for neurotypical people may be excruciating for those with autism. In these early days, after she learned to type, Carly's language was terse and staccato because of the formidable challenge; the pace was creeping.

To help her write her speech, I would prompt her with questions or thoughts, and she would respond with answers. We would then cut and paste these phrases together into paragraphs. I felt like we were building a house out of pebbles. But it was the first creative project we collaborated on, and I loved it. Not only was I helping Carly accomplish something powerful, I was learning so much about her. By the time the speech was complete, I would have a dramatically different view of my daughter.

Though progress was slow, she was exploring feelings, reflections, and self-knowledge that she had not yet expressed in her writing. In their afternoon sessions, Barb would work with Carly by prompting her with additional ideas when she seemed to stall and keep her on task with a series of reward-based goals. But soon we started to see that Carly had her own ideas of how the speech should unfold.

"I want to pick a Jewish topic to talk about," Carly told Barb one day when the speech was a paragraph or two long.

Barb went on to explain a concept known as *tzedakah*, the act of charity.

"I know what it is," Carly informed her.

"How do you know that, Carly?" Barb asked her, doubtfully.

"At your school," Carly retorted, referring to Northland, where the two had first met. At that time, Carly was at her most erratic and uncontrollable self. Although she participated in activities such as music, stories, circle time, and crafts, no one really considered that she might actually be absorbing the more subtle and intellectual concepts such as the spiritual value of kindness. That was seven years earlier, and we were amazed that she was able to comprehend the mature concept of charity—much less remember the Hebrew word for it—so many years later.

"What do you think of my idea?" Barb continued.

"I like it," Carly replied.

Barb suggested that perhaps, in preparation for the bat mitzvah, Carly could actually perform an act of altruism, not merely write about it.

"I want to make food for people who need it," Carly decided.

While it is not unusual to partake in such a project as part of the coming-of-age ritual, I was awed by my daughter's enthusiasm to help those less fortunate. Those *less* fortunate? Who could possibly be less fortunate than a girl possessed by a driving energy that produced destruction? A girl who was showing the signs of creative thought but who could not control the actions of her body? And yet in the following weeks she actively participated in baking cookies, shopping for food, and paying a visit to a men's homeless shelter to make the donation. As she sloppily mixed the cookie dough, my hand over hers gripping the whisk, I wondered what else was going on inside her head. Even as I felt a warm sense of pride at Carly's thoughtfulness, sadness clouded the moment. Despite our best efforts, she will always require someone else's hand guiding hers.

Sitting at my desk one morning in early October, I saw Carly sign onto her instant messenger. I instinctively smiled. "Carly has signed in," my screen read, almost like a cheerful accomplishment in and of itself.

"I want to write a letter with you," she typed.

"That's a good idea," I replied. I was thrilled that Carly was beginning to reach out and use her voice in ways that extended past requesting chips or popcorn. "You need to write a letter to Marty and Pop Pop," I reminded her. "To thank them for your new computer."

"I want to write a different one," she said. *"I want to write to Ellen."*

The time code at the start of each message on my computer screen taunted me. This simple request would take no more than thirty seconds coming from any other twelve-year-old. But Carly had to scan the keyboard and peck one letter at a time. She often needed breaks to stand up and jump around to release the eternal restlessness that haunts her body. This short conversation took an excruciating forty-five minutes. During the time she made the request, I had held a brief meeting in my office and written a memo of my own.

"Who is Ellen?" I asked. No response. Knowing that Howard would be sitting at Carly's side, I persevered. "Who does she mean, Howard?"

"The one I dance to," she continued, finally. *"I can't spell her last name. It's too funny."*

"It's Ellen DeGeneres," Howard informed me. "That's who she dances to."

"That's funny, Carly," I replied, shaking my head. As Carly never sits calmly in front of the television, I didn't immediately make the connection. "Okay. What do you want to tell her?"

With over an hour invested in this quest, I knew I had to press on. We had learned long ago to resist the temptation to write long responses or ask complicated, run-on questions.

"Howard says that she shares the same birthday with me."

"Cool. What do you want to tell her?"

"I want to make a wish."

"You want to tell Ellen your wish? What's your wish?" I was now thoroughly intrigued. If you were asking for something for the first time with a newfound voice, what would it be? Would her wish be for something frivolous like a computer game console or iPod? Simple, like a signed autograph from Ellen? Other than requests for basic needs or treats, I had never known Carly to ask for anything.

"cant say now will telll you later," she teased.

After taking a break for lunch, which allowed me to cram two hours of work into thirty minutes, Carly came back online and we started the letter. "I think you should start by introducing yourself, Carly," I suggested.

"my name is carly I am from Toronto," started the first letter my daughter ever wrote. *"I have autism I cant talk I can spell on myyy computer,"* she continued. I was struck by the fact that the onerous task of typing would make Carly's conversations so direct and to the point. Any extra adjectives, adverbs, even a simple article could add minutes to the task.

"its hard for me to sit still or play a game."

"How does this make you feel?" I suggested.

"it ok sometimes but I get sad and frusterrateted. I want to be like other girls."

This was not the first time Carly had made this painful admission, but it was still new enough that it stung. It had been easier to think that she was so intellectually challenged that she didn't notice how far she stood from the crowd. Those who make odd noises, flap their hands, walk in a shuffling run or a stiff-legged march, are they aware that others notice? Do they care what others think? How misguided I was to think they don't.

Carly had complained frequently, *"I need you to fix me. Fix my brain. My mouth feels silly."* She would then slam shut the computer and run from the room in a fit, crying and throwing herself to the floor. But now she was beginning to come to terms with her condition. Once Tammy asked Carly bluntly if she knew what autism was.

"It's something I have that other people don't like to see," she responded poetically.

After several weeks of slow progress, the letter was nearly complete. In it, she had introduced herself and made her request of Ellen but hadn't wrapped it up. During one of our evening routines—Carly freshly bathed and sitting at the kitchen table with Howard on one side, me on the other eating dinner—I told her, "It's time to get this letter finished."

In truth, I felt this exercise was a charade. I could barely get Taryn to clean up her room, much less convince a celebrity to read our daughter's letter, but with Howard's quiet confidence, Carly's steadfast effort, and Tammy's unwavering networking, I kind of went along with the plan. Carly was hesitating and wrapping up the letter had stalled. "Finish it with 'thank you' and 'yours truly,' " I suggested, trying to push it home.

Carly probably snickered at me inside. In hindsight, I think she was looking for a way to strike an empathetic chord. Finally, Carly added the last three sentences to her request.

Dear Ellen,

> *My name is Carly. I am from Toronto.*
> *I have autism. I can't talk but I can spell on my computer.*
> *It is hard for me to do things like sit still or play a game.*
> *It's okay sometimes, but I do get sad and frustrated.*

I want to be like other girls.

I like you because you make funny sounds like me. I like when you dance and act silly. You make me smile.

Howard told me we share the same birthday and I only know one other person that has the same birthday; she is my sister. I make a wish every year and it never comes true. If I tell you maybe it will.

My dream one day is to talk but I don't know if I will be able to.

So my birthday wish is for you, Ellen, to read my speech and be my voice at my party.

I'm sure you had a dream of being an actor and someone helped you out.

So can you help me out?

Love your fan,
Carly

Carly had mastered the centuries-old art of guilt and manipulation as she spelled out the closing sentiment of her letter. We marveled at how Carly was able to draw Ellen's experience into the situation to create empathy. "That's incredibly mature and sophisticated," I said, as much to myself as to Carly.

And the salutation was the first of what would become a signature trait of Carly's letter writing: personalized sign-offs, each one tailored to the theme of her letter. "Where did she learn the concept of being a 'fan' or how to write a letter like this?" I asked Howard rhetorically.

In the coming months, this would be a recurring theme in our relationship. Carly would dribble out small amounts of knowledge or observations, crack jokes and tease us. We hypothesized that although she didn't sit and watch TV or read newspapers, she likely picked up information. She seemed to take in information around her as if by osmosis. When I asked her directly about how she knew the definition of certain words, or where she had heard about various current events such as a particular politician's position on government-funded autism services, her only response was a coy, *"I know stuff. Duh."* There appeared to be an entire world spinning inside Carly that we had yet to discover—a world of imaginative thought far beyond the controlled, adult-managed one she lived in.

Although I wanted to encourage Carly in her goal of having Ellen read the speech, I had no expectations of being able to get the letter to Ellen—certainly not in the two months that remained before Carly's bat mitzvah.

Tammy was the one who was driven to bring about a miracle. As a friend once told her, "Some people don't take no for an answer. But you never even get no for an answer." With Barb's continual encouragement, Tammy engaged for battle—a compulsive warrior.

Carly worked on her speech and Tammy navigated the six degrees of separation that apparently linked us to Ellen DeGeneres. A search on Google led her to the name of Ellen's agent at ICM, a major talent agency in LA. Charles and Richelle Bolton, close friends of ours from graduate school, were living in Los Angeles and contacted someone they knew who also worked at ICM. "He's Jewish, too," Tammy joked. "He'll understand guilt. At least he'll know what a bat mitzvah is." By the time my wife's sleuthing was complete, we had contacted Ellen's agent, her manager, producer, and personal assistant. I think someone who worked for me at john st. even put in a call to Ellen's makeup artist, whom she somehow knew through the industry. Initial responses were not encouraging ("We can offer you a signed photograph of Ms. DeGeneres," said Ellen's manager). But compromise is the enemy of success, and Tammy continued emailing her newfound contacts and eventually, we successfully got Carly's letter through to Ellen.

By that time, several other leads we explored had also mentioned the request to Ellen and her staff. In an effort to persuade them, we got Carly to relinquish a draft copy of the "secret speech" to Tammy and me, so we could attach it to her letter. We thought if they could get to know Carly and the amazing strides she had made, perhaps we could move them as much as we were moved by Carly's unique voice and spirit.

Over the coming weeks, we would get occasional emails back from Ellen's agent. It might happen. It might not happen. It probably will happen. "My daughter told me I had to make it work. It's a chance 'to do good,'" he told us. All the while we kept this from Carly. Her life was a string of disappointments; she didn't need another. Maybe she would even forget about it, I deluded myself.

On a cold, dark evening in December, I received a call on my cell as I drove up Avenue Road from my office. Christmas lights adorned the shops and restaurants lining the city street. Traffic crawled. "Ellen will read Carly's speech on video," said Ellen's personal assistant, Craig. "She'll do it after she records her Christmas show, and we'll send you a DVD by the New Year. Will that be okay?"

I was stunned. What are the odds of this? I thought to myself. After thanking Craig profusely, I had to ask: "Clearly, Ellen is a very kind person, but I'm sure she gets thousands of requests. Why is she doing this?"

"She was very moved by Carly's letter and speech. And I have to tell you, you have quite the PR machine going there." He chuckled warmly. "We were approached by three or four people about this. No matter which way we turned, Carly's name was coming at us from all sides."

While I knew it was the confluence of strength, a group of strangers' and friends' desire to do good, I was equally becoming aware of the power of Carly's words to motivate people to action.

I called Tammy on my cell. "How should we tell Carly?" I asked.

"Let's take her out to Demitri's after dinner," Tammy suggested, referring to a dessert place near our house that Carly loved.

Later, as Howard, Tammy, and I sat around a table sharing an enormous slice of chocolate cake, we announced to Carly that Ellen had agreed to her request. Ellen would be her voice at the bat mitzvah. I had no expectations of heartfelt reaction, as Carly's face does not brighten and she will seldom spontaneously hug. With no way to vocalize her feelings, Carly is impossible to read. At best, she will look down and the slightest smile—almost a knowing look—will briefly cross her face.

The only way to understand what Carly is thinking is to persuade her to put it down in words. Her body fails to communicate what her brain thinks. "Tomorrow you need to write a thank-you note, and we'll send it to Ellen's assistant," Tammy told her.

This Carly did, with little persuasion.

> Hi Ellen. my mom and dad told me to write you a thank you two weeks ago. Before I knew that you had said yes. It takes me a long time to write my letters so I did it just in case.
>
> Last night my mom and dad took me out for a big big slice of cake and then they told me. They said you are going to read my letter. When I wrote my first thank you letter I did not know how excited I was going to be. So thats why I want to give you this also. You made my wish come true.
>
> Some times I think I would like a magic wand.
>
> So I could do what you did for me for other people.
>
> For my dad I would wave my wand and make him have lots of money so he does not have to go to work and he can stay home and read to me.
>
> For my mom I would make all the silly people understand about autism so she does not have to fight with them and be on the phone all the time.
>
> I would help Howard finish his dream and open his camp for kids like me so I could hang out with him all summer. I know it would be fun.

I think for taryn I would replace all the things I broke of hers and for Matthew I would get him a girl friend.

Wait I dont think any wand in the world could get Matthew a girl friend.

I know, I would wave my wand around and around so you would know how happy I am that you made my wish come true.

I need you to do me another favor. I need you to stop reading this letter and give it to Portia.

❧

Hi Portia,

Portia I am in Toronto and Howard showed me a map a long time ago and I saw that Ellen is far away from me. I want to give her a hug to thank her for what she has done for me.

But I cant.

So I was hoping you could give her a hug from me.

When you do hug her close your eyes and picture a girl whos wish came true and this way Ellen will know its from me.

I also would like to say I love your name.

You must have a cool mom and dad .

My parents just named me carly. But I like it.

Tell Ellen I say thank you and like I said in my thank you letter if she tells me her wish, who knows it might come true.

It worked for me.

Love,

Carly

With every letter Carly wrote, we got to know her more and more—her sense of humor, humility, and strength. I wasn't sure which I was more excited about: Ellen's commitment or Carly's response. This ability to inspire others through her words was the opening of a new chapter in Carly's life. Of course, we were all still working *for* Carly. But helping her reach out was a welcome challenge—and a far cry from that monotony of physical care, education, or therapy. Those efforts were one-way, tasks that offered little reward save for the knowledge that we were doing what was right.

Carly's inner voice had been trapped by the rough-hewn stone of her exterior for so long it was hard to imagine what she might sound like. The sharp edges of her behavior stood in glaring contrast to the beauty of what lay underneath. Coming to this realization was as disorienting and jarring as a jump in a frigid lake. And just as invigorating.

16

❦

That Is How We Learn

I am an autistic girl but autism doesn't define who I am or how I'm going to live my life. I have encountered many hardships in my life but slowly and surely I have been over coming a lot of obstacles in my path. There are many days when I think it might be easier to give up then fight. However if I give up if I don't try then who am I really. Because when it's all said and done I am Carly fleischmann a girl who needs to try to be the best I can be. I know its not easy I know I will slip up and temptation will win once in a while. But I am me and if I'm not trying to better my self then who will.

—Carly

A bat mitzvah for upper-middle-class modern Jews can become a weekend-long affair; more like a wedding than a coming-of-age ceremony. Family arrives from out of town. Dinners, lunches, party dresses, and makeup all threaten to overshadow the spiritual celebration that this occasion is intended to mark. For most, it is one of the happiest life-cycle events.

Carly had always been easily overwhelmed by big events and large crowds, so I was filled with trepidation as the weekend approached. Rather than withdrawing into herself, as is the stereotype of children with autism, Carly's reaction to stress was to explode. She would start by covering her ears and rocking, but this would quickly disintegrate into flailing, crying, and head banging. It had happened so frequently, I dreaded any occasion that included my daughter and anyone other than our immediate family or workers. Waiting for a ticking time bomb to explode is not my idea of fun. I had long gotten over the embarrassment of these public eruptions but would never overcome the anxiety of seeing my daughter out of control and trying to explain to strangers and near-strangers what was going on.

But when the day finally approached, I was relieved to see a different side of Carly. She had been remarkably engaged during the previous months—writing her speech, gathering food and baking cookies for a homeless shelter, and meeting the DJ to select music for the party that would follow the service.

"Mom says I can pick the song we come out to. Nothing by Soulja Boy. He sucks. I want to dance to Stronger. Kanye West. Will you dance with me? You should get glasses like his," she wrote to me.

I smiled at how playful Carly was inside but couldn't help but feel the creeping sadness that, while Taryn would be with her dozens of school friends, Carly would be with her workers and therapists. She had once complained, *"My friends are twice my age. And you have to pay them."* But Carly seemed to be putting aside any self-pity and recognition of her differences, and was getting into the spirit of her bat mitzvah with zeal.

Jewish law suggests that there are several times throughout the week when a bar or bat mitzvah can take place. Because of our special situation, we elected to go with a less traditional but simpler evening service on a Saturday night. Taryn would read from the Torah, we would say special blessings, and Carly would participate by opening and closing the *Aron Kodesh*, the special cabinet that holds the Torah scrolls. After the service would be dinner, dancing, and toasts. This celebration was as much an excuse just to be happy as it was a recognition of the girls' coming of age. We had had so many struggles over the course of thirteen years with Carly's challenges and Tammy's illness. The bat mitzvah celebration was to be a purely joyful event and was to exist squarely in the Autism-Free Zone— that social space Tammy and her friends had created where there was to be no mention of the "A" word.

The months of my wife's extraordinary planning paid off. On Saturday afternoon, a bright crisp winter day, the beautician Tammy had booked to do hair and makeup for the girls arrived at our house carrying a large case containing her tools of the trade. Our dining room was turned into an impromptu salon with hair dryers, straightening irons, and an endless array of boxes, brushes, and small metal contraptions that looked like they were borrowed from Dr. Frankenstein. As I held up one such tool in mock disgust, Taryn explained, her eyes rolling upward, "It's for curling your *eyelashes*," as if it were the most obvious thing in the world.

Taryn was the textbook teen on the eve of her bat mitzvah. She had been walking around the house for weeks chanting the section of the Torah and the accompanying prayers she was assigned. She fussed with the dress she would wear and what shoes she would get to match. She had attended many of her friends' bat mitzvahs and knew the drill. When it came time for her to have her hair and makeup done, she offered suggestions as though she were an expert herself and sat patiently while the woman cheerfully worked.

"I'm not sure how much you'll be able to do with Carly," Tammy warned the woman when she was finished with Taryn. "She generally can't sit for long and doesn't like her face being touched."

But what we witnessed was remarkably different from what we imagined. Carly sat perched on the high stool, ankles crossed. Although it was clearly a struggle for her to remain calm—she fidgeted restlessly—she sat for nearly twenty minutes as her hair was blown dry and pinned and a little makeup was painstakingly applied. This was her bat mitzvah, too, and it seemed she wanted equal treatment. We already knew she thought of herself as "cute and funny" from conversations she had with Barb's college-age son. "You're smokin'," I said to her when she was done. I think I detected a knowing smile.

We had asked the rabbi to respect tradition in the service while keeping it as short as possible in order to keep the stress levels down—Carly's and ours. Carly was able to sit through Taryn's reading with minimal squawks and slaps, and when it was time, she opened and closed the doors of the ark containing the Torah scrolls enthusiastically. Nevertheless, I was relieved when the focus of attention was no longer on us. I'm not sure who felt the pressure more, Carly or me.

After the service, held in a small ballroom on the second floor of a hotel in downtown Toronto, guests were ushered downstairs to a cocktail reception and ultimately, the dinner. The hotel had the festive elegance grand buildings wear particularly well during the holiday season. There's something about winter that suits formal occasions.

My son assembled a jazz trio with two of his high school buddies. They played in the lobby while guests mingled. Taryn's friends clowned around, reconfirming that while they were dressed like adults, they were in fact still kids. The photographer's flash popped while I sipped a scotch, letting the warm burn settle down the jitters that lingered from the preceding hour. "They both did great," Tammy and I agreed with relief.

As we entered the main ballroom for dinner, my wife and I were filled with an anticipatory buzz. We knew that the highlight of the evening would be the reading of Carly's speech and were thrilled to share this triumph with our guests. The room was a perfect venue for this accomplishment. The kids' tables on the left were adorned with candy-studded centerpieces, the adults' on the right with flowers and candles.

As the evening unfolded, I smiled with a happy melancholy. I knew my state of mind was hackneyed, observing that all my children were becoming adults. Dressed in a dark suit, my son acted as an emcee, introducing the family and friends who made short speeches or toasts, and instructing people to take their seats or join in a dance. He took his job seriously, standing at a small lectern with a microphone. "I'm not sure which one of you is the parent," my friend Phil quipped. I had to agree, Matthew looked so grown-up. At seventeen years old, he struck me as having become a thoughtful, caring person. Would he have become as sensitive and insightful growing up in another household? Was it nature or nurture? His voice choked with emotion as he noted that he would be leaving home for university in the fall and not be a part of his sisters' day-to-day lives anymore.

Although some siblings of disabled children feel resentment toward their parents for a lack of attention, Matthew clearly felt nothing but a loving attachment; he was as much a part of the team that kept Carly on track as her parents and therapists. Later that year at Matthew's graduation dinner, Carly would tease that when Matthew left for college she wanted his bedroom because it was larger than hers. *"But after we air it out,"* she said poker-faced. Exchanges of Matthew's kindness and Carly's sarcastic barbs had become a fixture in our family.

Taryn, too, spoke beautifully, and in a way that demonstrated the young woman she was becoming—yet with the charming sarcasm befitting a teen. Less heartfelt than our son but with a dry wit and a smile, she thanked Matthew for being a great brother. "I'll miss you when you leave for school this fall, Matthew. I don't just think of you as my big brother," she laughed, "but also as my IT manager. I will not only be losing a friend," she continued, "I will also be losing my chauffeur."

We saved Carly's speech for last. Tammy welcomed our guests and thanked the "village" that it took to raise Carly—all of whom had made what we were about to show a reality. "Here goes," she said, and took a dramatic breath before reading aloud a thank-you to everyone who sat at tables five and six—the twenty or so people who were part of our autism world. "I would especially like to thank our friends Charles and Richelle from LA for helping us pull off what you're about to see . . ."

These "thank yous" and "you're welcomes" are traditional fare at an event like this, but most guests were not expecting what was to follow. Less than twenty people knew about the video; fewer still had actually seen it. My heart kicked into high gear with anticipation. I wanted everyone to have the same reaction I had had when I watched Ellen reading Carly's words for the first time. I felt a surge of adrenaline; finally others would see Carly through a new lens. I was acutely aware that once her speech was read, Carly would no longer be the same person she once was. She would be publicly transformed from *the daughter with autism* into someone much more present and complex than anyone had known. We had described Carly's writings and conversations to friends and family during the past year, but there was no comparison to hearing Carly's words firsthand.

The room was briefly plunged into inky darkness before a shimmery light bounced from the projector screen. Ellen appeared, sitting on her set decorated for the Christmas holiday season. There was no audience in the studio, just my daughter's idol, in her signature chair, looking straight at the camera. "I received this letter from Carly," she said, and went on to explain that Carly had asked her to read the following speech. She was happy to do it, she said, because clearly, this was a very special girl. "So here we go, the words I'm about to read are her words. These are Carly's words."

"I am delighted to be here. I really don't know what to say but thank you for coming. It's been four months that I have been working hard on this speech and I hope you like it. I was hoping to read this speech to you. But I can't so I asked someone who makes me smile to read it for me.

"I have to tell you, I cheated and looked at some other girl's speech and she thanked everyone who came from out of town. I was told that people are coming on planes and trains just to see me.

"Okay, you can go now!"

At that, Ellen cocked her eyebrows and smiled. "*That's* funny." She continued:

"I know I might act or look silly to some of you, but I have autism that makes me act this way. A lot of kids and older people have autism, too. I am not the only one. Autism is hard because you want to act one way but you can't always do that. It's sad because people don't know that sometimes I can't stop myself and they get mad at me.

"I can't talk with my mouth but I learned how to spell and I can talk on my computer. It helps me sometimes to get things that I want like chips and candy. I like chips. My dad said that even though I can't talk now one day I might be able to. Two years ago I learned how to spell so who knows, one day I might be able to read this to you myself.

"If I could tell people one thing about autism it would be that I don't want to be this way but I am. So don't be mad; be understanding. I think people don't like things that are not like them or look funny. But we are not all the same and why would we want to be?

"I do want to be like everyone else but I think I would miss things about being me. Like when I spell for someone for the first time and see the look on their face. And that even when people are mad, if I cuddle with them they are happy again.

"When you grow up you might want to be a doctor or a teacher or just want to make people laugh. But I want to be a cook. When people are eating they look happy and I want to make people feel good.

"They say when you have a bat mitzvah you turn into a woman but it is not really true. I think a bat mitzvah is just the start. I think it is like me and spelling; it takes a long time to be able to get good at it. I don't think anyone can say they are the perfect woman. I am sure I will make lots of mistakes. But that is okay. That is how we learn.

"A bat mitzvah is funny. It says that now you should know all about being Jewish but it says that now you are old enough to *learn* about being Jewish.

"I was told that my sister has to read something in different letters and I can't do that. So my friend Barb told me to talk about something Jewish. What I am going to talk about really should not be just for Jewish people it should be for the whole world. It is called Tzedakah. It is when we are giving not just things like cookies, but giving of ourselves.

"If everyone in the world did one nice thing for someone other than yourself the world would be a nicer place. I can't say that we should be nice all the time because I think it's sort of like me. I can't help it when I do things, but I think we should try hard to be nice when we can.

"I was told at camp that when I smile everyone starts to smile so maybe just for today we should walk around with a smile on our face and then everyone around us would start to smile and it might just come back to us. I would like to make people in the world happier so I made cookies with dad for people who don't have food. It must be sad not to have food. I love food. I think I would be happy if someone took time from their day to make food for me; then maybe I would want to do some thing good for some one else. It was lots of fun and rewarding knowing that I made cookies for people who really needed them and that's why I did not eat all of them. I gave the men the cookies and they were happy to get them. The strange thing is even though it was my project, my whole family took part in it one way or the other.

"I have to say I like my dad so much. He is so nice. I am now a woman but he still reads me stories in bed.

"My brother Matthew is funny. He tries to be the boss sometimes but it never works. Sorry Matthew.

"My mom is always doing work for me and tells me I am a hand full.

"Which leaves me to Taryn. It's hard when you want to play the same games as her but you can't or when you break something of hers and you did not mean to. But even though all this happens she still loves me and I love them all.

"Lots of people have worked with me to help me get where I am. I want to say thank you.

"But one I have had for the longest time. His name is Howie.

"Every time I tell him my dreams he says one day it will come true. So I just want to say one day your dreams will come true too.

"Okay, I thanked every one for coming I talked about autism and my Jewish topic but how should I end this?

"I know.

"A wise woman once said that if you don't have anything else to say then you should just do one thing.

"Dance.

"Have lots of fun.

"I know I will."

Ellen's voice snagged with emotion, and she wiped her eyes. "Carly, you are amazing," she said. "This is for you," she concluded, before proceeding to dance her signature dance across the stage.

There was a pause in the room as the lights came back up and our friends and family absorbed what they had just seen. Then, as if breaking a vacuum seal, everyone rose in applause and cheers. I stood to the side of the screen next to Tammy, Matthew, Taryn, and several of the young women who worked with Carly through the years. As I watched, I slipped my arm around Tammy. Although I had seen the video numerous times to convince myself it was real, sharing it in a grand venue gave it an impact I was not ready for and I found myself winded.

Over the course of her speech, Carly helped people see sides of her that many of us had taken for granted. Instead of being bitter or petulant, Carly exhibited the same sense of humor that often kept our family from careening off the rails.

Carly had written this speech to be read by Ellen. The timing and cadence was that of Ellen's own monologues. Carly had never doubted for a moment that Ellen would be her voice.

Although I had watched her speech unfold over the preceding months, it hadn't occurred to me that Carly wanted to help people who were faced with greater hurdles than her own. In fact, it had never occurred to me that there *were* hurdles greater than her own. She did not see herself as "one of them" but as one of us. In fact, perhaps she was a better *one-of-us* than most. Despite the obstacles that kept her out of the mainstream, Carly was not looking for sympathy but rather for acceptance.

I looked about the ballroom. People were dabbing their eyes and blowing their noses as if we had all experienced some sort of collective catharsis. The waitstaff, bartenders—even a security person required by the hotel for such events—all stood statue-still, momentarily chilled with emotion.

"Okay," I said turning to the DJ, "you better play something lively. Now." Kanye West burst from the dance-club-sized speakers.

I had watched Carly throughout the reading. She sat on the edge of the dais, with one of her aides and therapists. Carly never looked up at the screen once. Rather, she sat unusually calmly with her delicate ankles crossed; her elegant taffeta dress billowing around her. She had the pensiveness and composure of royalty. She looked down at her hands clasped on her lap, blowing breaths through pursed lips. Clearly she was making every effort to sit calmly. Or was she basking in the knowledge that, after waiting thirteen years, she had finally been heard?

A friend of ours who had known Carly since childhood approached me later that evening. "I will never look at your daughter the same way again," was all she could say before she drifted back into the crowd.

And neither would I. Carly was standing just outside the group on the dance floor, those who were laughing, clowning around, and drinking. She stood apart but closer to the crowd than she had ever been, clearly content, even proud, maybe for the first time in her life. She smiled as friends grabbed her arms and danced her around in circles.

I observed the scene, briefly removed from the festivities and reflecting on a comment Carly once made about her ill-functioning mouth and her wish that we could "fix her brain." I watched my daughter that night—able to move people with her words—and I realized that not all that is broken needs to be fixed.

17

❧

Pilgrimage to the City of Angels

Hi Ellen.

They say that one of the greatest gifts in the world is someone's voice and I can't believe it but you lent me yours.

I know I have thanked you a thousand times. But I feel like I still owe you your birthday wish.

I was watching your show for the New Orleans party and I know your birthday dream is to give people without a place to live a home. It would be so sad not to have a home. I love my home.

I wish I could twirl my magic dream wand and give all the people without a place to live a home. Or I wish I lived closer so they could stay at my house. They can sleep in my parent's bed and my dad could read them stories. They might like that. His stories always cheer me up.

I might not have a magic dream wand but I want to make your

dreams and the people of New Orleans' dreams come true. I was given
money at my party and I was told I could do whatever I want with
it. I was going to use it to fly down and see you so we can hang out.
But I wanted to give the money to you and the people of New Orleans
instead so they can make it right.

I am sending you $550.50 since you turned fifty years old. I know
it's not enough to build a house, but I hope it's a start.

I think Howard was right when he says that if you believe in your
dreams it will come true. Maybe, just maybe, if we want it bad enough
all the dreams of the people in New Orleans will come true too.

I hope you had a great birthday with Portia and I hope I helped
make one of your dreams come true.

Keep dreaming.

Love,
Carly

Carly seemed to take the notion of her bat mitzvah to heart. After
her experience with Ellen and the emotional response she received
from the speech, Carly's writing—and so I assume her outlook
on the world—matured. She continued to have the same physical struggles such as disrupted sleep, paralyzing compulsions, and
mannerisms stereotypical of people with autism. But her voice was
transforming. We started to see more playfulness and a greater concern with the world around her, and the events of the following
months fueled this momentum.

Tammy had begun an annual ritual of taking Taryn to visit cousins in Los Angeles over Taryn's midwinter break several years before. It was a way of balancing out the time Tammy spent keeping
Carly's world spinning on its axis—time that could not be spent
with Taryn. I never really understood the enthusiasm the two
shared for the city. To me, LA was a sprawl, and other than a few

friends, I had little connection to the place. This year, however, we decided to take a family trip—something we hadn't done in several years.

Travel with Carly still stirred enormous anxiety in me. I had a flashback to the trip a year and a half earlier when Tammy, Taryn, Carly, and I had gone to New York to see a neurologist for Carly. Taryn and Tammy stayed on in the city for a few days and I flew back to Toronto alone with Carly. Although it was only a one-hour plane ride, the ordeal of customs, security, the flight, and luggage claim with Carly's unpredictable behavior made me so tense I wasn't eager for a repeat experience. Could a week in LA actually be called vacation? But Howard agreed to join us and as our Carly whisperer, he had an enormous calming effect.

In fact, the flight was uneventful with Howard keeping Carly occupied with her iTouch, games, and snacks. One of her compulsive actions—a means of calming her inner turmoil—was to shred paper. During the four-hour flight she pulverized three magazines. But we made it. Carly later told us she worked extra hard to hold her outbursts in check and to remain calm because she wanted to prove she was capable. She was particularly motivated because our friend Charles had helped us to get tickets to Ellen's show and the opportunity to meet her briefly before the taping. This vacation was not only a chance for Carly to be part of her family, but a chance to meet her hero.

We checked into the hotel and to our surprise, the two rooms overlooking the parking lot had been upgraded to a suite the size of our house. Charles's network of friends seemed to have no bounds; we learned that the hotel's general manager was a friend, and he went all out to make us feel welcome.

We settled into the hotel and the kids went for a swim in the pool with Howard. Tammy and I planned out the week's agenda. We had to balance squeezing in as much sightseeing and socializing as possible with the unknown of Carly's ability to handle it all. The yin and yang of life with Carly follows us everywhere.

Yet we had underestimated Carly, again. Through the week, she rose to the occasion. At Charles and Richelle's, where we went for dinner, she played hangman on her computer with Matthew, Taryn, and the Boltons' kids. She was in good spirits as we drove around the city and through the hills and canyons that characterize LA, later commenting, *"mom drove around and around so much I thought I'd throw up."* Our nights were uninterrupted and we were able to eat in restaurants without hasty exits or excuses.

During the week, we went to visit a small school started by a woman Tammy had met on a previous trip to LA. Patricia and her husband had been actively involved in autism advocacy since their son was diagnosed. The school consisted of four students and was run out of a carriage house adjacent to the family's home. Carly and Howard spent the afternoon with them, going on a field trip to the Museum of Contemporary Art.

Later that evening, Howard said, "Carly did great. She particularly seemed to like Lichtenstein and stood staring at his paintings for a long time."

I wondered how Carly's eyes might process the unique style of the artist: his use of tiny black dots in combination with comic book images. Did she view art the same way as I did? Her ability to absorb visual information was so different, perhaps she saw color and images uniquely, too?

"I see them in streaming colour and flashing images. Duh," she scoffed at me.

Howard smiled at her and I realized I was the butt of her joke.

"She got along great with the other kids," he said. "She was writing with them all afternoon."

Howard showed me a picture he'd taken of Carly sitting on a couch, her arm around a teenage girl's shoulder. At home Carly had no peers with a similar juxtaposition of talent and challenge. She had no kindred spirit with whom she could commiserate or even hang out, and I wondered why this was so. Was it that these kids were so unique? Or was it that kids with Carly's diagnosis in Toronto just don't typically receive the depth of therapy that she did and therefore never discover their voices? In LA, autism seemed more mainstream to us and the range of services more abundant. Carly finally had friends, but sadly they lived three thousand miles away from us and their continued connection would have to be online.

The highlight of the trip, particularly for Carly, was our visit with Ellen before joining the audience for her show. Carly sat on a couch next to Howard, all of us crowded into Ellen's small dressing room. The room was packed with clothing and a makeup table. Ellen's Guitar Hero game stood off to the side.

Ellen greeted us all warmly and introduced us to her mom, who attended most of Ellen's shows. Carly and Ellen sat on her couch, with Howard off to the side, while the rest of us attempted to stay out of the way in the snug room.

Carly had prepared questions for Ellen in advance in case her anxiety prevented her from typing. Carly was curious about what Ellen did in her time off and what it was like to be a celebrity. Ellen graciously answered all of Carly's questions, commenting that it was a pleasure not to be the one asking them for a change. I observed Matthew and Taryn watching their sister with an amused pride. As we shuffled out to our seats, Ellen gave Carly a hug, and invited her to come visit again. "You're an incredible woman, Carly," she said.

Our meeting with Ellen felt less like a brush with celebrity and more like closing a loop. Carly wanted to be able to thank Ellen face-to-face for "lending me her voice," as she described it. The reading of the speech was a very personal act and we all felt an enormous debt of gratitude, something that could not be paid off in an email.

We celebrated the day by having dinner at the Polo Lounge, an iconic restaurant in Beverly Hills. I thought we might be pushing our luck with Carly's ability to hold it together after a tiring day, but she seemed to be holding court.

"What would the lady like to order?" the waiter asked. I sensed he was from an era when being a waiter was a cultured art form and smiled at the respect he paid my daughter.

"Chicken strips and salad," Howard replied for her, and Carly's right hand went to cover her ear as she looked down and smiled.

Sitting at the large round table with my family, live music playing in the background, and the sun fading through the windows overlooking the shaded terrace, I realized I was actually having *fun*. Too often, events were to be gotten through—an accomplishment if completed without disaster. But here we all sat, enjoying ourselves. Carly's netbook computer lay open to the side of her place setting. Though she was too tired to write further that night, she was clearly happy.

I had given up hope that we could go away as a clan and all get something out of it other than a black eye. The logistics, squabbling, and feeling of walking on the eggshells of Carly's composure negated the pleasure of travel. With Howard's help, however, and years of waiting, Matthew and Taryn were finally getting their sister back and I was getting a complete family.

The trip, in fact the entire previous year, was as transformative for me as it was for Carly. I was coming to the recognition that Carly was a person independent of me. Dependent in need perhaps, but not in spirit. She was capable of having relationships and dreams, bonding with people and places outside her circumscribed world, and feeling pride and joy in doing so. As we headed back to Toronto, I was glad Tammy had convinced me to make the journey. It was easy to assume the worst and live within tight boundaries. Maybe LA, a city known more for eating dreams than making them come true, wasn't so bad after all. Our experience with Ellen was anything but superficial. Our friends were more welcoming and generous than we could have imagined. And we found a tight-knit community of families with similar challenges to ours who were open to new friendships. Maybe LA really was a city of angels.

Dear Ellen,

I am writing you because I need to give you a big thank you.
I know what you are thinking. Why am I thanking you?
A few weeks ago on your show you were talking to Oprah on Skype and she told you that you were going to be on the cover of O. That's very cool, by the way. Congratulations.
But that's not why I am thanking you. It's what you said after she told you that you were going to be on. You said set goals for yourself, that you can do any thing if you just try.
Well I took your advice.
I set two goals for myself. One was to be heard and the other was to help kids that are in the same boat that I was in to get their inner voices out. So again I have to thank you.
I remembered you saying that if you have something important to say, say it on CNN. So I looked for the oldest person there and I found him . . . Larry King. I wrote him a letter but Barb and Howard told me he gets thousands of letters a day. And if he is really that old I did not know how much time I had. I was stuck at that point so I thought I would ask all my friends to help. I knew if lots of people supported me, he would have to listen. So I started a petition to get on his show. I figured it would be something you would do but your petition would be probably to ban glitter. But mine's just as good, I think.
My goal was to get 5000 signatures in two weeks. Barb did not think I could do it. She even told me to lower it. Don't tell her but

I was going to listen to her. But I had a small feeling I could do it and you always go big. Why couldn't I?

After the first day and I went over my 1000 mark, I knew I was going to make it. By the third day I was at 3200 and Larry was knocking, well sorry, calling. I got to go on the show and I was even on with your friend Jenny McCarthy. I wrote a small message an hour before the show started and he played it on the show.

It was not the way I wanted to do it but it would have taken me way too long to write while the show was live. I still want to do a pre-taped show with him, so people can see me type.

I have to say I am sorry I stole one of your lines. I hope you don't mind, the one that you said people wont listen till some one stands up. Well I think Larry really liked it, so please don't tell him I got it from you. I really just want to say thank you for making me believe in me.

Your autistic late night guest,
Carly

Oh some one asked if I would do Oprah show and between me and you, you're the better one. Don't tell Oprah.

18

‹⟡›

Discovery

Q: *Carly, tell me about some of your favorite things? What kinds of books do you like? What kind of music? TV shows? Why?*
A: I love food. I like eating chips because they taste so good. It takes a lot out of me to read a book but i like when someone reads it for me. I like listening to Septimus Heap. It's fun because i can picture it all in my head from what Septimus looks like to the castle gates. I love listening to music i like songs that i can rock back and forth to. I like kanye west. I like tv but it's hard for me to sit in front of it some times. It's too overwhelming. I like to sit to the side of it and just listen. I love watching the Ellen Show. She makes lots of noises and makes me forget that I'm autistic some times.

—From a conversation with the producer of ABC's *20/20*

As I've said, Tammy is a news junkie. For her, news is something to be scoured over, clipped, and responded to. One Sunday in late January 2008, she was reading an article in *The New York Times* about girls with autism. The article explained that not only was the incidence of the disorder lower among girls than boys, there were unique aspects and abilities among females with autism. Unlike boys, the research noted, girls may have a greater sense of empathy and emotion, a concept known as "theory of mind."

"So this could explain why Carly seems so different from some of the other kids we know with autism," she said. "They're all boys."

Over the years, Tammy had tracked stories and research about autism. But this one stood out because it specifically addressed girls, who seemed to be the forgotten afflicted. One reporter whom she felt did an excellent job at advancing the understanding of the condition was a woman named Avis Favaro, the medical reporter for one of Canada's national television networks. Tammy had done an interview with Avis many years before, when Carly was four and we, along with many other families, were locked in a battle with the government for additional funding for autism services. So when Tammy read this pivotal article, she promptly called Avis to see if she would be interested in exploring the differences further.

"It's interesting, some of the things that Carly is telling us about what it feels like," she explained to Avis Favaro. "You might get some perspective on girls and autism."

"*Telling* you?" Avis was startled. Avis only knew the Carly of before. She had been a nonverbal, hyperactive whirling dervish with no means of communication other than the use of some basic sign language and a picture-exchange program.

"Well, *writing*," Tammy clarified for Avis. Tammy explained how Carly had begun her tentative writing three years earlier and was now communicating full and emotive thoughts.

"*That*," said Avis, "is the story."

Several days later, a news truck, camera and sound technicians, and a producer arrived at our house. It was a gray, snowy winter day, and Taryn and Matthew were at school. We had arranged for

Carly to be home with Howard and Barb to assist her in answering questions for the news producer and crew. Tammy and I were to be interviewed afterward.

Given Carly's tentative typing, we warned that there was no guarantee she would perform. She once chastised us, *"I am* not *a trained dog."* To reduce the stress, we asked Avis to send as few people with as little equipment as possible. And if possible, send a good-looking young cameraman. Carly loves to flirt. In addition, the producer provided us with some questions that she would ask Carly when she came to get the footage. This way Carly could think about her responses. It was critical, however, that Carly type on her own on camera, as people who had never seen her type were still skeptical that she wasn't being coached, facilitated, or assisted in any way. We understood their doubt, given the juxtaposition of Carly's behavior—her humming noises, lack of eye contact, and flopping—with her creative intelligence. For her own sense of self-worth, we wanted people to see the real Carly.

The day was slow and painful. Carly was rigid with anxiety at first, being filmed with a camera three feet from her face. She sat and rocked, her finger poised above the keyboard, unable to type a single letter. Barb and Howard sat to her side at the kitchen table or at her desk set up in the makeshift work area in our basement. Barb calmly and patiently encouraged her, knowing that it was important to Carly that people understand her for who she was, as she had said in her bat mitzvah speech.

The crew did their best to film from afar and keep out of sight, but it was late in the day before Carly finally began answering the questions posed by Avis's producer. Many of the questions put to her were ones we had had for years but in the daily grind had never been able to ask. So as the producer and the crew pressed on, we found ourselves hovering in the background, getting to know our daughter in real time. We were as naïve about Carly's inner psyche as the viewing audience.

"What is one of the hardest things you've ever had to do?" asked Elizabeth, Avis's producer.

"To tell you the truth," Carly began tentatively, *"I think I would have to say controlling my behaviors."* Howard sat several feet away, doling out a Lay's potato chip for each answer she completed, a reinforcement technique that for years had in fact helped motivate her to control those behaviors. To prepare for the day's recording, I had run out to the store to buy several jumbo bags and hidden them to avoid a power struggle with Carly.

She continued, *"It might not seem like I am at times, but I try very hard to act appropriately. It is so tough to do and people think it is easy because they don't know what is going on in my body. They only know how easy it is for them. Even the doctors have told me that I am being silly but they don't get it. If I could stop it, I would. But it is not like turning a switch off. It does not work that way. I know what is right and wrong but it's like I have a fight with my brain over it."*

We all shook our heads. Not so much in disbelief. We were becoming accustomed to being surprised by Carly. But she so calmly and intelligently scolded us for our short-tempered responses to her outbursts and destructive nature, her obsessions and compulsions. She went on, and in a few short sentences unlocked thirteen years of silence and mystery.

"Can you describe what it's like to have autism?" the reporter asked her.

In the few years that Carly had been typing, we had asked her few philosophical questions. We had focused more on the here and now—seeking to understand the issue that required tackling at the moment.

"Autism feels hard. It's like being in a room with the stereo on full blast. It

feels like my legs are on fire and over a million ants are climbing up my arms. It's hard to be autistic because no one understands me. People just look at me and assume that I am dumb because I can't talk or because I act differently than them. I think people get scared with things that look or seem different than them. It feels hard."

It took a reporter with the objectivity of an outsider to rupture the wall that separated Carly from her family—and the world. In the hour or two it took to write her pointed response, Carly helped redefine herself and possibly all people living with autism who had not yet found a way to communicate. At the same time, it raised a myriad of questions about how we might help Carly put out the fire.

For Carly, it was liberating to be able to unburden herself, to explain why she behaved the way she did. She helped us see her as a person locked in the box that is autism. For us, the afternoon was emotionally draining. On one hand, gaining insight provided us with perspective and hope; hope that we could find ways to help. But being confronted with the raw suffering our child endured daily for so many years was far more heartbreaking than receiving the diagnosis ten years before. Ignorance had been a gift.

As if to not leave us or the viewing audience with only the heaviness of her struggles, Carly went on to talk about her favorite memories of growing up. *"One thing I enjoyed the most,"* she wrote, *"is listening to my dad read me stories in bed. Some other memories I had was crawling in to my sisters bed at night after I woke up and she let me sleep with her. She cuddled me till I fell asleep. I am so lucky to have her."*

It had always been hard to know if Carly felt a real connection. In general, she only liked physical contact on occasion. She seldom initiated affection, although we felt drawn to give her hugs and kisses when she was curled up on the couch or when a mischievous look crossed her face. In particular, Taryn loved to jump on Carly at night and squeeze her in an embrace, telling her how cute she is and whispering in her ear.

I could tell from the satisfaction on Taryn's face, the way her large brown eyes smiled, how much it meant to hear that Carly adored her. While Carly had confessed how sorry she felt for stealing attention from Taryn or breaking her things, I have never heard Taryn complain about her sister's oddness or the impact she has had on our family life. Perhaps it's bottled up inside, but I prefer to believe that their love is greater than the burden of autism.

The day after the filming, Avis phoned to say they had looked through the rushes and were thrilled. The story would air later in the week. She told Tammy not to be surprised if we received a call from ABC, as the two networks often shared stories—especially those of medical breakthroughs and human interest.

With the filming done, the last of the bat mitzvah thank-you notes written, and life returning to a calmer pace, Tammy and Taryn took off for a visit to Los Angeles. Matthew plugged away in his last year of high school; Carly returned to her part-time respite and part-time homeschooling; and I returned to work. There was something utterly exhausting about the past month but also utterly stirring. Carly had written more than she had in the previous twelve years of her life, and we were seeing facets of her personality we had never imagined. We felt the CTV news report would be a fitting conclusion to Carly's coming of age that had started with her bat mitzvah preparations.

The day the CTV segment was set to air, Tammy was lounging by her cousin's pool. It was not hot yet in LA, but sunny and clear. With a hectic week planned of visiting friends and sightseeing with Taryn, she was enjoying the newspaper and a coffee and just not talking for a while. Her phone rang and she looked quizzically at the unfamiliar New York area code. Although it was very early on the East Coast, the medical producer for ABC's *World News with Charles Gibson* was phoning to get clarity on a story he had just picked up from CTV. He had not seen the footage yet; typically they receive only a typed transcript prior to the Canadian airing of shared segments.

At one point in the questioning about Carly's diagnosis, her breakthrough in writing, her inability to speak, and all the efforts we had made on her behalf, the ABC medical reporter John McKenzie said to Tammy, "I'll be honest. We don't believe Carly has autism."

Tammy snorted. "Well, why don't you tell me what you think she has and maybe we can fix this."

Tammy immediately phoned me. "They want to see a copy of Nancy Robards' and Dr. Stephensen's diagnoses. They're filed in the bottom drawer of my cabinet in the basement," she said.

I drove home from my office and rifled through Tammy's library of medical files. I found several reports from various doctors we had seen over the years, including the original diagnosis, "Carly presents as a child whose presentation in all three domains, stereotypic behaviors, communications skills and social interaction skills, falls within the spectrum of Autism—Pervasive Developmental Disorder. Carly is a child who avoids establishing eye contact, who is picky about the food she eats and will often spend her time spinning items and rocking back and forth. She makes sounds repetitively and flaps her hands. Carly continues to avoid eye contact and to resist physical contact with others. Developmentally, Carly shows developmental delays of global nature."

The reports were like finding a time capsule. Years flooded back. I remembered reading these documents carefully, analytically. I had scrutinized the language trying to understand what they had meant. I knew why I had had such little reaction when Carly was first diagnosed. Who could have known what *delayed* would mean? Who could have known the physical manifestations of autism? The grating, grinding, wearing effect it would have on our life? I'm glad no one told us. It was merciful that Dr. Stephensen's report didn't say how we'd spend years not sleeping, washing feces off walls, and praying for a real life, or death, or some way out. It was a life of filial piety in reverse—at times quite literally carrying our daughter on our backs. Unconditional love is a luxury; even parents have their limits. Ours was tested not in months and years but in seconds, minutes, hours, and days of physical labor, frustration, and heartbreak.

Later that afternoon, after ABC received confirmation that Carly's diagnosis was legitimate, the phone rang again. They had, by this time, also been given access to CTV's footage of Carly, her typing, and our interviews. They were intrigued and wanted to run their own segment. In fact, they believed Carly's story was of such interest, they would delay airing it several days in order to air promotional spots and recut a longer segment than the one that would be running on CTV that evening. I phoned Tammy, who confessed that while she was excited by the opportunity, she was a little disappointed that ABC's medical staff didn't come up with another hypothesis on Carly's condition. "I was kind of hoping they'd see something else in her. Something we could actually fix."

"Who knows," I responded. "Maybe someone will see the story and have some advice for us."

Tammy returned home from LA at the end of the week. She had watched the CTV story online and we sat in our den to watch it again, recorded on our PVR. "What do you think, Carly? How does it feel to be on TV?"

Carly sat rocking on the couch, her hands over her ears, and her shoulder-length hair hung tousled around her face, further closing her in. She made a blowing sound, lips pursed and vibrating. But there was a knowing smile on her face.

"What are you thinking, Carly?" I asked rhetorically. I knew that even with a large bowl of potato chips and the patience of Job, I could not get Carly to write for me. I had to be satisfied with the knowledge that in fact Carly was thinking something. Something wonderful.

❧

The ABC news story ran the next day. Public response was overwhelming and immediate. The network's website, which generally gets a few thousand hits for a good medical story, received tens of thousands of hits requesting the replay of the segment (several months later, the online story was still drawing viewers and had reached over two hundred thousand people). So many people were posting words of encouragement and questions, ABC asked if Carly would be prepared to respond to a few and they would broadcast the answers at the end of the news segment the following night. Not yet knowing how accurately Carly could read lengthy text from a computer screen, Howard read the questions the producer thought would be most powerful, and Carly set to the slow task of tapping out her short but perceptive answers.

Question

Name: *Anita*

Address: *Boulder, CO*

Millions of people saw your story on ABC News. Thousands have written letters of thanks to you. You are an incredible inspiration to so many families. Everyone is very proud of you.

How does this make you feel?

Answer

I am so happy. I got a big gift from people around the world.

Among so many kids with autism they chose me to be an advocate for autism. Where should I get behind a cause like this? I am so glad that I am able to help people understand autism.

Question

Name: *greg*

Address: *Erie, PA*

Hi Carly, after years of not being able to speak, what does it mean to you to be able to tell people what you want to say?

Answer

greg it feels so awesome to ask for things. So how do you speak?

Question
Name: *Ailyn*
Address: *Miami, FL*
Carly, I am so happy you found a way to communicate with those around you! My question is what was it like dealing with autism and coping with the frustrations of not being able to communicate your thoughts, feelings, desires and dislikes to your loved ones?

Answer

Ailyn it just sucks when I am alone. I feel very sad when mel goas away. I always yell when I feel like people so don't understand why I am sad.

Question
Name: *jerry and marieanne*
Address: *Ridgefield, NJ*
What can you suggest to me, as a teacher and a parent of young teens with autism, to help them?

Answer

be patient. Try getting a computer. Give them chips when they type.

Question
Name: *pgsad*
Address: *Chicago, IL*
What one thing do you think my autistic child would want me to know about him?

Answer

I think he would want you to know that he knows more than you think he does. He is lucky to have nice parents.

Question

Name: *mmfreedom*

Address: *Omaha, NE*

Do you believe the behavior therapy helped you and do you think intensive therapy has anything to do with you not only finding a voice, but knowing what to say now that you've found the means?

Answer

I think behavior therapy helped me. I believe that it allows me to sort my thoughts. Unfortunately it can't make me normal.

Question

Name: *Colleen*

Address: *Saltspring, BC, Canada*

Carly, you have come so far with all your success. Why do you think in the last year or so you've come so far and are able to communicate with more and more people?

Answer

because first Howard believed then dina [one of Carly's therapists] did. Believing helped. Then time went by and dina left and time went by. Then a miracle happened you saw me type. Then my therapist Mel helped me forget that I'm autistic. She treated me like I'm normal.

Although we didn't appreciate it at the time, Carly was transforming. Subtly, she was evolving from victim to spokesperson. We watched her intently typing out her advice, amused by the sophistication of the questions people posed to her. "She's becoming the autism diva," Tammy joked. "I'm not sure people realize she's just a kid." After the second broadcast, hundreds of questions continued to pour in from as far as India, the UK, Australia, and Israel.

I printed out the pages of text, putting it into a binder for her. "Do you want to hear more comments?" I asked her later that week.

"Eh ehss," Carly approximated. It was one of the few words Carly could still vocalize.

Although challenged to connect with the people in her everyday life, Carly was beginning to connect with millions around the world. People praised her, saying that in finding her voice, she gave them hope that their children or relatives, afflicted with autism, cerebral palsy, and numerous other conditions, would also find a way to reach out.

The emails continued unabated. How had Carly learned to write? Could she help them with their child? What kind of music did she listen to? What kind of computer did she use? Would she consider running for president? The two networks phoned to inquire whether we'd be willing to film a longer-format piece. It would run on CTV's news magazine, *W5*, and ABC's equivalent, *20/20*. "It's up to you, Carly," Tammy told her. "If it's too much, say so."

"Do the show," she replied.

It was agreed that ABC would be permitted to film all the footage for both networks in order to be less intrusive. Their producer, Alan Goldberg, and medical correspondent, John McKenzie, arrived with a film and sound crew. John spent two days interviewing Carly, Tammy, some of Carly's doctors, and me. Alan stayed a few days longer covering additional events that routinely occur in our family such as outings, meals, and conversations. It was like living with your mother-in-law for a week. But Carly seemed to connect with Alan. He had a dry, sarcastic wit that fit Carly's style. She responds well to humor. Taryn and Matthew hid from view as best they could, self-conscious with the camera. During the additional interviews with Carly, Alan posed questions and Howard, Barb, or one of Carly's other therapists sat nearby to help keep her focused and on task. The ever-present bowl of Lay's potato chips remained just out of camera range.

"What do you dream about?" Alan asked, picking up on one of the questions Carly received a number of times from viewers.

"I dream about a lot of things like boys. And food. I don't always remember my dreams, but I do like them."

"Are you autistic in your dreams?" he continued, genuinely intrigued. We found Alan took a personal interest in his approach. I felt like he was asking to satisfy his own curiosity, not merely to get a performance for the camera. He became our accomplice in helping us understand Carly; he asked so many questions for which we had never been able to find the answers.

"Yes and no. Some of my dreams I can talk and do things that kids my age do. But some I even have a hard time doing the things I can do when I'm awake."

"We all have those dreams," I assured her. "Like when you need to run but your legs won't move, or make a phone call but you can't push the buttons." Carly, it seems, had the same type of anxiety dreams we all do.

"What do you mean when you say you 'take over a thousand pictures of a person's face when I look at them'?" he asked. Carly had made this point a few times in recent months.

"It's the way I describe how we see. All the images come at us at once. It is so overwhelming. When I was young, I couldn't stare directly at things. I looked out the corner of my eye and even though you may think I wasn't looking, I was," she answered.

"Where do you get so much information about pop culture? TV? Magazines? Fess up!" Alan probed. We had all been amazed at Carly's awareness of the relationship status of movie stars, her knowledge of what musicians were at the top of the lists, and even an understanding of who was running for president in the coming fall's election.

"*I listen to every thing that's going on around me,*" she started. "*If a TV is on and I am in another room, I still listen to it or if people are talking I like to hear what they are saying even if they are not talking to me. Like I say all the time, just because it does not look like I am paying attention does not mean that's the case.*"

We were beginning to understand that Carly had more than peripheral vision. She had peripheral *hearing.* Although she seldom sat quietly in front of the television, if it was on in the other room, she was taking in the information and storing it away. Through the interviews she was now having, first with CTV and now with Alan, we were beginning to get a much deeper understanding of Carly's range of knowledge and how she had acquired it. Every day was like peeling back another layer of the onion. But rather than seeing more onion, we saw a completely different person.

Alan wanted to get to know Carly as a young woman and not just as an autistic teenager. "Tell me some of your favorite things," Alan asked her. This had always been a barrier for us. Most kids have favorite toys or hobbies. But Carly never had. Play was not intuitive for her; learning how to play games or do puzzles was a significant part of her early behavioral programming at school.

"*I love food,*" she responded. We all smiled because Carly has a diminutive frame. Although strong from years of rocking and constant motion, her legs and arms were still slim as saplings and her body willowy.

"*I like eating chips because they taste so good. It takes a lot out of me to read a book, but I like when someone reads it for me.*

"*I love listening to music. I like songs that I can rock back and forth to. I like Kanye West, but I'm told he is not better than the Beatles,*" she joked, teasing Alan about *his* favorite musical group. "*I like TV but it's hard for me to sit in front of it sometimes. It's too overwhelming. I like to sit to the side of it and just listen. I love watching the Ellen Show. She makes lots of noises and makes me forget that I'm autistic sometimes."*

As intrusive as the experience was, Carly was motivated and on a roll. We were learning more about our own daughter in a few short days than we had in the past thirteen years.

"If you could go on a date with anyone, who would it be? Why? Where would you go?" Alan wanted to know.

"Brad Pitt. Why? Are you silly? He is very, very hot. Even Barbara Walters agreed with me," Carly replied, referring to an interview Barbara had conducted recently with the movie star. *"I'd like to go to a restaurant. It's easier for me because most restaurants are loud. No one would look at me funny there."*

Alan smiled thoughtfully. Carly's self-awareness was becoming one of her most moving and endearing qualities.

Over the few days together, Alan observed Carly baking cookies with one of her therapists, going to the mall with two young women who had worked with Carly in the past, having a dinner at a Japanese restaurant with the family, and going through her daily routine at home. He witnessed the sharp contrasts of Carly behaving like a typical teenage girl, wanting to put on makeup and fix her hair—and then flopping on the floor and banging her head for no visible reason. Although Tammy and I quietly discussed this intrusion into Carly's privacy during the latter, in the end we felt it was more important for viewers to understand how hard her challenge is. We were concerned that the media would romanticize Carly, filtering out the struggle and showing only the success.

Carly found her brush with stardom uplifting. The only phantom that would haunt her for the next few years would be a handful of skeptics who didn't believe that Carly could in fact write for herself. Some believed her thoughts were being influenced by the therapists who were assisting her. Some cynics lumped her in with a group of people who had been tarred with the negative aspects of facilitated communication. The news stories only showed short glimpses of Carly's typing, which is an unfortunate aspect of television journalism. Furthermore, a number of psychologists had staked their careers on the false conclusions that those without speech and with severe autism could not possess advanced intellect, creativity, and "theory of mind." Carly debunked their years of work and challenged their professional being. For us, we never paid much attention to the naysayers, as Carly had frequently typed with accredited psychologists, doctors, teachers, therapists, and family. We had complete confidence in our daughter, as did all the professionals who worked with her. Although annoyed, we understood the sense of doubt some might feel given the gap between the internal and external Carly.

Alan was respectful and did his best to tell Carly's story in the *20/20* segment as directly as was possible in the sound-bite style of television journalism. After the segment aired, Carly sent Alan a thank-you letter and a volley of emails ensued over the following years.

Dear Alan Goldberg,

My mother asked me to write you however, I don't know who you are. See, I was on 20/20 and now I am famous and I have forgotten all my friends and family. I have let the fame and fortune go straight to my head. But wouldn't you if you were on a show like 20/20? Every now and then things come back into my head. I think I might have had a smelly brother, but I don't remember.

I do have to say I did not like having to wait through a segment about people eating soap to see me on 20/20. But I am famous now so I can say that. I liked the show but think your boss is crazy. The longer version is ten times better and I don't look like such a wild child.

I really like your work and when Oprah offers me my own show you will be the first person I offer a job to. You can get my coffee. Lol.

I miss you and just want to say thank you for doing everything you did.

> *Your famous super diva,*
> *Carly Fleischmann*

Oh, just to let you know, If you want to do a follow up that's okay, but I want my own trailer.

Sometimes it takes an outsider to help us see what's right in front of us. As invasive as it had been, I question how long it might have taken for us to embrace Carly for who she was had we not pursued the story. And without the microphone and camera, I wonder if Carly would have marshaled the inner strength she was beginning to show.

19

⸙

Coming Home

[11:24:56 AM] *Carly joins conversation*

[11:25:08 AM] **Carly says:**
can my house have a pool

[11:25:22 AM] **Arthur says:**
hi carly.

[11:25:42 AM] **Arthur says:**
well, mom and i have talked about putting a pool in at home.

[11:25:47 AM] **Arthur says:**
i know you would love that.

[11:27:55 AM] Carly says:

and a big bathtub

[11:28:20 AM] Arthur says:

I'll bet you would like a "hot tub." do you know what that is?

[11:33:29 AM] Carly says:

is it the one that the w ater shoots up your bum andfeet

[11:33:48 AM] Arthur says:

ha ha. you are funny. yes, you are right.

[11:34:01 AM] Arthur says:

a hot tub has water jets that shoot water. it feels nice.

[11:35:56 AM] Carly says:

i want one

[11:36:13 AM] Arthur says:

well, we'll have to see how it all works out.

[11:36:46 AM] Arthur says:

mom and I are working with Adam's parents.

[11:36:57 AM] Arthur says:

we are trying to arrange for a house in toronto.

[11:37:25 AM] Arthur says:

It would be much closer and you could come and go more frequently.

[11:37:42 AM] Arthur says:

the house we're looking at right now is closer to my office. it is down town.

[11:37:58 AM] Arthur says:
Shari lives two doors up the street from the house.

[11:38:19 AM] Arthur says:
but it may take us a while to work it all out.

[11:38:25 AM] Arthur says:
so you have to be very patient.

[11:38:27 AM] Arthur says:
okay?

[11:40:01 AM] Carly says:
can i see uit

[11:40:29 AM] Arthur says:
i will have to find out. right now, there are a few young men who live there, they will be moving out.

[11:40:37 AM] Arthur says:
then we would need to do some work to fix it up a bit.

[11:42:26 AM] Carly says:
can i put a hot tub in

[11:43:15 AM] Arthur says:
hmm. i don't know. it's pretty expensive!

[11:44:17 AM] Carly says:
and a big pool

[11:44:28 AM] Arthur says:
well i KNOW they can't put a pool in.

[11:44:32 AM] Arthur says:

the backyard is very small.

[11:44:39 AM] Arthur says:

in fact, right now, it's just the driveway.

[11:44:50 AM] Arthur says:

but I want to put in a patio and a garden if they will let me.

[11:45:06 AM] Arthur says:

i think maybe we should think about putting a pool in at our house though!

[11:45:14 AM] Arthur says:

and you would use it here.

[11:48:34 AM] Carly says:

i want a big pool

[11:48:45 AM] Arthur says:

I hear you. I do too!

[11:51:26 AM] Arthur says:

Carly, what else would you like to talk about?

[11:52:17 AM] Arthur says:

It's great that you are writing. I know you don't like it,

[11:52:40 AM] Arthur says:

but it is the only way we can all understand what you are thinking and what you want.

[11:53:01 AM] Carly says:

ellen had a woman on and she had a son like me and she fixt him

[11:54:00 AM] Arthur says:

Carly, I know that your challenges make your life very hard.

[11:54:06 AM] Arthur says:

But you do not need to be fixed.

[11:54:17 AM] Arthur says:

you just different than some other people.

[11:54:22 AM] Arthur says:

But you are very smart.

[11:54:27 AM] Arthur says:

You can write.

[11:54:37 AM] Arthur says:

And as you get older, you will have more control over your body.

[11:54:47 AM] Arthur says:

And you will be able to type very fast like me!

[11:55:00 AM] Arthur says:

Trust me, you will be able to do a lot of things.

[11:55:10 AM] Arthur says:

But don't give up hope. And be patient, okay?

[11:56:51 AM] Arthur says:

Mom, Howard and I are going to see Dr. Stein again in a few weeks and talk
about some changes to your medication.

[11:57:35 AM] Carly says:

he can now talk i want toooooooo talk like him

[11:58:03 AM] Arthur says:

i know you do. but promise me you will keep writing for now. we will keep looking for ways to help you speak.

[11:58:15 AM] Arthur says:

but you are so smart and have good things to say. so write them!

[12:01:59 AM] Carly says:

it is to hard and if I could talk i could stay home with you

[12:02:38 AM] Arthur says:

I know. But that isn't the reason you live at Cedarview part of the week.

[12:03:00 AM] Arthur says:

you live there because they have staff who can help you take care of yourself.

[12:03:10 AM] Arthur says:

they have lots of people who can help teach you.

[12:08:38 AM] Carly says:

if i could talk i would tell you i dont want to go i want to stay with you and mom

All good things come to an end, as the expression goes. Thank God, everything bad has an expiration date, too. Although Cedarview provided the services we needed, no one felt good about Carly's living situation. Even Taryn and Matthew pouted that we had sent their sister away—an accusation that was hard to hear. It was clear, however, that Carly was still not ready to live full-time at home if Tammy and I were to maintain a marriage and our sanity. But there had to be a long-term alternative to Carly's living many miles away four days a week and being homeschooled the other three.

We had become close to two other families through our years of litigation and negotiation with the government and schools over providing the needed services for our children. The families each had a child living part-time at Cedarview. They were equally eager to find a way to have their children be a part of their lives without losing their minds. After an exhaustive search of the options available to children and young adults and their families, we came to the conclusion that the area of the country we lived in was several decades behind other areas of North America. Our dream was to have a home in Toronto that was run by staff trained in ABA where kids could live full- or part-time, and have access to one of the two top private schools for children with autism in the city. It was a lovely dream. A $400,000-a-year-per-kid dream based on the estimates of the government agency that managed Carly's residential care. With that price tag it would remain a dream. Kids who are "in the system," as they are described, have a per diem amount allotted to them and none of the three families could get that kind of allotment. Nor were we in a position to fund it personally.

The families were used to hearing two words: *expensive* and *no*. Neither was daunting any longer, however. We learned that the only way to *not* get no for an answer was to ask a different question. So rather than asking for direct funding and purchasing our own property for the three kids, we took a slower, collaborative approach.

Peter McPherson, the executive director of the youth services agency we relied on to help fund Carly's per diem at Cedarview, was not the usual bureaucrat with whom we had worked before. While he maintained good relations with his government counterparts, playing by the rules as necessary, he had a creative bent and a progressive attitude. In him, we saw a kindred spirit and the hunger to do something radically different for kids with autism in Toronto.

"We want to start a program like the Eden II model on Long Island, New York," Tammy told Peter. We had regularly scheduled plan-of-care meetings with the social workers and Peter to assess Carly's living situation, and we used this as an opportunity to spring our latest idea on him. "We want Carly closer to home. And she needs to be in school."

We were sitting in the small office Peter shared with one of his colleagues. The offices, a rabbit's burrow of cubicles and nooks, housed the government-sponsored agency that was responsible for providing services for children who either were at-risk in their homes or required extensive support and intervention. Most cases were dire; many families involved single parents, welfare support, and a heartbreaking list of dysfunctions and catastrophes. We were an anomaly.

We were three relatively well-heeled families with good homes and good jobs. It would have been well within Peter's rights to show us the door and call us ingrates. Each of our three children had private rooms at a well-run group facility. Because of the government's philosophy that keeping children home was the first priority, there were limited facilities to support kids like ours. And those that got in were the province's most tragic cases. But we wanted more. While we were constantly pushing for better services for our kids, we were critically aware that our kids already had it pretty good. More than a few times I caught sidelong glances between social workers and administrators as we requested more funding, more services, and better settings over the years. I knew what they were thinking; it wasn't subtle. Rather than being cowed by embarrassment, Tammy and I chose to think of ourselves as Carly's advocates. "Why doesn't she deserve more?" we reasoned. Anything we asked for was to improve her quality of life.

"We want to open our own group home," our friend Rebecca told Peter. On the days the other families' sons were not at Cedarview, they attended Carlton Learning Centre. In fact, both families had been founders of the school. They had helped create something out of nothing, so the prospect of starting a new group home did not seem so far-fetched to them. "Perhaps we could do it in association with either Carlton or Autism Resources," said Rebecca, referring to the two programs the families were currently using.

Peter, a man in his fifties with the remnants of an Irish brogue and clear, blue eyes, sat and listened patiently. We had come to expect the litany of excuses that often poured out of the social service workers and bureaucrats we'd encountered over the years. But the request sounded reasonable, if not lofty, and faced with three earnest couples, Peter paid attention. He nodded, dutifully explained all the hurdles we'd have to overcome, and agreed to help. "But you'll never get your own license," he said. "The province stopped writing new licenses for youth facilities." Peter went on to explain the red tape we'd have to hack our way through to find an alternative. Tape of any color didn't discourage us given our collective skill at tackling bureaucracy.

"But I know there's a group home for intellectually challenged young adults in midtown," Tammy pointed out. "It's in a great family neighborhood about ten minutes from us."

"That house was licensed about twenty years ago," Peter interrupted. "There are no houses in those kinds of neighborhoods anymore." He wasn't being obstinate, but wanted us to lower our expectations. We would not be creating a group home in the rarified air of an affluent or even middle-class urban setting. Most homes were located on the outskirts of the city or well into the country where real estate prices were more modest and neighbors less troublesome.

In the coming months we had a series of meetings with various groups with the experience and licenses to run group facilities for children and teens. After meeting several and testing their interest for the task, we found one with the same enthusiasm as Peter. The group, Future Horizons, ran numerous group homes across the city.

It was important for us to find someone with not only the horse-power to get a program like this up and running, but the open attitude to allow parents to be involved in its design. Most parents of kids needing residential programs were in crisis themselves. They looked upon any help as a godsend and seldom challenged the form it came in. We weren't sure if not-for-profit groups were ready for our utopian vision and assertive manner.

While Dave, FH's director, began the search for viable residences, Tammy organized a trip to Long Island to meet with the regional director of the Eden II program. Both Peter and Dave joined her, as did Rebecca. The team returned from their two-day tour excited by what they saw. Eden II had been in existence since 1976 and was known as a model of excellence in providing living and education services to young adults and adults living with autism. The facilities were family homes in suburban neighborhoods. Residents each had their own room and participated to the best of their ability in the running of the house. During the day, the younger residents attended either local schools or schools for students with autism. Because the homes were located in the community, families were encouraged to be part of the household.

Our troupe quickly adapted roles that matched our personalities and skills. Rebecca, who was completing her master's in education, played the role of ensuring the program met the high standards they had created at Carlton. Ryan, a successful lawyer, had the calm, practical skills to help master the bureaucracy. His wife, Alyssa, was the daughter of two psychologists with a background in supervising residential group facilities. With my business background, I acted as project manager and sought out creative ways to get the house (if we ever found it) renovated and furnished. Tammy was Tammy—smart, connected, uncompromising, and tenacious. Any time a compromise was proffered in order to expedite the program, Tammy fought back. She reasoned that we had compromised enough. "Why should these kids get less because of their disability?" she continuously challenged. "Shouldn't they get *more* to help them overcome it?"

The families met regularly on our own to discuss who would provide training for the house staff. We knew we'd probably have to fight with FH on this issue, as they were accustomed to hiring, training, and maintaining all aspects of their facilities. But they had never run a home exclusively for residents with autism. And with a combined thirty-five years of experience in raising kids with the disorder, we were adamant about having input into the program design.

Our meetings were about twenty percent business and eighty percent support group. We rotated locations, but it seemed like Rebecca and Edward got an unfair share of hosting responsibility.

A bottle or two of wine and sushi often accompanied our discussions, which drifted from planning agendas to updates on the progress of our kids. My alcohol consumption increased alarmingly during the months of planning. Alyssa's mother and father would join us as counsel on the issues of group facilities. Although not always productive or well organized, our meetings allowed us to stay well-bonded as a team. Inevitably, everyone would be assigned a task to focus on until our next love-in.

"I think we've found two options," Dave said to me somewhat breathlessly one afternoon. "There's a large home downtown and one out in the eastern suburbs, in Scarborough. Probably our best options." We were looking for a needle in a haystack. We wanted a house in a good neighborhood that was already licensed. The three families lived somewhat centrally, and it was essential that any location not be in one of the eastern or western suburbs of the city—generally where most of the group homes were located. With traffic, getting to these towns took almost as long as getting up to Cedarview. Carly had already attended respite programs in the far eastern reaches of the city, and Tammy and I wanted to move forward, not back. Ryan and Edward made the trek out to Scarborough one afternoon anyway, as they had boys and felt that a suburban location might offer up more outdoor space for activities.

"Send me a postcard," I told them.

On a chilly fall evening all six of us and representatives from FH met at the second option, a house in Parkdale, a downtown neighborhood that's been in the process of gentrifying for about fifty years. This would be the meeting where we agreed to proceed with one of the two facilities—or pass on both and hope we'd find something more uptown.

Dave warned us that if we passed up one of these two opportunities, he could not be sure when or if another alternative would come along. It wasn't exactly a threat, but we knew that if we didn't take one of the two imperfect homes, our dream could be delayed by a year or even indefinitely.

My initial reaction to the downtown location was utter despondency. The house had been used as a group home for many years, and the bruising and battering was evident. It had the unmistakable air of neglect that characterizes publicly funded housing facilities. Tired, worn, and institutional. Currently, there were three residents who would be relocated within the coming months. I tried to look past the bare light bulbs, broken shades on the windows, water-stained ceilings, and cracked walls. It was a large home, enormous really.

In its day, Parkdale had been a grand neighborhood of large and imposing Victorian mansions. Its being located only minutes from Lake Ontario and the parks that line the shore, and a quick commute to the downtown core, made it an ideal affluent neighborhood. But through the 1960s and 1970s, real estate zoning changes allowed the conversion of many dwellings and apartments into halfway houses for those leaving drug and alcohol rehab. The crime rate in the neighborhood was higher than in the rest of the city, but as one policeman I asked told me, "Mainly petty theft. Addicts looking for their next hit." Not comforting.

However, in recent years, due to the explosive real estate market in Toronto, many neighborhoods had become unaffordable for young professionals and families. Thus, houses like the one we were considering rubbed shoulders with renovated, well-maintained Arts and Crafts and Victorian single-family dwellings. Even on the block on which this house sat, it was not unusual to see a nanny pushing a small child in a stroller down the street past gnarled men sitting in broken lawn chairs on the front stoop of their tenement.

"Can you really see Carly living here?" Tammy whispered in my ear.

"I can't see her living anywhere," I replied, trying not to lose enthusiasm after so many months of planning.

We huddled together on a few thrift-store couches in the basement, so as to stay out of the way of the residents and staff upstairs. The parents sat quietly, avoiding each other's glances. We had hoped for more. We always do.

Rebecca, the eternal optimist, broke the ice. "I think it can be fab," she said in her ironic post-hippy slang. "It just needs work. And it's only a few minutes to Carlton and downtown. You know, we're downtowners, so this kind of neighborhood doesn't really bother us." In fact, it was only fifteen minutes from the Annex, where they lived, but while it was close, it was light-years away. She looked up at her husband, hoping for his nod of agreement. Edward continued to look at his feet. The rest of us could only inhale and sigh.

"I gotta tell you," said Dave, "we can let this one go and keep looking. But you're not going to find anything else in the city. Certainly nothing in a nicer neighborhood," he reminded us again. "Let's at least take a look around."

We'd come this far and, after looking for four months, we were beggars. We plodded up the narrow, windy stairs, starting our investigation on the third floor. It was a maze of jagged hallways and rooms, but ample space for a few bedrooms and office space for the night staff. "Probably good for the girls' floor," Dave said. At least, I thought, the girls would have their own space away from the boys who were even more rough and tumble than Carly.

I closed my eyes for a moment to imagine my daughter sleeping here. Outside I could hear the traffic of Queen Street, the main thoroughfare just north of the house. Only feet away, through the thick, cracked brick walls, was a halfway house for old, drunk men. From their second-floor porch, they could look down into the paved backyard of what was to be Carly's new house. My stomach churned and I wondered why we were always in the predicament of making the best of a bad situation.

"We can try to get Karen to help us get the place renovated and decorated," Tammy added hopefully. She was referring to a friend who had a successful architectural design company.

"A designer group home, with hookers and addicts as neighbors. Maybe they'll come for a barbecue this summer," I replied sarcastically when Dave was out of earshot. I knew I sounded like a snob, but I was having trouble feeling gratitude just yet. Nevertheless, I forged on, resigned to making this work.

The rest of the tour revealed little to be excited about except the raw size of the house. It was dark and lopsided, like the bowels of a whaling ship. A few broken and stained (with what?) pieces of institutional furniture, bare floors, dripping faucets, and broken toilets. But it was in Toronto, licensed, and ours for the asking. It wasn't perfect, but it was about as perfect as you get when you're dealing with autism.

Dave agreed to keep looking for a few more weeks while we decided. He would also give the agency that currently ran the house a provisional statement that we were interested, just to get the paperwork going. We pretended we'd think it over, but we knew our decision was made for us. The kids couldn't stay at Cedarview another year while we kept looking. We were all weary at the thought of another winter of commuting and having our kids living in a different area code. Tammy and I were even more motivated; although Luc and Anton seemed happy enough at the residential program, Carly was miserable.

"I don't belong there," she said to us one night.

I felt my world cave in. I had fooled myself into believing, since she had never mentioned it, that somehow she didn't mind living up north for part of the week. We knew she liked Mel and one of the other women who worked with her. She never talked about the other residents, but that wasn't surprising since she didn't really have any friends in Toronto, either. Every Wednesday or Thursday when she made the trek up there, and on Sunday afternoons when I met the van at the truck stop to bring her home, my heart constricted and my skin tingled. I was nauseated by the situation. But she didn't cry or act up, so for months I could fool myself into believing she was happy. Recently, however, Carly made it obvious that this was not the case; I had to face the truth.

First, she made passing comments in conversations. When it was time to buy a dress for her bat mitzvah, Tammy asked her if she wanted to come out to the store to look for one. *"Can you bring it home?"* Carly asked.

"Why?" asked Tammy.

"I don't want to leave home ever. I miss it too much."

"Oh, Carly. Do you know why you go to Cedarview?"

"Because I act silly and you want me to be like Taryn but I can't"

She later wrote a note to Tammy just before heading up to Cedarview for the weekend: *"I am going to Cedarview. I am going to work hard there so I can stay with you."*

Eventually she was direct in her pleas, and began exploring guilt as a strategy—one in which she became frighteningly proficient.

"Hi Mom," she started one Saturday morning on instant messenger.

"Hi Carly. Dad's here too. How are you today?"

"I'm okay. But I want to come home."

"I know. You will be home tomorrow and now you stay home until Thursdays."

"You come today please. I want to come home."

"You will be home in just one day, Carly. We can't drive up this afternoon. I know you're disappointed, please understand we are doing our best to get you home soon. What are you doing today? Are you going to the mall?" Tammy tried to redirect her.

"Oh, I get it. You don't really want me there."

"You know that is not true! That's called guilt. You are getting good at it. We have to say no lots of times to Matthew and Taryn. They cannot get what they want the minute they want it either."

"You can come. You just don't want to."

"Carly, we can't. We have to take care of a lot of errands today. Remember, you are home more now; you just need to be patient."

"I guess I just, well, wish I were home."

"I know. I want you here, too. I miss you and love you so much. You know we are working on this. You have to trust me and just be a bit more patient. Can you do that?"

"yes. I guess."

"Thank you. I know this is hard."

"Bye."

"Bye for now."

It was becoming harder to ignore the fact that Carly was not a silent observer. She began telling her therapists that she was acting out because she hated living away from her family, and using manipulation to force our hand. But when she was home, she still lacked independence, sleep was challenging, and the complexity of managing her life frequently overwhelmed us. We could feel the walls pressing in from both sides.

After dinner one evening Howard and I were trying to get Carly to write with me directly. He quietly started to edge himself out of the room while Taryn sat across the table doodling on a pad and half paying attention. Tammy was out with a friend for a coffee. We had learned to divide and conquer and grab a few minutes for adult social time whenever we could. "Who's nice at Cedarview?" I asked Carly innocuously.

"The cows," Carly answered. She was learning teen sarcasm and I sensed attitude, even without the telltale facial expressions or voice.

"Who else?" I asked her, undeterred. I was perhaps prodding at a sore spot, but I was hoping to hear Carly talk about other residents or staff that she enjoyed spending time with.

"The ostrich too," she said with no evident sense of irony.

"Are the people nice at Cedarview?" I attempted to redirect her.

"They are okay."

"What is *not* nice about the place?" This was not going as I had hoped, but perhaps as I had expected.

"Being away from you," she said. Oomph. The plunge of the guilt dagger struck its mark. Of course, a child would rather be at home with her family, but we had become good at deflecting reality. In finding her voice, Carly was able to force us to face up to the truth.

"I know. It makes me sad too, Carly."

"You are going to have to fix me."

"You don't need fixing. You are not broken. You will learn to control yourself better in time. They are helping you learn to do this." I left out the part that it was also allowing Tammy and me to breathe, but I'm sure she could see through my ruse.

"but I can't," Carly said.

"You are already doing so much more than you did a few years ago. You are making great progress. Carly, you don't need fixing. Why do you say that? What do you think needs fixing?"

"My brain."

"You are not the only one like this, Carly. What do you think about the other kids with autism at Cedarview?"

"They make me feel sad."

"Why?" I asked. We had never broached the subject of her peers. Those with autism are supposed to lack social awareness. With this preconceived notion, we didn't overly concern ourselves with her thoughts about a community or peer group. We had made care and therapy a priority, balancing it with her integration into our family life.

"They are just like me," she responded with clarity. *"I want to be around normal people. I belong at home."*

I wasn't sure what to make of the hypocrisy. Did she not see the contradiction of despising those who suffered the same challenges as she? Maybe it wasn't so much that she despised them as the fact that they didn't uplift her. Misery in fact does not like company; it wants nothing more to do with it.

"Mom and I are working with Luc's and Anton's parents to create a house nearby. It would be a lot closer and you could come and go more frequently. You could be home more," I pushed on with forced optimism in my voice. "But there's a lot to do first. It's downtown, not too far from my office. And Shari lives right up the street," I said, referring to a woman who worked with Carly on occasion. In fact, knowing she lived in the neighborhood made the entire plan palatable.

"Why don't you just let her move home?" Taryn said with a pout, not looking up from her drawing.

"Please, Taryn, that's not helping," I heard my parental voice say, shooting her a caustic glance.

When Tammy came home, Carly was in bed. I showed her the conversation, which set us back in our usual spin of "what ifs" and "if onlys." We had debated the merits of trying to convert our garage, a large free-standing structure at the back of our lot, into a small apartment where Carly could sleep with the help of night staff. Or an addition on the house. But it always came back to the same conclusion. We were not equipped to run our own residential facility with the challenges of hiring and training staff. As it was, our life was always one phone call away from being in shambles when a worker called in sick or Howard needed a day off. No, the Parkdale house was our only alternative, and now we needed to get it going as quickly as possible.

The next day, Tammy called Rebecca and Alyssa to say we were "in" if they were. We were willing to trade in the ostriches and cows for indigent neighbors if only to get Carly back to the city and somewhat closer to home. Maybe we could even find a way to help the neighborhood improve once we got the kids settled in. Now with the parents' approval, Dave could begin the tiresome process of getting the license transferred to Future Horizons, and we could take on the onerous task of designing the ABA program. During the mudslide of paperwork and red tape, I would look for people to help me get the house renovated and furnished to decent standards as quickly as possible.

The goal of opening the house within a few months began to look like fantasy. While we had made some connections through our friends to replace the kitchen and bathrooms, drywall the walls gaping with cracks and holes, and redo the worn floors, no one would commit until they were sure FH would receive approval for its plan. FH needed to solicit both funding from one government agency and licensing approval from another. And no one would approve anything until a full education, staffing, and facility improvement plan was complete. The months slowly clicked by, and the Parkdale house remained empty with only the most rudimentary improvements completed. At least water was no longer draining from the third-floor washroom into the living room two floors below.

On good faith, our friend Karen had designers at her firm draft plans and make a list of items required to improve and furnish the home. She also convinced one of her suppliers to donate furniture for the dining and living rooms. A contact of Tammy's who owned a major lighting supply company offered to donate lamps and light fixtures. A national home improvement chain offered to come in and renovate the bathrooms and kitchen and provide supplies for us to complete many of the other improvements required to make the crumbling hulk inhabitable. They had initially turned us down, but David Legendre, a young colleague of mine, had a connection that he put me in touch with. As it turned out, the executive David knew also had a child with autism, and our wives were acquainted through the autism community. Through the back door we slipped and, without telling the department that had originally rejected our request for charitable aid, this executive was able to get us supplies and a construction team to do the work.

While we awaited final license and funding approval, FH and the families came to an agreement on who would provide the training and oversee the development of the ABA protocols and plans for the kids. Nearly a year past our original launch date, it looked like we'd have Parkdale open by the late summer of 2008.

With spring approaching, we began to make our plans to withdraw our kids from Cedarview. Carly would be attending camp during the summer. In the fall, she would transition to Carlton, the private school for kids with autism that both Luc and Anton attended, and move into Parkdale several nights a week. Far from a perfect life, it had the ring of stability and hope. We allowed ourselves a few moments of self-congratulation for the accomplishment and began the process of getting Carly ready for the transition.

❧

Excerpt from psychological assessment, 2008:

Dr. Susan Marcotte, PhD, C. Psych
Registered Psychologist

BACKGROUND AND OBSERVATIONS

Carly received Botox in January 2006 in her salivary glands for drooling problems. It was reported to be somewhat helpful. Her impulse control problems and obsessive type behaviors have been increasing. Carly has been prescribed a a variety of medications in the past, including Luvox, Ritalin and Celexa, however, Carly's parents found that these medications generally increased her agitation, constant movement and compulsive and repetitive behaviors. She also was previously taking risperidone due to anxiety and hyperactivity and Chlorpromazine to assist her in falling asleep. Carly is currently on Epival, Clonidine, gabapentin and, on occasion, chloral hydrate to assist in sleep. Overall, Carly's health is reported to be excellent.

Carly has been seen through this office since the age of 4½ for a psychological assessment. At the time of the assessment, it was felt that Carly was beginning to respond well to the Applied Behavioral Analysis therapy that she was receiving. The results indicated that Carly continued to present with Autism, a mild to moderate developmental disability and as ever communication disorder. In comparison, the results of her most recent assessment at this office in April 2006 indicated average non-verbal ability and receptive language skills. She also continued to present with Autism and a Communication Disorder. The current re-assessment is being completed in order to gain an updated understanding of Carly's progress to date and to assist with educational program planning, to ensure that she has the opportunity to learn to her fullest potential and manage behaviorally.

The assessment was completed over four sessions. The Wechsler Intelligence Scale for Children—Fourth Edition was used to assess Carly's intellectual functioning. Carly's abilities within the area of visual perceptual reasoning were within the Superior range (91%). These results were stronger in comparison to her previous Average score. She displayed categorical reasoning abilities within the Superior range (91%). Carly also demonstrated Superior range ability to find missing essential details in a picture (91 percentile). Overall, on the perceptual reasoning domain of the WISC-IV, Carly's performance was within the Superior range and continues to highlight her strong perceptual reasoning abilities despite her challenges. However, it is very important to note that Carly's behavior issues associated with her Autism often interfered with testing and the completion of each subtest often took a great deal of time.

The Peabody Individual Achievement Test—Revised was used to evaluate current levels of achievement in the areas of reading comprehension, spelling and general mathematics. On the PIAT-R Carly demonstrated Very Superior reading comprehension skills (98th percentile for age range 13 years, 1 month). Her math problem solving skills for language based problems were within the Superior range (95th percentile for age range +18). She received a High Average score on tasks assessing her Academic knowledge involving Science, Social Studies and Humanities, equivalent to a 16 year, 11 month level.

Overall, Carly's behavioral difficulties, such as withdrawal behavior, social problems and atypical behavior, continue to be related to her Autism. . . .

20

❧

Saying Good-bye

Hi Jonnie my name is Carly. My friend Howie told me I should write you. A lot of my friends are in L.A and I don't get to see them a lot. The friends I have here are really my twin sisters'. They rather play with her then me. Howie said you are really nice and wouldn't care that I am different then lots of people. I like doing lots of things like swimming, board games and just hanging out. I have to tell you I cant speak out of my mouth but I can spell on my computer to be heard. Howie said that you are going away to camp just like me for the summer. So I just want to know if you would like to hang out together before camp starts. You can email me or tell your mom to call Howie to set something up. Hopefully I will meet you soon

Your optimistic friend,
Carly

Hi Carly!

    I would love to get together with you before I go to camp! I will have my Mom call Howie as soon as possible!!!! Let me tell you a little bit about myself; I am 13 years old and I have a younger brother and sister. My best friend is moving to L.A. next year, and her name is Carly too!!!!! I love hanging out with friends (just like you) and I also like swimming and dancing. What camp are you going to?
    I can't wait to meet you!!! You seem like such a caring and interesting person. We can be email pals!

                    See you soon,
                    Jonnie

People on the autism spectrum are alleged to lack the social acuity to form deep emotional bonds. This is a gross generalization, in my experience. Underneath Carly's sometimes-robotic façade she is capable of great empathy and playfulness. In Mel, she found a confidante and buddy to whom she could open up. Carly had complained that there was no one at Cedarview with whom she could connect. None of the other residents spoke in meaningful sentences. Certainly none of them demonstrated the degree of self-awareness, humor, or power of observation that Carly did. We thought of Mel as a godsend, as she would open up to her in the same way she spoke with Howard and Barb at home.

    "Is there anything you want to talk about or ask about?" Mel asked Carly. At Barb's recommendation, we tried to give Carly many open-ended opportunities to start a conversation—an approach we use years later.

    "I am really down today."

    "Do you mean you feel sad?"

"Kind of."

"How come?"

"Really miss mom."

"I miss my mom too a lot. But you get to see your mom on Sunday . . ."

"I know but I'm sad."

"Well, did you know that lots of people get sad at this time of year? Do you want to know why?"

"Yes."

"'Cause its not very sunny at this time of the year. They call it seasonal affective disorder."

"Really."

"Yes, maybe you miss the sunshine, too!"

"Are you sad?"

"I'm not sad now 'cause I like working with you. I sometimes get sad in the winter. Most of the time I'm happy."

"Well I'm down."

"Is there anything I can do to make you feel better?"

"Well of course."

"What?"

"Give me a exlax."

"What! Are you feeling like you can't go to the bathroom?"

"No"

"Then why would you need an ex-lax?"

"Don't know."

"Do you know what ex-lax is for?"

"I think so."

"What's it for?

"To make you feel happy"

"Well, ex-lax helps you poop . . . I think you're thinking of Prozac or Paxil or something, those are called antidepressants."

"Are you on Prozac?"

"Nope, I don't need it. Some people really need it 'cause they're sad all the time."

"I'm sad all the time."

"Well, that sucks. Are there things that make you happy?"

"I like Ellen."

"Well, people who need Prozac feel like nothing makes them happy, even Ellen or seeing their mom."

"I know."

"Do you still think you need Prozac?"

"No. I guess."

People had been coming in and out of Carly's life as long as I could remember: Joanne, Colin, Amy, Ana, Paula, Yifat, Guerrette, Lori, Susan—a dizzying list of young people on their way to other careers, for the most part. Therapists who stopped in long enough to form a bond only to have it broken after a year or two. Before Carly could write and communicate with her companions, these relationships had an expendable quality to them. Some people were better than others in that they were more patient, more reliable, and more energetic. The relationships were defined more by what Tammy and I needed for Carly than by what Carly wanted for herself. As Carly emerged, she began to form her own connections with people well beyond the scope of our influence—and even beyond our view.

Mel had worked with Carly for two years and been her "Howard" while at Cedarview. But with plans for Carly to move to Toronto, Mel had found a new permanent job and tendered her resignation. It was time for Carly to start letting go of her friend. That Carly, too, would be leaving did not mitigate the sense of loss either of them felt.

"What's up?" Mel asked one afternoon when Carly was being particularly ornery.

"Just mad."

"Why?"

"I so don't want you to leave."

"I totally understand, I'm sad, too. But you have to realize that you will be going through a lot of changes in the next few months, good changes! Like going to camp, an awesome camp, then going home to Toronto and spending more time with your family. I have a family, too, and I have a house, and I needed a new job to pay for everything. So I want you to know I will always be around! Like on MSN, and when I come to Toronto I'd love to do lunch! What do you think?"

"Autism Resources I doesn't believe in me."

"Well, I work for Autism Resources and I believe in you, and so does Claire," Mel countered, referring to the program director and Mel's direct supervisor.

"No one knows. Just go be happy."

"Well, Miss Carly, you certainly know how to lay a guilt trip."

"I know."

"Well, I am so glad that I know you and I want to continue our friendship. If you want to?"

"Like I am best friends with Genna," Carly said.

Genna was another Autism Resources staff member who worked evenings supervising Carly's dinner and bedtime routine.

"Cool, I'm glad you are bff with Genna. That's great."

"Have you ever had a best friend?"

"Yes, I have, I was best friends with a girl Sandra and another girl Sandi in high school and university. My bff, though, is my cousin Jill, she's the best. Okay, so what should we do on Friday? That's my last day here."

"Have a party."

"What kind of party?"

"A pizza party."

"Do you read minds! That's what I was thinking, a pizza party would be so fun."

"*Just us.*"

"Okay. Should we watch a movie?"

"*I am finished writing.*"

"Okay, what's wrong?"

"*I am sad.*"

"I'm sad, too."

"*No Mel you are not.*"

"How do you know if I'm sad or not?"

"*Cause you got a new job.*"

"Do you know what the term *bittersweet* means?"

"*No.*"

"*Bittersweet* is a term used when something makes you happy on one hand but really sad on the other hand. Like when I left the show at Deerhurst, I was happy to be done but I was really sad to not work with my friends anymore. And now this decision was bittersweet 'cause I am really happy about my new job, but I am very sad that I won't be working with you anymore."

"*So you are sad.*"

"Yeah, I was really upset when I told Claire I was leaving 'cause I really like her, too."

"*Mel are you going to make lots of money?*"

"I'll make enough money to live comfortably."

"*Do you believe in me?*"

"Yes! I think you are very smart and you could change things and help people with autism, but you have to continue to work on controlling your body."

"*No way.*"

"I think when you live in Toronto, you will be happier and will be able to help people with autism. You can go to Queen's Park!" said Mel, referring to the location of our provincial government.

"Mel are you serious?"

"Yes, I'm serious, I think you have a strong voice and if you continue to work on your behaviors you will be amazing."

"Really?"

"Yes. I have never known anyone like you, you're so smart and so funny."

"For real."

"Yes, for real."

"But no one believes."

"Well, what about Howard and Mom and Dad and Barb and everyone like that?"

"Not sister."

"Who? Taryn?"

"Yes."

"She believes in you."

"Look, her best friend makes fun of me."

"I don't know if I believe you; you tend to lie about stuff sometimes, and I know Taryn would be really upset if anyone she knew made fun of you."

"No it's true."

"Which friend?"

"Yolanda."

"Are you telling the truth, 'cause I will verify this friend with your mom."

"No I'm lying."

"Why would you lie to me about something? You really shouldn't lie because then people can't trust what you say."

"Mel Autism Resources is stupid."

"Actually, I like Autism Resources, and you should remember that Autism Resources works really hard to help kids like you."

"Are you serious?"

"Yes, Autism Resources helps lots of kids with autism control their behavior and learn new skills. If places like Autism Resources didn't exist lots of kids wouldn't get the help they need."

"Cool."

"Do you feel any differently about Autism Resources now?"

"No I still think its stupid."

"Okay, well, you're entitled to your opinion. What do you want to talk about?"

"So Mel when are you leaving."

"Well, tomorrow is my last day of work. We're having a pizza party with a movie. Then I'll have to come back on a Saturday to train the new person."

"Bummer."

"I'm sad, too. Can we still talk on MSN?"

"Yes."

"You're going to a really cool camp this summer. Are you excited?"

"Yes."

"Will you email me from camp and let me know how you like it? I always want to remain friends with you. I think you're totally cool."

"Mel are you kidding?"

"No, I would never lie to my friends. I think you are amazing and I'd like to stay friends."

"Howard asked if he could make an important movie."

"What kind of movie?"

"A movie about Autism."

"Cool, so like a documentary?"

"I think so."

"Wow! That sounds great. Would you be the star?"

"Yes."

"Sounds awesome!

"Wanna play a fun game called M.A.S.H.?"

"*Yes.*"

"Sweet, I'm gonna read your future!"

On their last day together, Carly did not officially say good-bye. Perhaps it's too painful for her to close doors, even as others open. I am certain that Carly does not lag behind us in our world; rather it is us who are playing catch up. She has her own way of wrapping things up, creating order out of chaos. Unable to feel or share emotions? Nothing could be further from the truth. In fact, what better way to say good-bye than to hold on to a sweet memory.

"What's so funny, Carly?" asked Mel.

"*Mel you are so funny.*"

"What did I say or do that you found funny?"

"*Has been so nice knowing you.*"

"Carly, I'm not dropping off the face of the earth, I'm still gonna be around!"

"*Mel I remember a great thing you did.*"

"What's that?"

"*You made me cupcakes,*" Carly said nostalgically. With that, she gave the sign for "finished" and closed her computer with Mel for the last time.

21

❧

Staring Evil in the Face

"Have you ever stood up for any thing you believed in before, Carlito?"

"Yes," he replied with resentment.

"What was it?"

"You and taking you through the gauntlet."

"So then believe in me. I know what I'm doing."

I looked at her and replied, "really?"

"No. But you have to trust me."

Something in her voice made me want to trust her. Hooowie hovered in a spot and waited for us to come to him. "We are almost through the forest but it's getting dark and this forest has two faces to it," Carlito said.

"What does that mean?" Tareena anxiously asked.

"It's like humans. They can be nice one second and mean the next."

"I have had many teachers like that," Tareena replied.

"This is a lot worse tareena," Hoowie commented. "Come night fall this forest becomes crawling with the meanest and scariest animals in the world."

Carlito said, "Mean animals that's all this forest has to offer. I've looked the meanest animal in the eye and told him off and I'm still alive to talk about it. I'm not afraid of any animals."

—Excerpt from *The Elephant Princess*

A few days after Mel left Cedarview in April 2008, Tammy and I were attending an afternoon party for some friends. In the middle of the celebration we received a panicked phone call from the young woman working with Carly that afternoon. She informed us that Carly had made an accusation of abuse by a staff member. She read us the conversation she had had with Carly throughout the morning, her voice quivering with emotion.

There is no preparation a parent can have to receive news like this. I was numb. And incredulous. Abuse had been one of our worst fears when leaving Carly in a respite program. We had heard the statistics of mistreatment in residential homes but had convinced ourselves that the types of facilities we used were different.

Tammy and I rushed home from our friends' party to try to get Carly to speak with us directly online. On the drive home, neither of us spoke. We didn't dare. It wasn't until we saw Carly's words appear before us on the computer that we felt the full impact of the accusation. It was a slow, painful conversation. Tammy sat in our kitchen, Carly still at the facility with her therapist. At times minutes would pass as we waited for Carly to respond to Tammy's questions. We wanted to believe our daughter, but not believe this was possible. Carly had made up stories in the past—a fictitious boyfriend, an Aunt Rita, an attic full of books. But in all of these cases, she conceded that she had lied shortly after. She had a vivid and mature imagination that she flexed to counter the boredom of living at Cedarview.

The story slowly unfolded over the next two hours on instant messaging, with Carly miles and miles from home. I watched, in a gasping state, as if I were watching someone else's nightmare unfold. As Carly and Tammy spoke online, I paced the kitchen trying to walk away from the wave of panic and nausea. But the consistency in Carly's report, all the *whens* and *hows*, made her accusation impossible to refute. I was paralyzed.

Tammy had the clarity of mind to call Peter, the director of the government agency that funded Carly's residential program, at home to ask him what we should do. "Let me make it simple," he said. "With an allegation like this, I am compelled to phone the police immediately. It's no longer in your hands."

When Tammy hesitated, struggling with Carly's past stories and half-truths, Peter calmed her with his decisiveness. It didn't matter if we later found out that it was not true. When an allegation is made, the law favors the victim. This came with heavy-hearted relief; doing the right thing, either way, felt wrong. The police arrived that evening and we were not allowed to pick Carly up until the next morning. Late into the night, they attempted to question her and the staff that was on duty. With the police there, we knew her to be safe. Carly shut down immediately after the long and tearful discussion with Tammy. Exhausted, depleted, and terrified, Carly sat on a big couch with her therapist in the den at Cedarview, rocking. The officers left, agreeing to meet the next day with Carly, Tammy, and me at the local police station.

Even with a quiet house that night, we were sleepless. Tammy and I lay in bed, whispering so as not to alarm Matthew or Taryn. We broke Carly's story down into tiny increments, looking for breaks in the logic, praying it might not be true. Did the accused have access to her room at night? Where was the evening staff? Why would this just be coming out now? But why would Carly make this up? By morning it was clear in Tammy's mind that Carly was being truthful. "It just doesn't make any sense that she would lie about this. She knows she's leaving in June. Why would she make this up? And the description she gave . . ." Her voice trailed off.

That afternoon, as Carly recounted her experience, I watched something in my wife die. I bury hurt, but Tammy wears it like a second skin.

I was tortured by the devastation this would bring not only on the individual in question, but on all the staff and residents at Cedarview if her accusations were false. But I had to agree with Tammy. Carly's past fibs aside, she was neither cruel nor cavalier about others' feelings. The rest of her life was becoming more positive, not less so. Her voice was getting stronger and her confidence growing. If anything, it made sense that she now had the fortitude to come forward about the abuse she said had been going on for six months.

Early the next morning we phoned the police department near Cedarview. They would continue their investigation, they said, but we needed to try to get a statement from Carly in their presence. It was a rainy, raw Sunday morning and we headed north, playing the situation over and over in our heads, verbally wringing our hands. Carly would be home in Toronto with no support network, no staff, no school. Once again we were drowning in the whirlpool of autism. And now with a trauma to add to her already challenged life.

Carly was driven from Cedarview by two female staff members and we met her there along with Barb, who had driven down from her cottage where she and her husband were spending the weekend. We knew we needed all the help we could get if we were hoping to get a meaningful statement. In a dreary room with one-way glass and drab furniture, Barb and the police officers tried for two hours to elicit answers to their questions. Despite best efforts, the stress of the situation won out and Carly was unable to type her statement.

Instead, she rolled on the floor crying hysterically until we drove her home.

There was no time to feel the remorse that would ultimately worm its way into my soul. I could take a few days off work to come up with a plan, but by the end of the week we needed to create a new life for Carly in Toronto. After Tammy and Carly came home from seeing the pediatrician the next morning, we got on the phone desperately looking to put together a schedule that would include days, but equally important support for us at night given Carly's unpredictable sleeping patterns. It was triage. While we knew we'd need to deal with the emotional fallout the abuse would cause, we first needed terra firma. While we were tossing around the logistical hot potato of planning this next phase of Carly's life, my anger burned—though there was little time for revenge, much less justice.

Autism Resources, the team that managed Carly's staff and therapy while at respite, jumped into high gear. The founders and directors, a married couple who were both psychologists, also ran a day school for children with autism. Although Carly would be the oldest student, they created space and a program for her beginning the following week. Howard offered to come in the mornings to get Carly to school and in the afternoons to support her at home. This gave him time off during the day to be with his wife and young son. But that still left us weekends and holidays with no coverage. Even though she was thirteen, every moment of Carly's day required a plan and a backup plan. And we knew then that after this crisis, the Parkdale house—another group facility not so different from Cedarview—would never be home to Carly.

Again, Autism Resources came to our rescue. The cousin of one of the directors was a social worker who also had experience as a foster mother. These days, she mostly took in exchange students living and studying in Toronto for a few months at a time. Darlene had just moved into a large, modern house midway between the Autism Resources school and our house. She was experienced, having worked with young adults suffering from brain trauma. Despite the betrayal we had just experienced, we knew we were unable to live with Carly full-time at home and agreed to experiment with a night or two a week in Darlene's home. The house was a home; it was close by where we could easily supervise it; there would be no men present.

When Tammy and I went to meet Darlene, she enthusiastically gave us a tour, pointing out plans she had for improvements that would enable Carly to have room to work with her therapists, a fenced-in backyard, a deck, and her own bedroom and bathroom. Darlene had large, serious eyes and a demeanor that suggested she knew the drill. But along with a tough exterior, she showed tremendous empathy for Carly's situation and a keen interest to be more than just a landlord, but a mentor as well. Darlene had two grown children of her own, which I found somehow reassuring.

The school and respite plan looked perfect on paper. If I could compartmentalize the raw emotion of handing my child over once again to a complete stranger, then this arrangement looked plausible. A good thing, too, because it was the only option we had. A move like this would require a final stamp of approval from Dennison Children's Services, the agency that had been funding Carly's respite care—a stroke of a pen, we were assured. After a flurry of emails, phone calls, and meetings to review the proposal, Dennison Youth Services granted consent.

Carly had been home for three weeks now, and already we were feeling the strain. Once again the house was filled with streams of therapists, noise levels at the pitch of a dog kennel, and Carly's boundless energy. Any guilt at having Carly leave our sight was mitigated by the stress of having her home full-time. I didn't dare ask how she felt about being told she would still need respite. This wasn't a decision in which she had a choice. None of us did.

After a few overnight trials, however, we were pleasantly surprised at how easily Carly transitioned to the situation. Howard spent a few extra hours with Darlene and Carly, and we arranged for shifts of Autism Resources workers for evenings and weekends. Momentum built quickly and within weeks, Darlene and staff were taking Carly swimming and for outings to the country, shopping, and exploring the city. We noticed as the spring wore on that Carly seemed to *look* better. Not that she was ever heavy, but with increased activity and better eating habits, her body slimmed down. Her complexion looked smoother and brighter, her hair thicker. As best we could tell, she seemed happy.

We began thinking that if Darlene was up for it, this was a far better alternative to Parkdale in the fall when Carly got home from camp. Despite our months of effort to launch Parkdale, it was no longer a palatable solution. If Carly wasn't in our home, we felt better that she was in *someone's* home, not an institution. Darlene's house was host to an ancient dog named Abuksheesh, a huge aquarium of exotic fish, and her photographs and collections of artsy tchotchkes. And Darlene's elderly neighbors with tomato plants in their yard sure beat the ones in Parkdale, with track marks on their arms.

With a plan in place, Tammy pressed for justice. The police investigation of Carly's allegations crawled along. The detectives had interviewed all the staff at Cedarview. "Was it possible for the man in question to have access to Carly's room? Was she ever left unattended? Were there times when there was no other staff on the floor where Carly's room was?" We were not made privy to the responses, but all of the above were possible. Carly's room was at the end of a short hallway, out of view of the other bedrooms. Night staff did not routinely stay on the floor where the bedrooms were; they were responsible for doing laundry and other chores after the residents were asleep. In our minds, with staff often attending to other duties during the evening, we were confident that the accused could have had access to Carly's room without anyone else knowing. In fact, when we spoke with a staff member the day we took Carly home, she encouraged us to pursue the matter with police. We took that to mean she knew something.

The investigation, which required looking for DNA on Carly's bedding (which had been washed frequently), took several months. Not surprisingly, none of the employees had witnessed anything, and the forensic work turned up no evidence. The staff member who had encouraged us to call the police entered an official statement that she did not see how the man could have had access to Carly's room.

A month or two had passed, and Carly was sufficiently calm to broach the topic of her abuse again. She agreed to speak with police, if they came to our house. The investigators, a man and a woman, arrived and sat in our kitchen alongside Tammy and Barb and repeated many of the questions they had put to Carly at the police station. Again, she gave the same description of events she had recounted to Tammy and her therapist several months earlier. In between typing her answers, she cried and slapped the table, clearly in distress. But over several sessions, she persevered. Her description was consistent, and it sickened us every time she recounted it.

The victim in these types of abuse cases, we were told, is not a reliable witness—and one like Carly who has autism and is non-verbal is particularly problematic. Tammy and I were infuriated, as Carly was in fact the only one who *could* speak up and right the wrong. She could not only be an advocate for herself, but in doing so set an example for other victims. And yet it seemed the law could not protect the most vulnerable. As the case weakened, our conviction to support our daughter grew. In removing Carly from Cedarview, we had pulled the knife out, but the wound would take years to heal. Since she had returned home, Carly had been plagued with nightmares and bedwetting, both of which her doctors believed to be consistent with trauma. We encouraged her to write about her experience and talk to a psychologist.

One of the specialists we sought help from was Dr. Nancy Robards. Nancy, one of Canada's top experts in autism, had recently agreed to start seeing Carly again even though much of her time was absorbed by her role as researcher. We had consulted with Dr. Robards and her team many years earlier when Carly was first diagnosed and had kept in touch. Parents like us know the value of networks and connections. Sometimes it's all we have.

Carly had a fondness for Dr. Robards. It was easy to see why. Nancy's warmth and commitment was apparent from the first moment we walked into her offices years before. She had a patient manner of listening to Carly and a thoughtfulness that gave us hope when we were feeling especially hopeless. We never left an appointment without a clear action plan. On the rare occasions we had to call her on her personal cell phone, we were never made to feel like we were intruding, although sometimes I wondered if I would be as accommodating.

One afternoon after a particularly restless night, Carly wrote a note to Nancy.

"*Dear Cool Doctor,*" Carly began. She had taken to calling Dr. Robards the "Cool Doctor" because she spoke directly to Carly, treating her as an ally in her treatment, not a patient. She continued,

> *I need your help. Last night I had a really bad nightmare. I did not feel safe the whole night afterwards. Even though it was a dream it reminded me of what happened at Cedarview. I started freaking out and I could not stop.*
>
> *My mom came in the room and told me to stop and even told me I cant go to L.A if I act like this way. But how do I tell her it's not my*

fault. She has a preconceived notion that it's easy to behave or that it's in my power to stop it. If only that was true.

I wish I could turn my dreams off. But I can't. And I am too scared when I wake up. I don't find I sleep well any more. I find when I'm not in a deep sleep the dreams come.

I need new night time medicine. The liquid meds don't work. They make my body silly.

My dad does not think you will be able to find any thing else to help me sleep but I can tell you this one is not working.

I have faith in you.

Barb thinks I should talk to a professional about my dreams and what happened to me.

I am scared to, but I agree.

Please, please, please help me.

Your cool patient,
Carly

Through Dr. Robards we met a therapist who had helped victims of abuse and, in particular, young adults with autism. Beth was a godsend. She would come to our house and meet with Carly, Howard taking a backseat on the couch while the two women talked. These discussions were private—a piece of our daughter's world we would never see. In the months that followed, the therapy helped Carly find some peace and she seemed more relaxed. Her sleep improved, although an uninterrupted eight or nine hours with Carly is something we never rely on, even now. Over the coming months, she complained less frequently of nightmares and moodiness.

While Carly worked hard to make sense of and peace with her trauma, we found little satisfaction in the delivery of justice. About eight months after Carly left the respite program, Tammy and I drove up to the local court handling the matter for a meeting with the Crown Attorney. We met together with the judge assigned to the matter and the police for a case review. They said upon examining all the facts that there was insufficient proof to proceed with an indictment. The witnesses were inconsistent, our daughter would be seen as unreliable, and there was no DNA or physical evidence. "Unless anyone else comes forward or new evidence is found, I don't have enough to prosecute," the Crown Attorney concluded.

While the case may be legally closed, it will never be closed for me. On good days, I can forget that I dangled my daughter in the mouth of the lion. On the bad ones, the guilt rises through me, a vapor burning my insides. Several years later, Carly told us she would one day be able to come to terms with the hurt and move on. Despite the betrayal and torment, she loved us and forgave us. Once again I realized how much I had to learn from my daughter. Perhaps one day I, too, will forgive. But just now, I'm the last on my forgiveness list.

Just a Girl at Heart

November 18, 2008

Hi Gaby

What yoga studio do you go to
I have been doing yoga for a month and a half and I am getting really
good at it
I can't wait for our sleep over
I had a movie party with my sister Taryn and it was so much fun
We had lots of food and the cool thing was I got to spend time with my
sister
Don't tell her but she treated me like a normal sister at it and I even
forgot I had autism
What kinds of foods should we have at the sleep over

I just got a really small computer that i can take any place and look
normal
Do I need to bring any thing to school

Do we go on any trips
I really can't wait to see all of you

your computer savvy pen pal
Carly

❧

November 28, 2008

Hi guys

I really want to celebrate my birthday with you three
I dont have that many real friends here and I thought it would be cool
to celebrate with all of you
I have never done that before
I normally have to celebrate with Taryns friends or family that rather
hang out with Taryn then me. I thought this year it was going to be
different. But its fine as long as my mom is ok.

Eric I have to tell you the fiz in my body went away. My cool doctor
put me on a new medication and I have not been feeling the fiz any
more. It sill might be there but I cant feel it. I don't know when I am
going to see you so can you get skype on your computer so we can talk?
Its so cool and I am really good at it.

Gaby I would love to meet your yoga teacher. I am getting taught
by my O.T she is good but I think I want a real teacher soon. when
I eventually come to LA can we go to a yoga studio? I also want to
do yoga on a beach. We don't get to do that here all are beaches are
covered with snow and its cold outside. Oh, ya Gaby i love pizza
and when i do come we for sure have to have it at our sleep over.

*I am going to ask my dad to get the book you guys are reading. He and
I read a book together at night and it would be cool to read that one.
Maybe I can do some of the work you guys are doing here.
I'm hoping I get to see you soon*

> *Your overly patient waiting friend,*
> *Carly*

∽

December 25, 2008

Hi guys

*I hope you are having a good Holiday. I am having a great time.
I went to see the movie Madagascar 2 with my brother. It was ok.
I went horseshoeing with Howard and his wife. Howard fell down and
could not get up it was so funny.*

*Eric i dont know when I am going to come to LA. now. i was hoping to
guilt my mother into just taking me for my birthday but she is really
sick. I heard my mom talk to Carol her sister in the kitchen and she
told her that she is sick and she is going to lie to my sister, brother
and me. I was sitting watching tv and i heard the whole thing. No
one thinks i can hear them if they are whispering but i can hear every
thing. You know what i mean, Eric. I have been thinking about it a
lot at night and i even have been waking up because of it. I know she
will be ok but I am still a little scared.*

*Gaby when do you leave Cogwheels? Can you give me your new
email? Whats the other school like that you go to? I have been using
a weighted blanket and it's been helping me sleep at night. Ashley*

my OT is getting me a bigger one and that should help me sleep even better. How big and heavy is your blanket?

Neil the beaches here have snow all over them and some have ice. I really want to do yoga on a beach but its cold out side. I did do something cool today called snowshoeing. You put metal bars on your feet and walk on the snow. I liked it and i went tobogganing down a tall hill. It was scary but lots of fun.

> *Your overly patient friend that was wishing she was with you,*
> *Carly*

22

❧

Good Enough, Isn't

Q: BarryV @CarlysVoice: *sometimes when u set high goals and dont achieve them it hurts more than when u set a small goals.*
A: That is true but if u don't set high goals for your self you will never meet your full potential. I would of never spelled.

The years on the hazy cusp of adulthood are hard for most teens. Being fourteen or fifteen is an abstract phase of life, with neither the independence of adulthood nor the carefree freedom of childhood. Carly was finding this limbo to be particularly trying.

With Carly home from Cedarview, settled at the Learning Center, and a respite program in place, Tammy and I thought the rest of 2008 would be a time to catch our breath. Although we knew she might resist the full-time ABA school program, we knew Carly was not prepared for the rigors of a mainstream school—even if we could find one that would accept her with all of her exceptionalities.

"It doesn't matter how smart you are if you can't control your outbursts. The other kids find it too distracting," I explained.

While she would head off to school without too much resistance, once there, she refused to type and made fairly lame efforts to comply with the program the team had put together. Since Carly was unable or unwilling to use her computer spontaneously, the staff created a curriculum with multiple-choice solutions. At least she could point to the correct answers. We attributed some of her listlessness to the fact that she didn't want to be in the school in the first place. *"I want to go to school with Taryn,"* she would tell us.

"Taryn goes to Hebrew day school!" I tried to explain. "She takes Hebrew, French, and a full curriculum. It's not the right place for you." I wondered where exactly *was* the right place for Carly.

"I think she's bored at school," reasoned Tammy. "Why don't we ask them to give her an academic assessment in a classroom setting so she can see what level she's at, and if she can handle a class environment."

It seemed like an intelligent idea to all of us except Carly. At least we would know what kind of curriculum she could handle at the Learning Center and perhaps she'd be able to sit for a lengthy period after all? If so, maybe she *could* handle a public school at least on a part-time basis.

Despite the logic, Carly had a lengthy, circular conversation with me one afternoon that spring that left me both annoyed and bored. I ducked in and out of my office for meetings in between staving off Carly's rebuttals of why she shouldn't have to take a placement test.

[2:20:52 PM] Carly says:
i dont want to go to school and take the assessment test tomorrow

[2:22:37 PM] Arthur says:
why not? It will help them come up with a better program for you.

[2:23:38 PM] Carly says:

i want to go to the public school nearby

[2:24:50 PM] Arthur says:

you are getting too old for that school. and they don't have the right type of class for you. Carly, PLEASE try tomorrow. Please try to work with the teacher and students. we are trying to understand what you are capable of doing. so that we can find the right type of school and class for you. do you understand?

[2:25:49 PM] Carly says:

that school is not for kids like me

[2:25:58 PM] Arthur says:

No? why not?

[2:27:35 PM] Carly says:

they have some thing wrong wi th them

[2:28:30 PM] Arthur says:

they need a special way of learning. but many of them are just as smart as you are.

[2:30:07 PM] Carly says:

no it makes me sad to see them. i don't want to go. i am not going. Howard said they have normal kids but tell them to come here i am not going. i am going to write Claire and tell her i am not going.

[3:46:49 PM] Arthur says:

i know. you have been telling everyone that. but i think you are being very stubborn. you want to be like other kids and learn. the only way to do that is for us to assess how much you can do.

[3:51:57 PM] Arthur says:

are you still there?

[3:52:51 PM] Carly says:

i never get a choice in what I want to do. you said go to cedarview, i went. i don't want to go to that school.

[3:53:30 PM] Arthur says:

okay. i understand how frustrated you must feel. will you let me explain something?

[3:53:55 PM] Carly says:

no

[3:54:23 PM] Arthur says:

if you won't have a conversation and listen to me, then i cannot help you. i need to explain something!

[3:56:05 PM] Arthur says:

tomorrow's session at the school is what's called an assessment. it is Marion and Claire's way of seeing what the best way is for you to learn. then we can figure out what school program will work for you.

[3:58:46 PM] Carly says:

ok they can do it here. i dont want togo to the school

[4:02:25 PM] Arthur says:

i understand that. but they cannot do the assessment in our house. we cannot ask 5 or 6 people to come over just because you don't like to see other kids with autism. and Carly, I think you are being selfish—you don't want other people to avoid you because you are autistic!

[4:05:29 PM] Carly says:

why not we have done it beforeeeee. i never ask for much and i am askinggg

[4:26:34 PM] Arthur says:

I know, you do not ask for much. you are not a greedy person. If you really refuse to go take this assessment, we will not make you. But, if you do not do the assessment, we cannot figure out what kind of schooling you are capable of. So where does that leave us? That is why we are doing the assessment.

are you still there?

[4:34:23 PM] Carly joins conversation

[4:36:51 PM] Carly says:

I can t work in a sad place.

[4:37:44 PM] Arthur says:

you will be in a class room. i think if you have a good attitude, you will do fine. and then we can discuss your options for education. but this is an important first step

[4:43:06 PM] Carly says:

it's just too sad for me to go I will cry

[4:45:10 PM] Arthur says:

why will you cry? you will be with a boy and a girl who are your age. They do not have autism. you will work with them.

[4:49:07 PM] Carly says:

i will still hhhear them

[4:49:39 PM] Carly says:

iiiiiiits sad

I could see this would go on forever. "Maybe she should be a litigator," I told Tammy later. "She'd just wear the other side down till they were like, 'Fine! I'll pay anything, just please let me out of here.'"

Seeing that she wasn't getting anywhere with me, the next day Carly sat down at her computer with Howard and Barb and drafted a letter we later termed *the rant*. It was directed at the program director of her school, but I think it was more of a cathartic explosion of pent-up emotion. In her note, she continued to refuse assessment, but also gave us a better understanding of why. Teens are often a mystery, but when we could get Carly to open up, she gave us excellent perspective. Her note read in part:

I do want to go to school but I cant

Its not that I cant do the same work as all the other kids

I went to school before and even did well on tests

But I could not stay in class because of all my behaviors

I was hard for me to sit in the class without banging or screaming or standing

I tried so hard to control it

But it is too hard to do when I need to spell and do other things at the same time

My dad said that is why we see the doctor in the hospital she is trying lots of medication to see if she can help me

You say you to want to help me

But how can you when you don't know what its like to be me

You don't what it feels like when you can't sit still because your legs feel like they are on fire

Or it feels like a hundred ants are crawling up your arms
How can you help me when you don't know?

My dad and mom say that every one takes tests to help let people know
what level they are at
But I have taken lots of test and I know what I can and cannot do
You want me to be in a room with three kids and concentrate on
playing a game I probably cant do in the first place and at the same
time try to control my behaviors
You don't have to be smart to know what is going to happen
I wont be able to play the game
I will end up scaring the other kids and I will feel bad inside and you
will make me feel this way for a test
How does that help me?
Don't tell me it shows you what level I am at because you know what is
going to happen

I try so hard to stop my behaviors but it is too hard
I can't walk by food without having a fight with my self
You want me to spell but it takes a lot of concentration just to hit one
letter on the keyboard

It is so hard to be me
And you would not even understand
I wish I could put you in my body just for one day so you can feel what
its like
All my friends are double my age because it's hard for me play with
kids without scaring them
I was asked why I like MSN so much. It's because I can talk to people
without them seeing me hit the table or screaming

*I want to clear something up. Just because I am hitting the table or
 screaming does not mean I am not reading or listening.*

*I wish I could go to school on MSN.
I could do the work but no one would have to be distracted by my
 behaviors.
And I could pay attention more to my work*

*I hate when people ask me to do things that they already know I can
 or can't do
Like ask me to spell "chips" for a chip
It makes me feel like I am stupid
"spell your name." Good have a chip
"spell your name." You did not get it right I guess you are not
 smart
How does that make you feel?*

*My mom asked me a question that no one ever asks me
What do I want?
I want not to feel what's happening in my body
I want to stay at home
I want to be like every other kid*

*I cant sit for long times or even walk past an object with out having
 fights in my head
I know I can't take the object but my mind is fighting with me*

*I want to be able to go to a school with normal kids but not have to
 worry about them getting upset or scared if I can't help myself and
 I hit a table or scream*

I want to be able to read a book by myself without having to tell
  myself to sit still and not close the book and follow each word and
  concentrate

I want to sit at a table with my mom and dad and not be worrying
  about what my body might do that I might not be able to control

I want to be able to talk to people and have them understand me the
  first time
Not respell over and over again
It's too hard

What I want is to have some one programming for me that knows what
  I am feeling inside

What I want is to be like taryn
But I cant
Because I am Carly

Carly's words were a painful reminder that no matter how much effort it took for us to manage her life, it took twice as much for her to live it. There was a limit on how hard we could push her, knowing the magnitude of her internal struggle. But it was always hard to tell where her OCD left off and either her autism or teenage manipulation began. I didn't want to misconstrue gripping pain for teenage stubbornness.

The assessment was scheduled and canceled several times before we finally scrapped the idea. No one had the heart or stamina to force the issue, and in the end, Carly could control the agenda by just not typing.

In fact, Carly's OCD *had* been getting worse since the incident at Cedarview. The outside world only sees the manifestations of autism and OCD. I could not imagine what it looked like from the inside, and she had not been able to articulate it very clearly. OCD is an anxiety disorder, her doctor told us. The first step is to bring the anxiety down. Despite our trying various medications and therapy, however, it continued to be her prison.

Some months later, Carly would give us a peek into what lay underneath her flailing.

"I feel the pain course through my body and its unbearable," Carly complained when Barb asked her to discuss her tumultuous outbursts she had been having at school and home.

"Does hitting your head make you feel better? It's very dangerous. You can injure your skull, your brain," Barb said, referring to Carly's tendency to flop to the floor or stand next to a wall and bang her head. Rooms in our house were pockmarked with dents from outbursts that came on quicker than we could restrain her.

"It helps me cope"

"What can we do to help?" Tammy interjected.

"Back off and let me be. Most of the time I am having a power struggle with myself."

"What does that mean?

"I tell myself to stop but I can't. Have you ever yelled at your boys to clean up their room but they don't. It's like my body. It does not always do what I want it to. It feels like my insides are being ripped out of my body and the longer I don't do it or get it, the more it hurts. The pain is unbearable. That's why I cry and bang on the floor. I wish it would just go away. I try the breathing [exercise] but it doesn't work. I act up because I feel so trapped inside myself. I don't spell not because I don't want to. I just can't get myself to and I act out because I can't explain or communicate what I need."

As Carly's therapist suggested, Tammy and Barb reminded her of the relaxation techniques she could use to convince herself that her mind was playing tricks on her. Given the severity of her outbursts, however, this remedy felt like we were putting a Band-Aid on a compound fracture.

It seemed to me that Carly's existence was some grand-scale Whac-A-Mole game. No sooner would we tackle one challenge, the next popped up. I was beginning to agree with Tammy; it wasn't Carly's autism or even her lack of voice that was the real trouble—it was her obsessive-compulsive disorder. It plagued her every waking moment and inflicted physical pain.

"It's not fair, I know," Tammy told her.

"You're telling me," Carly replied.

Howard had become adroit at helping Carly de-escalate from her outbursts. He could quickly spot the telltale signs, such as Carly's back going rigid, her bleating *uh-huh* sounds, and the possessed look in her eyes. If we were home, he'd rush her down to the family room, where she would lie on a thick foam massage mat that would vibrate when activated. I had created meditation playlists for her iPod, and the sounds of pan pipes and the perfume of scented candles wafting through the house indicated Carly was in the basement attempting to re-enter the stratosphere. The frequency and intensity of Carly's obsessive bathroom ritual in particular was driving me crazy—and it was growing. By this point in Carly's life, I had hoped to be well beyond this kind of struggle, but I was cast as a supporting actor to this hellish drama, particularly in the middle of the night.

"Go by yourself, you're a big girl. You have been going to the bathroom by yourself for seven years," I would complain to her. "You don't need me. Just go to the washroom and get back in bed," I'd say, my temper rising.

But no.

"Dad you do it," she seemed to say. "Dad you do it. Dad you do it. Dad you do it. DadyoudoitDadyoudoitDadyoudoitDadyoudoitDad youdoitDadyoudoitDadyoudoitDadyoudoitDadyoudoitDadyoudoit

DadyoudoitDadyoudoitDadyoudoitDadyoudoitDadyoudoitDadyou
doitDadyoudoitDadyoudoitDadyoudoitDadyoudoitDadyoudoitDad
youdoitDadyoudoitDadyoudoitDadyoudoitDadyoudoitDadyoudoit
DadyoudoitDadyoudoitDadyoudoitDadyoudoitDadyoudoitDadyou
doitDadyoudoitDadyoudoitDadyoudoitDadyoudoitDadyoudoitDad
youdoitDadyoudoitDadyoudoitDadyoudoitDadyoudoitDadyoudoit
DadyoudoitDadyoudoitDadyoudoitDadyoudoit."

On one occasion that spring, after our third excursion to the
bathroom, I helped her back to bed and sat on the edge, my back
turned to her. I heard her breathing deeply to calm herself. "Oysh,
Carly. I know you're fighting it. Sorry I scolded you." How often
had I said that over the years? Then I added, "I know you'll win
one day." My back was turned to her. I felt a soft, small hand on my
T-shirted shoulder. I thought she might be comforting *me* and I swallowed hard.

Without a clear understanding of Carly's academic strengths and
deficits, the staff at the Learning Center continued to take a hit-or-
miss approach to a grade-appropriate curriculum, mixing behavioral therapy and academics. It was not a perfect situation but the
best we could do at the time. Tammy's lymphoma had recurred and
she was going through another six months of treatment and all the
anxiety that comes with the condition. "It isn't as much fun this
time," Tammy deadpanned.

Other than the placement test, Carly had rarely put up resistance to the decisions we made regarding doctors, therapists, tests,
and activities. She went along with whatever plan we had come up
with without complaint. School, however, was a different matter,
and as 2008 wore on, she took a scorched-earth approach. Carly
turned a deaf ear to my entreaty to work hard in the hopes that one
day she *could* go to public school.

"Dad does not know what he is talking about," Carly griped to Barb

and Howard one afternoon. She had been in a cranky mood all afternoon and Barb was trying to understand what set it off. *"I know I don't know everything,"* Carly continued, *"and he is right, I am not trying hard at school. But I said many months before I did not like the Learning Center. But he puts me there any way. All the kids at my school are younger then me. I want friends. I want to be challenged by kids, not by silly staff. I want to be with typical kids."*

"Whoa, Carly. You have a chip on your shoulder. Dad is trying to get you a good education," Howard rose to my defense.

"I do not have a chip on my shoulder. I want him to get it. It's always his way. He says I have influence, but I don't. He's got to stop. Or I'm going to stop caring. He's never seen the school. He's talking out of his ass."

If Matthew or Taryn had spoken to me that way, they would have spent the rest of their teenage years in their room. I cut Carly much more slack, just happy that she was willing to voice her opinion at all. Besides, I was more amused than offended with her proper use of slang. And she may have had a point—what teenager wants to go on field trips with seven-year-olds? Carly saw her twin sister Taryn styling her hair, painting her nails, and going out with friends while her time was spent in the company of children, being monitored and cajoled by therapists. It *was* unfair. But Tammy and I saw no other option, and we felt we had already run a marathon when it came to providing the right schooling for our daughter. So we steeled ourselves to Carly's stubbornness and left her in the patient hands of the staff.

Although we didn't have the fortitude to begin exploring new schools for Carly, we did finally get around to contacting Ashley Evans, an occupational therapist Barb had been telling us about for a few years. Ashley would be able to help Carly master some self-care skills she found challenging due to her motor-planning issues. We had always wanted to bring Ashley onto the team, but it was one more task that kept slipping to the bottom of an endless to-do list. As a teen, Carly wanted to be able to do some of the things other people could do naturally—like tie a shoe, fasten a bra, or make cookies. Ashley worked with Carly to painstakingly teach her muscles to cooperate with her brain by breaking each step down into minute increments.

Ashley's secret weapon, however, was her yoga training. At the end of her weekly session, Ashley spent twenty minutes teaching Carly basic yoga poses and meditation. Tammy and I fully supported any means of relaxation that didn't come out of a prescription bottle. I came home some evenings to find the basement lights dimmed, the scent from an aromatic candle wafting through the house along with the sounds of new-age music. I could hear Howard, Ashley, and Carly's short, raspy chants of "ommmmmm." A few months later, the OT introduced Tibetan singing bowls to the routine. I just looked at Tammy and shrugged, happy to have another inventive and caring spirit working with Carly.

Although Carly's scholastic progress stalled during 2008/2009, her emotional progress was undeniable. After our successful trips to LA, we began including Carly in the family's extended trip to Cape Cod for our summer vacation. Carly had spent July at Extreme Sports Camp in Boulder—a camp for teens on the ASD spectrum. There she amazed all of us by learning to rock climb, knee-board, traverse a ravine on cables, and zipline; yet another breakthrough Tammy and I witnessed via video. The week after returning from camp, the family—Howard and his wife and toddler son in tow—headed to Cape Cod for two weeks. The Cape had a magnetic pull on my family since my childhood, and Tammy and I had been spending time there together since we started dating. We wanted Carly to experience the Fluffernutter-soft sand dunes and salt air of the beach community we visited each year. Although we stay active when we're there, Cape Cod has a sleepy quality I wished I could bottle up for the remaining fifty weeks of the year.

Our friends, the Gillmans, had been joining us for the prior five years, so each summer we rented the same large home. The sprawling colonial was host to family, visitors, dinners around the huge dining table, and a lot of teasing. With Carly maturing and Howard's help, we could now have Carly be a part of this tradition.

Carly was thrilled to hang out with the Gillmans' kids, who were seventeen and nineteen, and Taryn and Matthew. Howard, true to form, kept them hopping from parasailing to Ski-Dooing, making my credit card sweat. Tammy was recuperating well from her cancer treatment and found she had the energy for long bike rides—which the adults were keen on, the kids not so much. The town we stay in had preserved its sweetness without being cloying. Friday night there were concerts at the band shell in town—a main street lined with centuries-old inns, the Ben Franklin Five and Dime, a few pubs, and an ice cream store on every corner. It was one of those perfect holidays so memorable it feels like a physical possession.

As the late summer evening sky went deep purple and the parents sat on the back deck talking, our kids crowded around the dining room table to play Monopoly. Carly engaged in banter with her brother and our friends' son, who was one year older than Matthew—playfully flirting.

"Would you have imagined this five years ago?" Karen asked, having known us since Carly was an unstoppable swirl of energy. It was a rhetorical question.

On a day-to-day basis it was often hard to see just how much Carly *was* growing. But when we would string together all the small accomplishments—conversations, letters, camp activities—it was a dramatic trajectory. For my birthday that summer she wrote me a letter; something I told her I valued far more than presents.

Dear Dad,

You have been bugging me for almost the last two weeks to write something funny or comical for your birthday. But what if I don't want to write that now that your older you have to stop dancing with your old man butt or sleeping in your underwear? I want to let you in on a big secret about autism. But don't tell anyone. Promise. When you sing no one with autism will ever be able to audio filter you. But I still love you.

I love when you read to me. I also love when you just chill in my room and say funny things and I love that you believe in me.

I have made you and mom use all your contacts to get Ellen to read my speech and have even stressed you out about school. But somehow you always come through. I know I am not the easiest kid in the world. However, you are always there for me holding my hand and picking me up.

I heard some one say on the radio that a wise person learns from a fool, but a fool learns from no one. So you must be the fool and I must be the wise person. LOL.

I just want to say happy birthday and I love you.

Your little Elephant Princess,
Carly

Oh, by the way you better tell the readers in your book you called me an elephant.

Carly's sense of humor was a fuel source that kept us going through much of the drudgery and frustration. In one of her final sessions with Barb and Howard before the summer break, she responded to Barb's question of "What would you like to talk about today?" by saying, *"I want to talk about how cute I am."*

"Okay, Carly. How cute are you?"

"I'm so cute blind people stop and stare."

As 2008 progressed, we watched Carly mature and we felt more restored. With renewed energy, Tammy and I once again weighed the option of conceding to Carly's wish to leave the Learning Center. We reconsidered sending Carly to Carlton, the school our friends Rebecca and Edward sent their son to. We likely should have looked into it when Carly first came home from Cedarview, but in the urgency of the situation, there was little time to think. Furthermore, Autism Resources ran a world-class program and we wanted to maintain consistency with the therapists and directors.

It made me feel like a nomad—each year a new game plan, a new location—but there was no point in keeping Carly in a program where she was unmotivated and refused to make an effort to participate. Carlton was a school for kids with autism, similar to the Learning Center, however, many of the students were teenagers. It was housed in a former public school, so while ABA was used to teach the students, the building was roomy and bright, with classrooms, desks, and computers. At least Carly would no longer be the oldest student at the school or have to work in a small office by herself.

As space had opened up, we were told, Carly could start in September. Based on our friends' endorsement and Carly's desire to leave the Learning Center, we agreed to make the move. Although Carlton was not a mainstream school, we thought perhaps Carly would find a kindred spirit. We were doing our best to balance Carly's desire for normalcy with her need to learn the skills to achieve it. I was well aware that life with teens is often a battle of wills— balancing doing the *right* thing with doing the *popular* thing. But the decisions we had to make regarding Carly were often more painful than those we made for our other kids, with compromises no parents should be forced to make. Sending Carly to Carlton, I hoped, had the potential to make both Carly *and* her parents happy. Or was I once again talking out of my ass?

23

⁓ঙ৶⁓

What She Always Wanted

@Carlysvoice: Today was my third time sitting in a real high school class. It is so cool and I love doing real work. Oh just want to say hi to the girls.

In early spring of 2010, Carly sat with Howard in a classroom, doing her best to answer a teacher's question. Her typing was so slow that the class had moved on to another topic by the time her sentence was completed. Carly, her classmates, and her teachers were all still figuring one another out. The school buzzer sounded. Howard closed the computer and grabbed Carly's jacket, encouraging her to get a move on.

Carly made her way through the crowd at Western Secondary, a high school of 1,800 kids in midtown Toronto. Howard was close beside her to be sure she wasn't trampled in the mad rush of students racing through the enormous, rambling building en route to their next classes. She seemed to hold her head high despite her signature gait that swayed side to side slightly, due to scoliosis of her spine. She had a bounce in her step, her battered red knapsack slung over her shoulder as Howard toted her laptop in its Desert Storm protective case. Carly went through laptops the way most teens go through running shoes.

That Carly was there, if only for one class three times a week, was nothing short of a miracle. She would say it was all her doing, but the army that surrounded my daughter knows that nothing comes easy when it comes to progress.

Carly had been at Carlton since August 2009. Changes for Carly could be like disturbing a hornets' nest, but some nests needed disturbing and we transitioned her cautiously and with tremendous planning. By now we had had too many "fresh starts" to try it any other way. I no longer had much enthusiasm for new years and new approaches because they often went south fast, leaving me feeling more desperate as the options dwindled. The first semester at Carlton had unfolded relatively smoothly, however, and I faced the year with guarded optimism.

Working with the school's staff, we had developed a new IEP, Individualized Education Plan, to replace the one that had grown outdated in the past months of academic turmoil. The plan included a list of targeted behaviors to correct—sitting for periods of time without slapping the table or making loud noises; resisting the urges to shred or dump materials in front of her or to flop to the floor and bang her head; fetching and eating her lunch independently. Tasks one would expect of a fourteen-year-old but that for Carly required microprogramming. In addition to the behavioral therapy, Carlton created an academic curriculum, hoping to satisfy her keen interest to learn. But with Carly's history of not being able to type with strangers, I was skeptical about how far this might progress before the school would give up.

During the first month, while Howard was there to ease the

transition, Carly seemed happy. She sparred intellectually and conversationally with the staff assigned to her. Carly would type, her teachers and therapists would respond, and, when they had the time, they typed what they wrote so we would have a record of the conversations. They began her English literature module by reading *Death of a Salesman*. *"Do you think our economic downturn is like a distorted mirror image of after World War 2?"* she asked her therapist, showing off.

The young woman assigned to work with Carly didn't know how to respond, which was probably Carly's intention in asking.

She connected well with some of the staff, particularly the ones willing to engage in the types of conversations Carly was interested in—the ones about pop culture or, more important, about boys.

"Do you have a boyfriend?" she asked Kendall, a petite twenty-three-year-old who worked with Carly in the mornings.

"Yes. But we broke up," she replied.

"Did you brake his heart?" asked Carly.

"No, it was a mutual break-up."

"Was he cute?"

"Yes. Very."

"Was he not considerate?"

"Yes, he was."

"How did you meet him?"

"Grade 11, class. In school."

"Are you on internet dating?"

"No. But my friends are."

"Can I put you on and write your profile?"

"Can I hear what you would write first about me?"

"She's a blond bombshell looking for an adventurous and old fashion valued man to treat her right."

"I'm not sure I'm ready to go on online dating."

"But I will get you lot of guys"

"Have you ever written a profile for online dating before?"

"no but im sure i can do it"

"If Howard weren't married, what would you write for his profile?"

"He's not worth it ladies. Lol"

"What do you think of school?"

"It's cool."

"Do you think any of the boys in the class are cute?"

"They are cute but no brad pitt."

"What about Angelina Jolie?"

"We can just push her out of an airplane."

As Carly got acclimated to her new school, so did I. On the surface, everything looked like a smaller version of the typical school our other children had attended. A low-slung brick building abutted by a tidy parking lot and slightly worn-looking sports field, a candy-colored play structure of tubes and ladders, and a line of self-sufficient shrubs lining the pathway up to the side entrance—all gave the impression that nothing more complicated than mathematics and civics went on inside. Entering through the heavy double doors ("Keep doors secured at all times!"), I looked down the long hallway lined with student and staff photographs, artwork, and crafts projects. Once I was through the foyer, however, all the similarities to a typical grade school ended. Students transitioning from one room to another seldom roamed the halls unescorted. Staff, generally young women in their twenties, walked just a few steps behind, occasionally redirecting their students with a gentle nudge or quiet reminder of the task to be completed.

"This is Mr. Fleischmann," said one companion to her student on an afternoon I was visiting. "What do we say when we meet someone?"

"HellomynameisStevenit'sapleasuretomeetyouwhatisyour-name," the boy said, with a rehearsed precision and flatness of a foreign actor reciting his lines phonetically. The boy's eyes darted anxiously at my torso or the wall behind my head.

"Hello, Steven." I smiled, knowing how many months of therapy it must have taken to elicit that response. "My name is Arthur. I'm Carly's dad." Sometimes I would offer a hand to shake. But after a young man a good foot taller than me and twice my girth had once squeezed my fingers so hard they nearly popped like sausages on a barbecue, I was tentative with the formality.

"Oh," he replied, looking down the hallway and wandering away, his therapist turning back to smile at me.

Despite the enthusiastic beginning, however, Carly's friendly chatter with her therapists ended within a few months. Much like she had at the Learning Center, she refused to write or do work for any of her teachers or therapists with the exception of completing some multiple-choice answers on worksheets. It was always hard to tell whether her refusal to type was intentional or beyond her control—and this was a constant source of frustration for everyone.

But it wasn't just the lack of spelling that stymied us; it was her regressive behavior. We saw Carlton as an interim step toward integration into a mainstream high school. Carly needed to demonstrate her ability to remain calm and still for the duration of a traditional high school class period before we could unleash her on the chaos of a public high school. We explained to her that as soon as she was able to sit for periods of time, focus without tantrums, and cooperate with the teachers, we would be able to try part-time days at a local high school. We knew by now what she was capable of, and she knew we knew. Yet we continuously received reports of urine accidents that seemed intentional, refusal to cooperate with simple requests, and an increasing number of tantrums. Despite Carly's intellectual ability, the school eventually moved her into a classroom of *lower-functioning* children because she was disturbing her classmates.

"What's happening at school that would explain why you're acting up so much?" Barb asked Carly one afternoon, after about six months at Carlton.

"I can't explain it," she replied.

"Well, what happens inside you when they ask you to answer a question?"

"They don't. They ask me to spell "carly" or "dip" like a moron."

In fact, the teachers had tried to get Carly engaged in schoolwork, but when she wouldn't type, they moved to simpler tasks, hoping it would help her overcome the anxiety of typing in a new environment.

"I don't even have to ask you how that makes you feel, but if you can tell us what you would like us to do, maybe we can help fix this," offered Barb.

"They moved me to a lower class and never really gave me a chance in room 7."

"How did they not give you a chance!" interjected Howard. "You were in there for six months and never spelled. How is that their fault?" The frustration was clearly wearing on his nerves.

"I did well at The Learning Center just answering multiple choice boards. It was rare I got a question wrong and Audrey saw me do it."

"It isn't just the lack of spelling. You were moved because your behaviors were disturbing the other kids. They were all trying to do their work. That's why they moved you into the other classroom. And you are going to have to do more than multiple choice if you want to convince them that you're ready to fit into a mainstream high school," Howard told her. He wasn't insensitive to her struggle, but he wanted her to take some ownership of the situation.

"I don't need to convince them. They're treating me like I'm dumb. When was the last time I had a legitimate pee accident? They are the real morons."

"This tactic is not working for you, Carly," Barb pointed out. "You have to have find another way of communicating your frustration."

"I am only as good as my environment and when I am treated low it's hard to be anything else. Don't u read my tweets?" she asked, referring to her more frequent use of the social media network. Carly continued the irritating and circular discussion; her behavior was so Carly, but her language was so teen.

"Part of growing up is to learn some self-restraint. If someone does something not nice to me, I don't lower myself to their level but try to rise above it and be the best person I can be," Barb counseled her. "Peeing in the classroom is not demonstrating the best that you can be."

"It's funny that my dad can go on national TV," Carly huffed, referring to an interview I had done a few years earlier on ABC News, *"and says he believes in me but he doesn't believe in me enough to let me pick my own school. I just want a chance."*

She then closed her computer to shut down any further lecturing.

"She is such a diva," Howard fumed.

We persevered. The rest of our family ecosystem was in relative balance, something we had craved for years. Audrey, Carlton's director, seemed almost apologetic for their inability to connect with Carly, but we were just happy to have an environment that was willing to keep trying and a school with the resources to counter Carly's jabs. Our family fell into a solid routine. Matthew was away in Halifax at university and Taryn had entered high school only a few blocks away from our house. Carly's school was in the west end of the city, but Howard offered to come to the house in the mornings and help get Carly ready for school and then drive her to Carlton. He could then spend the day with his family and work on the plans for the residential summer camp he was developing for young adults on the autism spectrum. After school, Howard came back for Carly and worked with her at our home until nine or ten, when she went to sleep. It was a long day for him, but he never seemed fatigued.

Our weekday morning routine was hectic, but probably no more so than in other homes with teenage girls getting ready for school. With some guidance from Howard, Carly would now wash and dress herself for school and was learning to prepare her own breakfast—significant accomplishments.

Tammy would shuffle in bleary-eyed for coffee, and Taryn, who vacillated between chipper and sullen in the manner of teenagers, would come downstairs, where she would have to pass my daily wardrobe inspection. I often shot Tammy a look to see if she approved of the amount of skin showing below Taryn's neckline. Taryn and I had entered that phase between a father and teenager that sometimes felt like radio silence. Like an astronaut, I prayed we'd resume communication when the obstacle blocking our frequency cleared the path.

"Is leftover shepherd's pie okay for breakfast?" Taryn asked one morning, poking through the fridge.

Now it was my turn to roll my eyes. But compared with our daughters' childhood—a time of flying food, banshee screams, and two hours of sleep—I was in heaven. I had begun to view managing Carly's life as a marathon, not a sprint. There would be times we could surge with energy and change. But, there had to be periods of stasis, too. In a life filled with so much turmoil, lack of change was refreshing. So while Carly may have resented her predicament at Carlton, she would have to struggle through good days and bad. My back hurt at the thought of exploring any other options.

Although school was not a high point, Carly was becoming more engaged in her role as an autism spokesperson.

"Barb, should I go on Larry or Oprah?" she asked. Early in March of 2009, Carly had gotten it into her head that she'd like to be on *Larry King Live*. She had been getting messages on her Twitter page from people who thought she should try to get on a talk show to inspire others with her story of finding her inner voice. Not that Carly needed encouragement to dream lofty dreams anymore, but her followers were fueling her ambition nonetheless.

"Which one would you prefer to be on, if you had a choice, Carly?"

"I want to do Larry."

"Why Larry?" Barb mused. To her recollection, Carly had never expressed a real interest in Larry King.

"He's so old it takes him forever to ask a question. Even at the speed I type, I can get my answer out before he speaks three words."

Howard laughed his silent laugh, more of a nod, smile, and look of parental amazement. Barb shook her head. "Carly, you are one funny kid."

Carly wrote a note to Larry King that we passed on to one of his producers we had come in contact with some months before. As would become a recurring theme, once Carly gets something in her head, we all end up part of the plot. I also noted that Carly seldom shared with us much of her experience with autism—despite our questioning. However, when she wrote for strangers, or responded to questions on Facebook, she shed light on mysterious and hidden aspects of her life. I was all for that.

Dear larry king

> *My name is carly grace fleischmann I just turned 14 years old and ever since I can remember ive had autism. I am non-verbal but have found amazing way to communicate my thoughts and needs.*
> *CNN showed my story a year ago and so did other news stations.*

Since then I have had an apifany [sic]. I hate or maybe a better word
is dislike the way so called experts try to explain the world of autism.
    If a horse is sick you don't ask a fish what's wrong with the horse.
    You go right to the horse mouth.
    I want to do something I have never done before
    I would like to sit down and educate you and your listeners on
autism
    I am not the fastest typer in the world but if you pre tape our
interview you could edit my response to match your questions
    But I want people to know that know one is telling me what to
say and I don't have a hand up my butt like a puppet I would love to
answer any emails question your audience might send

                              your true autism expert,
                              Carly fleischmann

We received a call from the show's producer on April 3, the
day Larry was covering the topic of World Autism Awareness Day.
"Would Carly like to participate in this evening's broadcast with
Jenny McCarthy and several doctors who specialize in ASD?" she
wanted to know. "We'd set it up on Skype and she could be our autism expert and guest blogger."

We had about two hours for Carly to prepare a statement to be
played via computer. Carly would then stay online for the remain-
der of the show to answer questions that audience members posted
on Larry's website, if she was able to sit and focus. It wasn't exactly
the full-blown interview Carly had imagined, but with her growing
desire to share her experience more broadly with the world, it was
a coup.

Racing home, we called Barb and asked her to come over. In particularly anxious situations, it made Carly feel more relaxed to have
both Howard and Barb at her side. She now had just over an hour

to write a message about what she called the "truths and myths" of autism. We then had to send it to the producer for vetting before airtime. The next few hours were chaos—like a war room on election night. Howard and Barb sat with Carly while she wrote in the dining room. Tammy and I worked out the logistics of using our computers for a remote hook-up and did a video and sound check with the producers in Atlanta and Los Angeles. Matthew was away at college at that point so we called him to let him know to tune in. Taryn weaved in and out of the kitchen, dining room, and den, not sure what to do with herself. Even our dog seemed to be pacing.

We were told approximately what time Carly's segment would air and had to stand by for the phone call from the producer in the studio telling us to take our places and be cued to start the reading. My stomach was in knots. Asking Carly to comply was always a risky proposition; we had never put her under the kind of pressure live television created. Carly, however, was adamant that she could handle it and wanted the world to hear from "the horse's mouth." I paced one end of the kitchen, behind Carly and Howard, so as not to distract them; I had the phone in my hand waiting for the call. Barb, Tammy, and Taryn were on the sofa watching the show as if it were the last heat of a race.

The call came about thirty minutes into the show. I gave Howard the nod as I heard Larry from the TV in the den: "I'd now like to introduce Carly Fleischmann, our special correspondent." Carly pressed the space bar on her computer, the trigger to start WordQ, the latest type-to-voice software she was using on her computer, and she sat, somewhat noisily, with a proud smile, rocking back and forth on the kitchen chair. On the screen was her written text:

For as long as I can remember I have had autism.
I overheard Jenny McCarthy say that her son commented that he felt like Dory from Nemo [Disney's *Finding Nemo*]

because he didn't remember things when he was autistic. However I have a great memory for many things. I also know many autistic kids that are exactly the same way. Parents know what I'm talking about, kids that can tell you the name of every subway line or that can memorize line for line different movies and tv shows.

Doctors would like to tell you that we have a hard time processing information. Its not really true, our brains are wired differently. We take in many sounds and conversations at once.

I have learnt how to filter through some of the mess.

Her piece was abrupt, as she had had so little time to prepare. I knew it was not the entire story she hoped to share. But it was a start on her road to becoming the self-described "autism advocate." Appreciative of the opportunity to get her message out to a wide audience, Carly emailed a note to thank Larry, but told us that she still wanted to do a *real* interview, as she had so much more to say.

Larry's producer called us a few days after the show aired, to thank us for participating. "Tune in for the Sunday night rebroadcast of the show," she said. "Larry reads part of Carly's thank-you note and addresses her."

We huddled around the TV at the appointed time, watching the way some people await election results. "And now an update on our special correspondent, Carly Fleischmann, who was on this program last week to talk about living with autism," said Larry in a piece added to the end of the original segment. "She wrote me a letter, which read in part, 'I would like to thank you for having me on your show . . . Children with autism need their story told. We need help. We need people to believe. We need people to understand. We need people to listen. In three and a half days people believed in me enough to have almost 5,000 sign my petition to tell my story. I still think it's a very important one. I love the fact you had me on your show and by doing this I believe that you believe.

"'I was told once no one will ever listen till someone stands up. Well I am standing and I was wondering if you would stand beside me. It's been a hard process for me to get to the point that I am able to spell. I believe we all have an inner voice. We just need to find away to get it out.

"'You said that there are a lot of things about autism you have not gotten to but you will try to touch on a fair bit. Let me be the first to open those doors. Your optimistic and able to back it up believer, Carly Fleischmann. Oh Thank you again for everything.'

"Well, Carly," Larry closed, "we thank *you*. And look forward to hearing again from our *optimistic believer*."

Tammy and I were keen to encourage Carly's newly found purpose, believing it would be good for her self-esteem. There had been a lot written about teen depression in general and the higher incidence among those suffering from ASD. A healthy sense of self-worth, we felt, might counterbalance Carly's struggles. Though her transformation was as slow moving as cold molasses, it was undeniable that Carly was indeed growing. Our daughter was determined not to be seen as the autistic girl without a voice but rather as the voice of autism.

Partway through the school year at Carlton, Howard cautiously tested the water with us about public school once again. "What if we could find a school near Carlton where she could go to one class per week. Just to try it," he mused.

"Howard, you are like a piece of sand in an oyster," I said.

He smiled, knowing it wouldn't take much for Tammy and me to get started again. Howard has an uncanny sense of timing, allowing us to rest just long enough to catch our breath before whipping us up the next hill.

Over the next few months, while I mulled over the possibility, Tammy got to work. "What about Western?" Tammy asked, referring to the large high school within our district. We had heard positive reports—despite the complaining about public schools that was in vogue. This particular school had a broad range of resources including an inclusion program for kids on the autism spectrum, though to our knowledge none of the students at Western dangled so far off the edge of the spectrum as Carly.

Looking at the school's website, Tammy noticed that Dennison Children's Services, the government agency that had helped provide respite and funding support for Carly over the years, had on-site counseling services for students at the school. She immediately called our social worker at the main office to inquire if they could help.

Within a few weeks, we had a meeting scheduled with a counselor, and the principal, Elaine Abrams, as well as a special education representative from the school board and one of the special education teachers at the school.

"Okay, now that we have a meeting, we need to figure out what we're going to say," Tammy said to us several days after she spoke with Steve.

"I have a game plan. You will have to wait and see," responded Carly.

Tammy looked at Howard, inquisitively.

"She's fine," he said. "She's writing out her request."

On a warm fall day in 2009, just after the start of the traditional school year, Howard, Tammy, Carly, and I walked through the front entrance of Western feeling like the Little Rock Nine. We had not often felt welcome in the public school system in the past, so despite the encouragement of Western's principal this time around, we remained on guard. Carly was assured a place in public school by law. That wasn't the concern. She wanted to be in a mainstream school, and the school board was required only to provide a placement *they* deemed appropriate for her abilities, possibly in a developmentally handicapped classroom. With Carly's intelligence and willingness to learn hampered by her behavioral constraints, finding a spot that made all parties happy had proven impossible in the public school system. Unlike the U.S., Canada does not pay for private placement when a public classroom is unavailable. Getting Carly into a mainstream high school with the right support network had been our dream and our main struggle of the past ten years.

Western, a large gothic building, is often used in the filming of movies and television shows, as it is the quintessential city high school: imposing and a bit scruffy, but full of energy. As students drifted from their after-school activities, we waited in a converted classroom that was used by school staff for conferences and meetings. The air in the room was heavy with the day's heat and lack of air conditioning. I looked distractedly around the room at the mismatched furniture. The west wall of the long room was a bank of impossibly tall windows covered with blackout curtains of a mysterious green synthetic material. They sagged in sections, clinging to the curtain rod for dear life. The tables were arranged in a horseshoe and we took our seats to one side as our hosts shuffled in.

Elaine strode in last, and with great purpose.

"I'm so sorry to keep you waiting. It's commencement next week and we have diploma packages to prepare for almost five hundred graduates," she explained breathlessly. Not a tall woman, Elaine nevertheless commanded presence. She introduced the staff with a confident formality, her posture straight enough to pass a grandmother's inspection.

"How can we help you?" she asked from her seat at the head of the table.

I suggested that perhaps the best way to articulate what we were hoping to accomplish for Carly was to let her present her statement. She had been fighting a cold and was not feeling well. In the heat of the room, she looked like a melting ice cream cone. "Is that okay, Carly?" Howard asked.

"Ess," she replied sleepily as Howard opened her laptop and turned it toward Elaine and her colleagues. Howard opened the document and booted up the software that breathed voice into Carly's words. The prepared statement was delivered from the computer in the familiar monotone:

"It's funny because I feel the schools are using labels to hold people back. I am autistic but does that mean I can't be a part of the same education that someone who is not autistic gets? If Albert Einstein was around in this century, fifty out of a hundred doctors say he would be diagnosed with learning disabilities and ADD. The other fifty say he would have been on the autism spectrum. When Albert went to school he was in a one classroom school house and was given a chance to learn. His teacher was quoted saying that Albert did not pay attention to any of the lessons that she taught him. She went on to say that he had to wear the dunce hat more times than she put logs in the fireplace. Yet she still gave him an education that led us to $E=mc^2$. What if he was born in today's time and put in a segregated school? Would we know what $E=mc^2$ means?

"Stephen Hawking was seven years old when he lost all oral ability in his mouth. He made lots of sounds but could not talk. Thanks to some amazing teachers that saw the potential in him, Stephen stayed in a mainstream class and is now one of the smartest men in the world with a PhD in science and many papers on black hole phenomenon. But what if the teachers did not let him stay in school? Do you think he really would have met his potential?

"I am not saying I am going to come up with the next E=mc^2 or write a dissertation on black holes but I would like the one thing these two individuals and many more like them had and that is a chance. School is about teaching young minds knowledge and I have proven with my IQ test that I take in all the information that is given to me. So please help me fill my head with knowledge. I am eager to learn and eager to put my own stamp on the world. Please help me do so.

"Thank you for listening to me I am willing to answer any questions you may have now."

A silence hung in the room. The broad metal venetian blinds, hanging awry, swayed slightly in the stingy breeze.

"Well," I heard someone say, and I looked up. Howard had the sheepish smile he wears when he knows Carly has won her point.

It was the end of a long day for everyone and we could see that Carly was fading fast. "We need to think this through," said Elaine, finally. "I have a few ideas, but I need some time."

She continued, looking directly at Tammy, "I want to make this work. There is a teacher here who has experience with students on the spectrum. Mostly Asperger's. And she teaches a class for our advanced pupils; it's in our *gifted* program. The course is on modern thought and philosophy. From what I've read from Carly, that might be of interest? If we can make it work out." She gave herself the wiggle room.

"How cool is that?" asked Tammy. "Would you like that?"

Carly was slumped against Howard, clearly feeling unwell. But her eyes brightened, her trademark half smile of self-satisfaction.

"That would be amazing," she typed. I smiled at the thought. From an ABA school to a gifted program; that *would* be amazing.

~§~

Over the coming months, Elaine worked through the details of how Carly might attend the class without contravening board or union protocols, which are rigid in Canada. Carly seemed to draw upon all her resolve, and while she was still not able to write with her teachers at Carlton, her freak-outs at school dramatically lessened. It was quid pro quo. We trusted in her to attend high school, and she redoubled her efforts at controlling herself.

It took until spring 2010 before we finally had permission for what we termed *the experiment*. Carly would attend Ms. Liko's advanced philosophy class that was just embarking on a module about psychology—one of Carly's areas of interest. Two or three times per week, Howard would pick her up from Carlton and drive her to Western. "If this goes well," said Elaine, "over the summer we can talk about whether Carly might be interested in enrolling at Western full-time." You could almost feel Carly's body vibrate with anticipation.

"How'd it go?" I asked Howard after their first day in class. "Did Carly hold it together?"

"She did. She was amazing. Not a peep. And the class is over an hour long."

"Were the kids freaked out by her?"

"Not at all. We showed the *20/20* video to help them understand. And these are mature kids. Bright. Mostly grade ten," he said.

When Barb showed up later that day, she asked Carly about her first day at school.

"It was very hard and Howard kept on bugging me asking if I wanted to go."

"We were only supposed to be there for fifteen or twenty minutes for the first day," Howard defended himself. "I felt like I had to ask you if you wanted to go."

"Do you accept that explanation, Carly?" asked Barb.

"If I have to," Carly snipped.

"Carly, what strategies did you use today or what were the situations in the class that made it work today? Knowing may be helpful in the future," Barb asked.

"I think it was just the fact I kept on telling myself this is my way out of ABA schools."

"Given that this was hard for you and you had to keep telling yourself to focus, were you still able to listen to what was being said? Could you still learn?"

"yes," Carly replied.

"Did you count at all in your head?" asked Howard, referring to a calming strategy they had learned to help Carly sit quietly.

"yes"

A few weeks later, Howard reminded Carly that she had to write a letter to the teacher to give her feedback about finally being allowed to attend a mainstream school. With a bowl of chips as her encouragement (why isn't Carly three hundred pounds?), she girded herself for the task of typing out a letter to her new teacher.

Dear Ms. Liko,

I would first like to say thank you for giving me an amazing opportunity to be a part of your class. I enjoyed listening to all the presentations today. Howard pointed out that I had my back to the presenter. I am sorry about that but I have a hard time processing overwhelming visual input for long periods of time. I will try to work on it.

I haven't decided on my topic for the assignment however I have a few ideas. I would also like to thank you for talking directly to me. A lot of people stop talking to me or start talking to Howard

because I don't look directly at people, but I can promise you that
I'm listening.
    I'll e-mail you soon about my assignment.

                                Your proud and excited student,
                                Carly

I needn't have worried about Carly rising to the challenge of school. Carly was motivated by the intellectual stimulation and by the opportunity to be around typical teenagers. We could feel her enthusiasm despite her narrow range of emotion she demonstrated physically. She was eager to share her experiences with people in her social network on Facebook and Twitter.

    "Working on high school homework. I always wanted to say that," she posted one afternoon. I wondered how many of the other kids at Western felt as enthusiastic about schoolwork. Carly had always been a hard worker. Even the simplest tasks took her months of practice to master. Now, spread out at the dining room table with articles and textbook chapters to read, she was finally working on what she wanted. And while it still took her weeks to type out what some students could do overnight, her enthusiasm never waned.

    Despite the energy required to produce relatively terse output, Carly devoured her assignments with gusto. It was a chance to demonstrate to the world that despite appearing disabled, she had plenty to say. As the class turned to Freud and the psychology of dreams, Carly noted on her Facebook page, *"Is it just me, or does anyone else think Freud was a pervert? Lol."*

    Every afternoon that she wasn't working with her occupational therapist or going swimming, Carly worked on her first major high school assignment. She had not let on how she planned to tackle it, proudly feeling the need to prove that she was capable of producing work without anyone's help.

"*Freud was obsessed with dreams and their meaning,*" she typed out for her teacher. "*But if he was alive today I think he would be fascinated by the bond and relationships between a nanny and the children she cares for. This song is written for a nanny to sing to the children she cares for. It's a good thing Freud wasn't around to psychoanalyze my song,*" she concluded before typing out the words to her lullaby.

I was a little perplexed by the topic, as Carly had had two nannies in her lifetime, neither of whom was a theme in her previous conversations or writings. "Okay," I said to Carly, "will you show me what you've written?"

Wishy Dishy

Wishy dishy I'll fold your clothes,
and then I'll tickle your little toes.

Wishy dishy I'll make your food.
That should put you in an amazing mood.

Wishy dishy I'll hold you tight
and stay with you til the pale moonlight.

Wishy dishy let's wash your hands.
Then I'll tell you a story I promise you'll understand.

Wishy dishy dinner's almost done
and then we can have some real fun.

Wishy dishy time to close your eyes.
It's time for your nanny to say her good-byes.

Wishy dishy you'll never know how much I love you so.

"I love it, Carly," I said enthusiastically, and gave her an unrequited hug. I was moved by the simplicity of the lyrics as well as the maturity of thought.

The time Carly would get to spend in class was short that spring, only about eight or nine weeks, as classes ended early for exams. But she soaked up every minute and proudly told everyone who cared to listen about her experience in school. It was the ultimate "I told you so," as she had been asking to attend a traditional school for years.

As a final psychology assignment, Carly was required to describe three of her dreams and then analyze them using the basic psychological principles she was taught in class. I waited expectantly. Would her dreams be conflicted and anxious to match her internal tension? Or would they be lofty and exciting—a reflection of a vision of some future self? Over the years of receiving notes from fans and followers, Carly had been asked repeatedly about her dreams. Though she confessed to vivid visions, she had never described any in detail.

When her assignment was complete—or as complete as she could make it given the creeping pace of her typing—she wanted to share it with both the teacher and the principal.

Dear Ms. Liko and Ms. Abrams,

I just would like to thank both of you for giving me the amazing opportunity that you did by letting me participate in the Dream Class. I enjoyed being apart of the class and school. You both may never really know how much it meant to me that you believed in me. I hope I made both of you proud and I hope that I will be able to see both of you in the halls next year.

Your hard working and eager student,
carly fleischmann

Carly then spread her dreams out in front of us like a patchwork quilt. Each one seemed to represent a shard of her experience among us. In one, which she referred to as a recurring dream, she was invited to speak to an audience about her experience with autism.

I am in a dark room. I can't see anything but hear voices. At first it's little whispers but then the voices appear louder and louder. I start turning around and around to see who's talking but because it's so dark I am not even sure if I am actually turning. I stop moving and right at that moment over a hundred lights turn on and I am blinded once again but this time not by darkness but by lights. The voices start to fade lower and lower. I can hear hushes like people trying to silence a crowd. My eyes start to show images, foggy images but nonetheless images.

I start to see blurry faces that seem to surround me. When the fog finally dissipates I find myself on a stage in an auditorium. This stage is not a normal stage. It's round and the audience surrounds you. You can feel hundreds of eyes looking at you from every direction.

I start to pan around and as I complete my 360 a voice suddenly talks over a loud speaker. Because the voice comes out of nowhere I jump back. Startled, a man in the front row gives me a weird look and I turn away from his gaze and begin paying attention to the voice.

The voice is announcing me as Carly Fleischmann, an autistic girl, who found her voice by using a computer to communicate. The voice of the announcer goes on to say I will be talking about autism and ways to cure it.

I can't believe my ears. I remember thinking if I could cure autism wouldn't I be the first person I'd cure? Finally the voice says "without further adieu, Carly Fleischmann."

I look around this small round stage and I notice my

computer is nowhere to be seen. I start to panic and I can feel thousands and thousands of eyes looking directly at me. I start to scream and notice something strange. I have control of my voice. I look out in the crowd and try to say a word. At this point my view changes and I can see myself. With my lip quivering I manage to say the word "hi." Shocked, I say "My name is Carly Fleischmann." Then I start talking more and more. All of a sudden someone from the audience says "Aren't you supposed to be using a computer?"

I tell him "I don't need it anymore."

The man stands up and says "I'm not paying good money to see a girl that can talk" and he starts to walk out.

The rest of the audience starts to agree with him and walks out. I am left all alone on the stage thinking I just was able to do what I've not been able to do for many years, that is talk. And now I'm being punished for it. Then all of a sudden the lights go off all around me and I wake up.

Most people see only Carly's external conflict, the battle to control the outbursts and urges that govern her interaction with the world. Beneath the skin lies deeper conflict. For years she had been writing that the world must believe in people with disabilities, believe they have an inner voice and purpose aching to get out. I assumed her proselytizing was for our benefit: We will be better people if we believe in those who are unlike ourselves. But Carly's dream gave me a peek into what it must feel like to be someone under constant scrutiny and doubt. She once said in an interview that she has never used facilitated communication, and bristled at those who were skeptical about her ability to produce original creative and emotive thought. She reminded people that no one had a hand "up her butt" telling her what to say. We laughed at her words, but their meaning was pivotal to her.

At some point, we all have anxiety dreams: showing up unprepared for an exam or arriving at school in our underwear. Carly's dream showed a more complex set of anxieties. The media—social and otherwise—had portrayed her as a thought leader in autism ever since she started communicating the experience of autism. She often seemed to relish the role by asking people on her Facebook page to send her questions about autism to "get it out in the open." Is there a paradox here? The more she yearned for the limelight, the more stress she felt.

Worse than the weight of responsibility is the snare of cynicism. Who is the man who scoffed at her in her dream? He is everyone that has doubted Carly all her life. Carly learned that if she did not communicate, she would be thought of as intellectually delayed, the disabled person her doctors had predicted she would be as a child. But if she *did* communicate, she is a sham because people who fit her description, according to many psychologists, are thought to be incapable of creative thought. Tammy and I had seen the accusations online before. That Carly must not really have autism if she can articulate her feelings so eloquently. Or that her writings must somehow be facilitated or coached. Carly found herself playing Cassandra: screaming the truth to the deaf ears of disbelievers.

And a new worry laid on the pile of parental neurosis was the fear that Carly would give up trying. If communicating is a monumental task and yet met with skepticism, was Carly's spirit sufficiently strong to persevere? She once wrote her friend Gaby, *"Do you ever feel misunderstood? I do all the time."*

Carly's dream project continued, revealing other facets of her inner sanctum.

My next dream takes place at a school. I find myself walking the hallways to get to my class. The bell has rung and I know I'm

late but even though no one is in the halls I feel like I am working my way through a crowd. In the hallway I see a clock. The
hands start moving around and around. I'm trying to make my
way to the stairwell but it feels like it is taking forever. I look
down on the floor and notice I am standing on a floor escalator
the kind they have at the airport and I am going the wrong way.

I start to run and manage to make headway. I get to the end
of the hallway and start to ascend the steps. Then I notice them
start disappearing behind me. Afraid they might vanish in front
of me, I start to run and run. I make it up the stairwell and turn
the corner to my classroom. I put my hand on the door and
the bell rings. The class empties and the crowd from the class
knocks me and pushes me all the way back to the start of my
dream.

I see this as an anxiety dream. How many times have I dreamt
of trying to make a phone call only to have the buttons on the hand-
set disappear or to run like a cartoon character, my legs pumping
but covering no ground. I am not surprised that Carly would have
feelings of stress as she begins growing from a girl, protected by
the confines of her disability, to a young woman entering the mainstream world.

Carly completed her project with a dream that made me smile,
although I don't believe she saw it as a lighthearted vision.

In my last dream I was on a beach with Brad Pitt and Justin Tim-
berlake and we were sitting together talking.

We started to laugh and all of the sudden a reporter started
asking me questions and then another and another. I looked
over at Brad and Justin for help but I could not see them and
was surrounded by reporters. I tried pushing my way out of the

crowd but kept on getting knocked back into the middle. A man with a deep voice said, "Carly, I'm coming to get you."

The sea of reporters started to sway and I saw a large, dark hand appear in the crowd. Another one emerged and just like a parting of the sea, this man opened his arms and cleared a large passageway through the people. I started to follow him into a small building and the crowd of reporters began to follow us. We started to run and run.

And the man said, "Do you see the room at the end of the hall? Go in there and lock the door."

So I headed to the door. When I finally got there I put my hand on the door and it was locked. I turned around and saw the reporters running at me. They came closer and closer like a freight train. Just as they were about to run me over I woke up.

Even without her assessment of what she thought this dream meant, I was left with a melancholy smile—amused by the presence of her two longstanding crushes and concerned about the presence of the media. I wondered if in fact her public attention hadn't been a double-edged sword. Carly has had more public involvement with press and social media fans than most teens. While she had voluntarily put *herself* out there, I wondered if it was taking a private toll on her. But Carly has her own mind and a steely determination. She had found a calling in life—to share the truths and debunk the myths of living with autism—we let her steer the boat through those waters believing it would build her self-esteem.

Many aspects of her dreams were, I'm sure, typical of a teen growing from childhood. For Carly I am sure they were heightened, as all of her senses seem to be, electrified by the voltage that surged through her body. I am reminded how far she had come. How far we had all come. I thought of something Carly had once written, *"Living with autism has been hard at times and the gains are great, but challenging to get to."*

How simply she captured a decade and a half of struggle, but her dreams told me she was only partway to her ultimate goals. "How far do you want to go?" I asked her at a team-planning meeting.

"To be honest I don't know yet. I would like to travel. I would like to go to university. I would like to date."

"How wonderful," everyone told her.

I closed my eyes and tried to imagine what it would take to make that wish come true.

A Final Dream

We are sitting around the dining room table. But we are not eating. We're having some sort of meeting. Tammy, Carly, Howard, a therapist Carly works with to help her with her OCD. And me. We are talking about Carly's future and where she sees herself. We are talking. Carly is writing.

She tells us she understands that she is not the easiest kid to bring up, yet how hard she tries—every day.

We acknowledge that we know and are very proud of her.

She ponders what life will hold for her. Whether she will ever be independent, be free of torment. Regardless, she says, she has plans.

Carly writes that she loves us and forgives us for the things that she has had to endure. Things that a child should not be asked to endure, I think to myself. Not by her parents.

I am moved and proud and tearful.

But in this particular dream, I am awake.

24

~~~

Take a Bow

I was asked if I had to pick another disability other then autism to be
what would it be?
My answer to that is: I was once told a blind man wanted to be deaf and a
deaf man wanted to be blind. But its always better to be your self.

—Carly, May 2009

Carly's experiment—attending a class for gifted students at a local high school during the 2009/2010 school year—had been largely successful. Although it was a few months by the time Carly was successfully registered, she had proven to the school and to herself that she could sit reasonably quietly and complete several of the assignments. More importantly, she won the hearts of her teachers and fellow students. Rather than return to Carlton in the fall, Carly would be attending Western on a full-time basis.

Before our summer plans got under way, Carly was invited to introduce Temple Grandin at a conference being held at a university an hour north of Toronto. Dr. Grandin was diagnosed with autism as a child in the 1950s, when it was generally accepted that those afflicted with ASD would spend their lives in institutions. Through her mother's dedication and her own creative problem solving, Dr. Grandin progressed through school, completed a Ph.D., and embarked upon a career in animal husbandry. Dr. Grandin was a vocal advocate for those living with autism and sensory integration issues, and she had been invited to speak at the event slated for late June, the weekend before Toronto hosted the G20 Summit.

Carly confessed to being very nervous about the task. Temple was a hero, and introducing a hero is a daunting task. With only two weeks to prepare the opening remarks, she wore the pressure like a lead blanket. Each time Carly sat down to write the address, she would close the computer before Howard could save her work, intentionally deleting it.

"It was really good," he said. "But I guess she doesn't think it's good enough."

We encouraged her to just put it down and we could edit it later. Eventually Carly was able to finish her speech and we saved it before she could deliberate further. Her mood seemed to brighten and her anxiety lifted.

Days before the event, she joked on Facebook:

So when i was on 20/20 they had a thing called a trailer that they ran over and over. It was something like 'Autistic nonverbal girl with what seemed like no hope found her inner voice and now has a bright future. tune in at eleven'. So I decided to write a real one for this Thursday. I am about to post it so tell me what you think of it. 'This Thursday great political minds are going to sit in a room and talk about absolutely nothing at the G20 summit. One hour away two autistic ladies are going to be presenting and changing the way people view autism. Temple Grandin and Me, Carly Fleischmann, this Thursday. Straight from the horses mouths.

Carly had now made several presentations of this nature—though none as auspicious—yet she still got very nervous about her ability to control her behaviors. She needn't have worried. Tammy and I sat in the front row and watched Carly seated on the dais with Howard to her right. Mustering all of her energy, she sat calmly, swaying slightly, her right hand on her ear—a gesture she would eventually tell us helps her alter the sounds around her. The digitized voice from her computer echoed through the university gymnasium. Carly's written text scrolled across two enormous screens for the audience of eight hundred people:

For those of you who don't know me my name is Carly Fleischmann. I am a fifteen year old autistic girl who, as you can see and hear, has found her inner voice. I feel honoured and privileged to be introducing a woman that really needs no introduction, but don't tell her that or I might be out of a job. Rumour has it I'm getting paid in potato chips. Yum yum.

Let me go back to being serious for a moment. I have been doing a lot of research to prepare for Temple's introduction and I couldn't believe similarities we both seem to have. Just like me and many children with autism, Temple's mother sat in the doctor's office when Temple was a little girl and she was told that Temple had autism. Temple's mother asked what caused the autism. The doctor responded with a response that many doctors told mothers up until 20 years ago. He looked right into Temple's mother's eyes and said it is caused from bad parenting and lack of love from the mother. Temple, like me, was nonverbal at the time and her mother, like my mother, could not accept the fact that her child would never be able to communicate. Temple, from that point on, went through an intense therapy program. It was not ABA but some people would argue that it could be considered the first ABA program ever made.

With intense speech therapy, a nanny working non-stop on social skills, and a mother with a will to educate her daughter, Temple was able to communicate. Even though Temple was able to talk, it did not mean the fight for her was over. Temple, like me, was given an opportunity to attend school but challenges and skepticism lay around every corner. Temple was able to do what a lot of doctors and educators thought would be impossible. She graduated school with a PhD in animal science. She has gone on to write books on a variety of subjects including animals, social skills and of course, autism.

Living with autism, myself, has been hard at times and the gains are great, but challenging to get to. However, being able to see someone who is able to walk a mile in the shoes I'm already wearing, gives me more than hope for myself and for the hundreds of thousands following with, and behind me.

I have to be honest with all of you here today. I usually am able to write a speech or a story in my head, and then type it out. However for this speech today, it has been a hard process for me. I thought it was because of my autism but I realized it's my admiration for Temple Grandin that made it so difficult. A wise man once said to dream of greatness is just the first step but actually attaining it is, like they say on tv, priceless. Most children my age would say that they look up to pop stars, reality tv stars, and sports stars but I'm proud to say the person I look up to is Temple Grandin. So without further adieu the woman who really needed no introduction, my idol, Temple Grandin.

I seem to hear Carly's voice for the first time on each occasion I read what she has created. It's been six years that she's been writing and with each epistle, I'm still left somewhat speechless myself. Carly and Howard stepped down from the stage and Temple made her presentation, but I was so busy playing and replaying Carly's introduction in my head that I only half-listened to Dr. Grandin's speech.

Carly was finding the perfect opportunities to share her message. Technology helped ease the burden of communicating—software with word prediction, more sophisticated image-based programs, the iTouch, and then the iPad all improved Carly's ability to converse. With the growth of social media channels, Carly was able to reach people in ways that would have been impossible just five years earlier.

And the public wanted to be reached. The media's interest in autism was growing, sparked by startling statistics of one in 110 children being diagnosed with ASD every year. The condition was being likened to an epidemic.

It was through this confluence of technology and public interest that we came to meet Holly Robinson Peete. She and her husband, ex-NFLer Rodney Peete, had started a foundation known as HollyRod that provides funding and services to those affected by Parkinson's disease and autism. Their son RJ was diagnosed with autism at age two and Holly had become a passionate spokesperson for the cause. Holly began following Carly on Twitter and the two had exchanged a few emails. On one of our trips to LA, we met with Holly and her son. We had lunch at an outdoor market on the kind of bright afternoon that reminds you why everyone in LA has a smile. Holly was passionate about her work at HollyRod and completely down-to-earth.

Shortly before Carly was to introduce Temple Grandin, we received a call from the executive director of HollyRod, informing us that Carly had been selected to receive a Youth Champion award from the foundation at their annual gala, DesignCare. The event was to be held in July, just before Carly was to leave for sports camp. Tammy graciously thanked them and said she would see if there were any way to attend, but she wasn't optimistic. One trip to LA with Carly every year was about as much logistical juggling as she could handle.

Tammy and Carly checked out the DesignCare website later that evening and realized the magnitude of the honor. The annual event draws hundreds of donors. "Carly *could* go straight to camp from LA if Sheila comes with us," Tammy said, referring to the young woman who was to be Carly's aide at camp that summer.

I reflected on the effort it would take to coordinate and make the trip. Wasn't summer supposed to be a break? On the other hand, I knew Carly felt honored—as did we—for the recognition. Furthermore, I looked forward to hearing the acceptance speech Carly would inevitably have to write. Her desire to be a voice for those who couldn't communicate combined with her unfailing perfectionism resulted in an eye-opening experience each time she undertook such an effort. I was getting to understand and appreciate Carly more from the writing she did for strangers than in all the conversations we had and all the sessions with Barb and Howard. I knew many families with children living with autism who never heard meaningful language from their kids. I considered us fortunate in our misfortune; although Carly's life was a daily battle, her voice was a gift.

"So, let's do it," I exhaled, somewhere between a sigh and a statement of resolve. Missing opportunities such as this only breeds regret later.

Taryn would be at camp. Matthew, who was entering his junior year of university, had to stay in Toronto to work at his summer job. He was doing research in a psychology lab at the Hospital for Sick Children. Relatively speaking, Tammy, Sheila, Carly, and I were a small crew to transport.

During the flight, Sheila was able to calmly talk Carly through one bout of bleating, back arching, and head banging in her seat. Even with Carly's growing sense of self-awareness, to this day she cannot articulate what sets off these eruptions. Otherwise, the flight was uneventful, though I didn't dare relax until we arrived at the hotel. I don't think I'll ever be totally calm when I travel with Carly.

Tired from the trip, everyone slept through the night. The next morning, we spent our one free day walking by the beach in Santa Monica and Venice. Sheila had never been to Los Angeles, but we wanted to keep the pace calm and save our energy for the event the next day. At Holly's suggestion we stopped by the venue for the gala to give Carly a chance to see where she would be sitting and to walk up on stage. Practice doesn't make perfect, but it does take the stress levels down just a notch. The event was taking place at the estate of a prominent businessman and friend of Holly and Rodney's.

"The award show and entertainment is taking place on the tennis court," the event manager directed us. "It seats six hundred with room for a double stage and a runway for the fashion show."

I looked at Tammy, giving her a silent "holy crap" look. Sheila, Tammy, Carly, and I found the section in which we would be seated and practiced walking up onto the stage several times. Carly seemed calm, her stimming and noises almost nonexistent, but my stomach tightened at the thought of everything that *could* go wrong in the few feet between our seats and the stage where we would stand to accept the award.

Having cleared the hurdle of the rehearsal, we went over to our friends' house to hang out. Their son was also nonverbal and yet wrote beautifully using a keyboard. He had sent Carly a poem about living with autism earlier that year. Tammy and I wondered aloud why we couldn't seem to find anyone similar to Carly in our city. Would Carly have to move to LA to have friends?

The next day passed peacefully and quickly. Tammy ran out to buy a new pair of shoes, feeling somewhat intimidated and under-accessorized by the magnitude of the event. Sheila and I took Carly sightseeing, relaxed by the pool, and napped. My niece Sydney, who was in LA for the summer for an internship, joined us with her boy-friend, Ben. Getting ready for the formal affair brought me back to my wedding day. The women were in one hotel room blow-drying, nail painting, hair straightening, and getting dressed, while Ben and I were in the other quickly putting on our suits and waiting impa-tiently.

When we arrived at the event, Carly, Sheila, Syd, and Ben found a quiet spot in the garden where dinner was being served while Tammy and I wandered around the silent auction and said hello to the handful of people we knew. I had hoped to gaze longingly at Eva Longoria, who I heard was going to be there. I didn't notice her until much later in the evening, and by the time I realized it was her, my celebrity crush had walked past.

As darkness fell, we were asked to make our way down the hill to the tennis courts, which were now fully festooned for the enter-tainment and award show. Carly's award was to be one of the first of the six awards being given out, and I calculated how we might make a run for the exit immediately after if she couldn't hold it together for the rest of the evening.

Just before Carly was called up to accept the award, a short video about her was played. It was neither melodramatic nor su-garcoated, but seeing the film the production company had artfully edited using our home video, family pictures, and excerpts from the *20/20* segment had a jarring effect on me. In reality, Carly's life had come together in small increments over the past fifteen years like a mosaic, one tiny tile at a time. All within three or four minutes, her struggles, her breakthrough, and her dream of being a voice to autism all played out. I felt as if I were a witness to my existence, as were the hundreds of strangers sitting around me. I reached over to hold Carly's hand and could tell she was focusing hard to keep her composure.

The video ended and we were called up. Holly and Rodney

hugged us as if we were long-lost relatives and thanked us for making the trip out. In all the excitement I had forgotten to think about how I would express my appreciation in that short moment on stage before Carly's speech. Holly turned to the audience and told them that Carly had prepared a short acceptance speech and the lights dimmed slightly as the screen filled with her words, the stadium speakers giving life to the voice of her computer:

> I feel deeply honored to be receiving this award tonight. I just have one question. Does anyone know if I can trade this award at a convenience store for a bag of chips? I love chips. L.O.L.
>
> Ok, I'm ready to be serious. Are you? I don't think many people thought when I was a young child that some day I would be getting my first A in a mainstream advanced grade 10 English class or introducing Temple Grandin to over a eight hundred people or even finding my inner voice and being able to share it with all of you tonight. In the last four years of my life I have found, and I am proud to say, started using my inner voice to type and to share the truths, secrets and myths about autism. I was asked, a while ago, if I get sick and tired answering questions to my over 15 thousand fans and followers on Twitter Facebook and my blog. The way I see it, how is anyone really going to know the truth about living with autism unless someone with autism talks about it? They say autism is one of those things that even doctors and experts don't really understand yet. So, like I tell my readers, why go to a duck to find out what's wrong with the horse when you can go right to the horse's mouth?
>
> It hasn't always been a smooth road for me to travel and I still find myself traveling over many bumps in the road to get to where I want to be but luckily for me, I have many caring people traveling beside me. I would like to thank my mom who has

taught me to fight for what I believe in. She does this by helping me fight and helping other families with autism get what they need to give their child the opportunity to find their inner voice.

I would like to thank my dad who would climb a volcano oozing lava or swim across the ocean just to read me a story or spend time with me.

There are two other people in my life I would like to thank, Barb, my speech pathologist, who has been with me for longer than I remember and Howard, a man who every child with autism should have stand beside them. I owe a lot to these two for believing in me so much that I started to believe in myself.

Ok, enough with the mushy stuff. I promise I am almost done. Just 112 more pages to go. LOL. I believe it's time that children and adults with autism have a chance to find their inner voices. It is time that people around us get educated about autism and what it is really about. It is time that we all start believing in the possibilities. Because of this, I would like to share my award tonight with everyone living with autism. Many small steps have been started in the right direction but maybe it's time for us all to take that one big leap.

I would like to thank Holly, The HollyRod Foundation and Lori for giving me the opportunity to be here with you tonight. Their generosity and caring has made me feel like a real celebrity. I would also like to thank all of you for this honor and award tonight on the behalf of people living with autism everywhere.

Thank you.

While the speech played, I stood behind Carly, who pursed her lips, putting her right hand to her ear in the pose that was her trademark. I wrapped my arms tightly around her waist to make both of us feel more secure and Tammy wrapped her arm around me—the three of us stabilizing one another.

When the speech was done and we had thanked our hosts one last time, we returned to our seats, receiving pats on the arm and smiles from audience members as we walked by. Despite her lack of broad expressions, I could feel Carly was basking in the glory. She sat quietly for the rest of the awards ceremony and when the music started for the entertainment that followed, Carly rocked in her chair, a small, pleased smile on her face.

We departed early the next morning—Carly to sports camp, Tammy and I to return home. At the airport, I watched Carly and Sheila pass through security and waved as they disappeared into the throng. Carly had on her worn knapsack and pressed through the mob with her impatient, swaying gate. Sheila walked quickly to stay next to her, guiding her through the crowd. I thought to myself, since Carly's first tentative words five years earlier, her voice had become strong and distinct. Her actions, though often sidetracked by uncontrollable compulsions, were directed and purposeful. I knew that while she would always need someone at her side to guide her, she had a newfound momentum to her life.

"How far up the ladder will she climb?" I had asked Carly's doctor, years before.

"We'll just have to wait and see," she had replied.

I turned, slinging my carry-on over my shoulder, and walked the other direction toward my gate.

25

❧

I Am Carly

Q: kpm @CarlysVoice: Do you think you'll ever be independent?
A: I don't know if I will be fully independent. I still am working on lots of my
issues. but I surprise my self every year so u never know.

The 2010–2011 school year started with the hope and promise and tingling nerves of a first date. Carly came downstairs wearing close-fitting designer jeans and her favorite Pink by Victoria's Secret T-shirt. Howard had learned to iron her hair, allowing wisps to spray forth over one eye. I took to calling him *Mr. Howard*, with mock affect.

"Morning, C," I said. I had already walked our dog, Nelly, and was sitting at the table, sun streaming across my newspaper.

Carly flopped heavily onto the kitchen chair next to me as Howard brought over the whole-wheat tortilla with low-fat mozzarella I had prepared minutes before. This was Carly's favorite breakfast.

It's actually her only breakfast thanks to her need for repetition. For the first time in her life we had to watch her weight. Carly had gained nearly fifteen pounds due to a medication her doctor was trying in an effort to decrease the OCD outbursts. "No dip today, okay, Carly?" I told her more than asked.

After a summer that included receiving her award from Holly-Rod and two months at two different summer camps, Carly was about to start high school as a ninth-grade student.

"Let's start with five classes," Elaine suggested when we met over the summer. "And we'll try to stagger them so they don't all require lots of writing and don't all land on the same day. One will be a resource class; like a study hall where she can catch up on some of her work."

Western Secondary has three levels of education: gifted, academic, and applied. Carly was enrolled in two gifted, the most vigorous of the three levels, and one of each of the others. In the coming weeks, we would settle into a schedule with two assistants escorting Carly to school. Sheila, who had been working with Carly for over a year, had recently finished teachers' college but agreed to put her job search for a full-time teaching position on hold to work with Carly in the mornings for the school year. Howard finished the day and stayed on until bedtime. Carly only went to Darlene's house on the weekends now. I am nothing if not practical and know that despite her gains, Carly's erratic sleep patterns, her obsessive compulsivity, and the string of therapists that accompany her fifteen hours a day are too much to have in our house 24/7. I love my daughter, but I needed some space if I was to continue to do so.

She was not happy about the respite situation, but told us that she understood why we needed a break from her and she loved us despite the circumstances. Guilt is a powerful tool Carly had mastered with the deftness of a Jewish grandmother. But when she told us this, this time, her sincerity allowed me to cut myself some slack.

The fall was filled with Carly highs and Carly lows. She participated in activities and events at school along with her classmates, but her OCD continued to imprison her. Carly attended her first school dance at Halloween dressed as a skeleton, the only costume we could agree upon. She wanted the Sexy Ladybug; we wanted modesty. Howard escorted her and watched as her classmates beckoned Carly to the dance floor, holding her hands and swinging her around. Such a simple act of acceptance no one might have dreamt of a few years earlier.

> Ok so Friday night I went out to see a movie with my friends. I was amazing at the movie and love not needing my parents or anyone like that beside me. I had a really good time but fell asleep 10min at the end. But really the movie was No Strings Attached and everyone really knows how its going to end. lol. After the movie we went out for dinner and I had a surprise birthday cake show up. It was so cool.
>
> —Facebook posting, November 2010

Class assignments stacked up as Carly was unable to type fast enough to complete them. "This was never about getting the academic credits," I said, "it's about getting started." For reasons only Carly knew, her mornings with Sheila were more challenging than her afternoons with Howard. Even after a year together, Carly seldom typed for Sheila and struggled to keep the compulsions in check. There were days when Sheila's main task was getting Carly from home to school. Any pretense of class work was cast aside in the pursuit of survival. Why Sheila endured the punishing task I would never know. It was a testament to her character and a product of the spell Carly casts on people.

Howard continued to be the "autism whisperer"—often able to help Carly down from her explosive compulsive episodes faster than anyone else. And though Carly was making great strides in typing more independently, she was still more capable if Howard was in the vicinity.

One afternoon as the two of them moved from English to philosophy class, Howard stopped briefly to talk to one of Carly's teachers in the hall. In the rush of students, he didn't notice that Carly had wandered away. Looking around as the crowd thinned, Howard was filled with a wave of panic. Running down the hall, he burst through the doors of the stairwell to find Carly standing with two classmates, tapping out a conversation on her iPad.

"Carly! Don't wander off like that again," he said, exhaling in relief.

But when Howard called me at work later that afternoon to tell me what had happened, I heard pride rather than remorse in his voice.

> So i have big no huge no massive news. Today I participated in a class play reading. The play was call One Of Them and i was girl number 2. It was so cool howie programed my ipad with my lines & I was able to deliver them. It was so much fun being able to do what my class were doing. They all clapped and came up to me to tell me i was great. I love my ipad and thanks to it I'm participate in class in a whole new way.
>
> —Facebook posting, April 2010

It has always been Carly's vision of what *could be*, her drive, that kept us all moving forward. "When I first met Carly, she was about two years old," Barb once told a reporter writing an article on Carly's communication breakthrough, "She was very active and had a really short attention span. I would see her at her preschool and I remember for circle time they would sit her on top of a cube chair so she wouldn't take off. My goal with her then was to create the best communication system possible, and that included speech. Even then everyone at school had the sense that she had a spark. There was more going on inside."

It was this spark that could bring Tammy and me back from the edge so many times. Carly had the devastating ability to bring us to our darkest places—deep caverns of hopelessness, exhaustion, and sadness. But her determination, good humor, and considerate nature lifted us back up.

On the occasion of Tammy's fiftieth birthday, Carly asked Howard to take her shopping for a special gift. They stopped to get a card first and at the store she spied a paperweight—a snow globe with Cinderella's glass slipper on a pink cushion inside. On the base was the aphorism "Even miracles take a little time." Carly wrote Tammy a note saying that she thought the quote aptly described both mother and daughter. The gift sits on the bookshelf in Tammy's home office, and I stop to look at it every time I go in. Never before has a tchotchke had such meaning.

By nature I am an optimist and try to feel some measure of gratitude in whatever is dealt. So while my heart will always break at Carly's suffering—the shackles of OCD and the tangles of autism—I remain hopeful that her life will bring her happiness and a sense of meaning. In the autism community, we are among the fortunate ones. Through years of hard work, constant intervention by some remarkable individuals, and perhaps luck, Carly has found her voice and with it has come accomplishments that others afflicted with ASD will not achieve. We have been given the opportunity to understand our child, where so many others have not.

Tammy and I have been asked how we do it. What keeps us moving forward? Sometimes it's just inertia. But we keep sight of Carly's dream to be accepted. She wants to live life fully, accomplish great things, and not be pitied. She just wants to be understood. What else can we do? We get up in the morning when the alarm goes off. And never accept "no" or "maybe."

Still, there are days where one step forward is met with two back; I have not yet returned to the days of peaceful sleeps, awaking in laughter. That is the real price of autism. It's not the money required for education, therapy, and staff. Or even the forgone opportunities. The real cost is the lack of security we feel in our lives together—as if we are perpetually stepping onto slick ice for the first time, never sure of our footing and what catastrophe may await us.

It's been fourteen years since Carly was diagnosed with autism and cognitive impairment. We were warned that she might never develop abilities beyond those of a child and would likely spend her life in a group home. Carly has defied most predictions and lived a life out loud, to paraphrase Émile Zola.

These days, I think more about what's still to come than what might have been. I tiptoe into Carly's room and whisper in her ear as she sleeps, "Everything will work out. Everything will be fine." Then closing her door gently, I slip into bed next to Tammy and pray that I'm right.

Epilogue

The world looks beautiful when we walk with our eyes open.
—*Carly, June 11, 2009*

From the Horse's Mouth

(Grammar and spelling edited for clarity.)

Wow, I can't believe you made it all the way to my chapter of the book! So tell me the truth. You really didn't end up reading all of my dad's boring writing, did you? There could only be three explanations for how you ended up at the end of the book, reading this chapter.

Okay, so option one is you bought the book and while you were opening the book, it fell to the floor and landed on this chapter. THANK GOODNESS FOR YOU.

Or option two, you started reading the book and got so bored that you just wanted to know how the story ends and you turned to the last chapter and found out who wrote it. Now you're so happy that you are not going to put down this book until you finish this chapter.

Or option three, you read the cover jacket of the book that says my dad will pay you $100 if you read the whole book from top to bottom and fill out the online quiz.

Ha ha, made you look at the cover jacket.

All joking aside, I love my father and feel so honored to have him share my story with you, the reader. People have always called me a miracle child, but the truth is, as you read in the book, my spelling really did not come overnight. It took lots of hard work, time, and devotion to get where I am today. My father and mother have always been there for me and thanks to their hard work and dedication to me, I am able to share with you my inner voice.

So, why do I call my voice my "inner voice"? The truth is ever since I was a young child, I talked. The words never flowed out of my mouth or came out of my head to be shared with the outside world, but I talked to myself in my head. The earliest thought I have of me talking in my head and wanting to share something with the outside world was when I must have been five or six years old and my nanny was in the kitchen making some food for Matthew, my brother, and Taryn, my sister. She was asking them what they wanted to eat. I remember my brother replying first and then my sister yelling in her idea. I recall telling her in my head that I wanted Kraft Macaroni and Cheese. My nanny at the time repeated the orders back to my brother and sister but never repeated mine back to me. I think that was the first time I really realized that my outer voice wasn't like Matthew's or Taryn's. I remember thinking at that point in time that I was different. I kind of knew it, I guess, but never really realized it until that day.

So, as you can see, I always had a voice. It was just inside of me. I would talk to myself and even reply back to people sometimes even though they couldn't hear me. My voice was always special to me even though it was only for me to hear. I remember thinking that if I could get my inner voice out and share it like Matthew or Taryn, then maybe I wouldn't be so different. However, my inner voice stayed inside of me for over ten years of my life. I do believe we all have an inner voice and it's just trying to find its way out.

The day after I realized I was different I also started to see other small differences between my sister and myself. She would be able to sit in front of a TV for hours. I couldn't understand how she was doing it because when I attempted to do that, I would have information overload.

Sticking a brush through my hair felt like someone was ripping my hair out strand by strand. Yet my sister would sit and brush her hair like it was no big deal. Occasionally, my mother or father would have to yell at her to do it, but she was still able to do it without any problems.

The smell and sensation of different foods would always present problems for me. However, it never seemed to be an issue for my sister or brother. One of the biggest things I noticed was that they would always want to be touched or hugged or to roughhouse with each other. However, any time they tried that with me, it felt so constricting and overwhelming that I needed them to back off. I could never understand how they were able to do all those things I couldn't.

Life at that point started to even seem more different than my siblings. I realized that I had therapists come to my house every day getting me to do things that seemed to come so natural to Matthew and Taryn. I remember thinking that I wished that I would be good at something that they weren't, so they would have to have a therapist come in to teach them something. I used to share a room with Taryn, and every morning she would get dressed all by herself and run into the washroom to brush her teeth, when she remembered to. I can remember for me every day one of my therapists would come in and work on how to put on clothes. It felt so hard. I hated the feeling of taking off my clothes and the feeling of putting on cold clothes. During one of my sleepless nights I remember turning on the light in my room and trying to put on my clothes all by myself. I think I forgot my underwear and couldn't do up the button to the pants and had my shirt half on as I started to wander down the stairs to see if I could find some food. I think that's when my mom found me and sent me back to bed. She was so tired and didn't even realize my makeshift accomplishment.

Later on in life I started to realize that I was taking in information a lot different than the typical children around me. I always had a hard time understanding what people were saying. Even as a young child I would only be able to understand one or two words in a sentence that someone was saying to me. I now realize it wasn't that I didn't understand the words, it was that my brain couldn't focus directly on the conversation.

Let me break it down for you and set a picture up in your mind like they do on *CSI* and those other TV shows. Picture yourself in a coffee shop with just one other person. The person starts talking and you are able to focus directly on what they are saying. For me that is a different case altogether. The woman who brushes along our table leaves an overpowering scent of perfume and my focus moves. Then the conversation over my left shoulder from the table behind us comes into play. The rough side on my left sleeve cuff rubs up and down on my body. That starts to get my attention, as the whoosh and whistle of the coffee maker blends into different sounds all around me. The visual of the door opening and shutting in the front of the store completely consumes me. I have lost the conversation, missing most of what the person in front of me is talking about. With more scents to smell, more overwhelming visual input coming in from the coffee shop, and more audio conversation from people talking at other tables in the room, I find myself only hearing the odd word the person in front of me has said.

So I know what you are thinking. With all those things going on, how do I drink my coffee? Just joking. How do I understand what people are saying? About a year and a half ago I coined a term called *audio filtering*. Lots of people with autism do it and it's something we learn to do on our own. I don't even think doctors, scientists, or psychologists even know we do it.

Audio filtering is hard to master, and some people who audio filter only manage to use it a little bit in their lives and might not be able to control when they are doing it. The best way to explain audio filtering is to bring you back into the coffee shop. Imagine having a DVD remote control programmed in your brain and when the conversation starts you can pause, slow it down, rewind, or skip things. Now just because you can do all those things does not mean you understand the conversation. You now have to be able to pick out and understand everything that is going on around you, including other conversations, before you start to understand yours.

For lots of people with autism, this can take days weeks, months, and even years. For those parents, educators, or doctors reading this book, think of one person you know with autism. Have you ever seen them, in a room, start to laugh or cry or get mad or even scream for no reason you can pinpoint? The reason you can't pinpoint it is because they are audio filtering. I have learned to audio filter a minute to two minutes after a conversation has started. It's harder being in a big hall or movie theater or a stadium where it can take longer and can become very overwhelming at times.

Let me clarify something. Audio filtering isn't just for sorting out audio input. It also helps sort out smells, physical touch, like a rough shirt cuff, and also visual input. I think audio filtering is ingrained or hardwired into the brains of people with autism. We just have to figure out how to use it and control it.

Communication was a big goal of mine, but at the same time it was a big goal for everyone around me. Barb, my speech pathologist, was working on many ways for me to communicate ever since

I could remember. I recall having popsicle sticks jammed in my mouth and being taught how to use my hands and fingers to do signs for sign language. It was always hard and, to tell you the truth, frustrating at times. I can almost picture the first time I was introduced to using picture symbols. I remember thinking, Wow, I point to a picture of chips and someone just hands it to me. That, to me, was amazing. The first time I communicated, I asked for something and I got what I asked for. Now the hard part I understood, but with everything going on around me how do I duplicate it or do it again? I took a while to get the hang of it. At first I found it was hard to stop my impulses to pick other picture symbols that weren't the ones I needed at the time. For example, I would want to tell someone that I needed the washroom, but the chip picture always looked too inviting to ignore.

As the years went on I was introduced to Howie, who would become an important person to Barb and me. I think Howie, like Barb, always believed I had something important to say and wanted me to find a way to get it out. Howie and Barb would always come up with neat ideas for me to communicate. One of the things they came up with was a big binder that they made me carry around my house and school that had picture symbols all throughout the pages. The picture symbols didn't only have pictures on them, they had words streamed across the top. Those words would lead me to spelling, but that's for another paragraph.

I recall Howie asking Barb in my classroom what was the ultimate goal for me to communicate? Barb turned her head at me and then back at Howie. She began to say, "Carly is six and for now, I think we need to focus on picture symbols because I think the long-term goal is to have Carly use a voice output device."

Howie had only worked with me for a couple months at this point and I think he wasn't too sure of me, at first, but when Barb mentioned a voice output device, something must have clicked in

Howie's head. That day, and for the next weeks and months, Howie pushed picture symbols over and over again. A lot of my days at school had to do with programs that taught me the meanings of the symbols or how to use the symbols to express my wants and needs. I was always good at identifying pictures, but because I wasn't fully able to audio filter, I didn't always understand the full label for the picture.

The way I understand it is, my mind works differently than most people's. When I see something, I take a picture of it and it stays in my head. This is why I have trouble looking at people's faces. When I look at someone I take over a thousand images of that person's face in less than a minute. Now think of my brain as a digital camera. The more I look at someone's face, the more pictures I take. Because I take so many pictures, my brain or, as in my example, the camera gets full. I am no longer able to process the pictures or images and I am forced to turn away. That is why, for most people with autism, you will see their eyes wandering or face moving in a different direction when you are talking to them.

Because of my ability to take pictures of people, objects, and images, the picture symbols Howie introduced every day stuck in my head. My progress was not slow but not fast. However, midway through the school year, Howie convinced Barb and the school board that I was ready for a voice output device. I think the day I got my voice output device was a big moment in my life, and I did realize how much work and effort I was going to have to bring to the table. Looking back, I worked over and above what most children do in a day. Using ABA, Howie and Barb worked on their own program to teach me how to master the voice output device. From day one, Barb and Howie would only hold my hand to teach me where the symbols were. Once I learned the location of the symbols, Barb made sure no one would help or assist me when I used my voice output device. Even though my fine motor skills prevented me from holding a pencil, I was always able to point and target images. Barb and Howie wanted people who were around me to know and to see that I was able to do this all on my own.

My first voice output device was big and only let me use eight symbols at a time. Howie made a book with over a hundred symbols and categorized them to put on the voice output device when I would be in different situations. Wow, to think about it, Howie had no life. Just joking. He had a girlfriend at the time, who he later married.

A little bit after I got my first voice output device, I was already growing out of it. My parents, with the guidance of Barb and Howie, ended up getting me a computerized voice output device, which changed my life. The voice output device had words scrolling at the top of the symbols. My photographic memory started taking in those images/words.

A couple of years later, Howie and Barb started coming up with a spelling program. The program was really clever and I recommend it for anyone wanting to teach someone with autism. They showed me pictures with text and would first get me to match Scrabble letters to the text. Once I was able to match, I then had to spell the word without seeing the text. It was all sight learning. There is something I never told Howie or Barb: I already had over two thousand words in my head that I was just processing and their program started getting me to understand what to do with those words.

I find it weird, but I have never been asked what was going through my head the first time I spelled. The truth is, as you probably read in my dad's chapters, I was feeling sick that day. Oh wait, I forgot you haven't read his chapters. So, I was feeling sick the first time I spelled. Howie pulled me over to Barb and I just felt achy all over. I remember thinking I didn't want to use my voice output device, so why are they making me? I knew Howie wasn't going to let me go without getting me to say something. I just wanted them to know I was not in a good place and then, in my head, I saw the word *help*, a word that had been on the main page of all my voice output devices since the beginning. I started to spell it: *H E L P*. I then pulled away to lie back on the couch when Howie pulled me back. I think they were shocked and I, well, I didn't really process my accomplishment yet. I felt really nauseated and threw up a little in my mouth when Howie pulled me back to spell. I was placed in front of the voice output device again and, well, you know, I wrote "*teeth*." In my head, I was just trying to think of a word that would describe what just happened in my mouth. In hindsight, I should have written the word *mouth*, but I was just a kid.

I didn't fully understand what I had done until a day or two later. It took time for me to process that part of me, again. I was proud of my accomplishment but did not know how really big it was. It would open a world for me I really wasn't sure I wanted to be in. Don't get me wrong. The ability to communicate my wants and needs is great; however, with great abilities come greater expectations.

A month after I started typing, all new and creative programs emerged. I remember my silly brother Matthew running around my house with a label maker labeling everything. Howie made me look at every word I walked by. Just to tell you how crazy my brother and Howie were, they labeled the toilet and every time I sat down, Howie made me point to the word. It was really crazy but helped me start to audio filter the label with the word.

As the months went by, I started to get new voice output devices that would help me showcase my newfound skill. I started using a device called a Lightwriter that made me feel like I was even more different than everyone else. All my other devices always piqued people's interest with all the pictures and their shocking talking ability. Because of that, I never felt different but with my Lightwriter I never got the same reactions, and I got more strange looks than curious looks. After I kept pushing away these devices, Howie looked into getting a computer for me. He found an amazing program called WordQ that had word prediction and also had the feature of text-to-speech so I could have a conversation with anyone in a room or around the corner.

Sitting at a computer brought new *and* familiar challenges to me. I have been quoted as saying: *"My body feels like a can of Coke that has been shaken for hours."* Now sitting down at a table and writing a sentence took all of my concentration and strength. I would find, after talking for only five minutes, as soon as I would stand up, it felt like someone opened the can of Coke and I would just explode. I would have to get out all this built-up energy by jumping, running, and rocking. To look back at it now, I wonder what my mother and father thought about it. Here I was, a girl that was now able to spell but freaking out after sitting so calmly?

More challenges always seemed to present themselves. I had a hard time using both hands and if I would bring my left hand up to help me type I found it got in trouble. So I would concentrate not only on typing but on keeping my hand down and out of trouble.

My ability to keep the amount of focus and concentration I needed to type was always a challenge. There were times I would just refuse to type for days and months. I never thought of it as giving up or quitting but more of taking a small break or rest. I know what you're thinking. How would I express myself or get my needs met if I couldn't talk? The fact of the matter is I found not talking a challenge, but I think it was also easier in ways. I was able just to run in to the kitchen and grab what I wanted or just point to something and people were so glad I pointed, they would just give it to me.

If I had to pick a point in my life that really made me excited to be able to type it would have been my bat mitzvah. My sister had her bat mitzvah speech all ready to go and no one really knows this, but I had mine made up as well. I write all my work in my head and regurgitate it onto the screen. I even knew who I wanted to read my speech for me. At one of my sessions with Barb and Howie, I told them my goal. I told them I wanted Ellen DeGeneres to be my voice. Barb was shocked, and Howie said, "Okay, let's talk to your parents and see what we can do."

I started to write Ellen a letter and every time my finger hit the keys, I got more excited. Like I said before, I had the whole speech written in my head, but getting it on the computer seemed to take forever.

A couple of weeks before my bat mitzvah, my life changed forever. All my hard work, all the hard challenges I had to overcome to write my long speech felt worth it. My mother and father sat me down and told me that Ellen saw my letter and agreed to read it. There is no greater feeling than knowing you can do something that may have seemed impossible. From that day forward, I welcomed challenges.

My life had changed. I started to write on social media websites and writing my own blog. I felt that I needed challenges in my life so I challenged myself to be on *Larry King Live* and to even be invited to a conference called the Annual International Technology & Persons with Disabilities Conference at CSUN in San Diego. These challenges kept me thinking and knowing that I am capable of doing anything and everything I set my mind to. Well, I mean of course, my whole life I was told I wouldn't talk and here is my voice talking to you.

My recent challenge has had to do with me attending a typical high school. In case you're wondering if I succeeded with that goal, all I can tell you is the principal has chased me around the school and I broke the captain of the football team's nose. Just joking. I made lots of friends this year and had my first real party at my house. I even went out to a movie with a group of friends and didn't need a worker. As for schoolwork, I got A's on a lot of my assignments and had a fun time learning.

A wise man once told me that a seed needs love and nurturing to become a flower and a caterpillar needs time and persistence to become a beautiful butterfly. So that's why I say everyone has an inner voice that is waiting to come out and all they need is you.

Thank you for reading my dad's book about my life, and I promise my book, written by me, will come out soon so you don't have to read my dad's chapters. Just joking.

Or am I?

A Conversation with Carly:
The Truths and Myths About Autism

I'm not sure what to make of the fact that I've gotten to know my daughter more by conversations she's had with others, answers to questions posed by strangers, and her blog posts than by any direct dialogue. I guess I'm just grateful for the opportunity, however it comes. What I am certain of is that even at the young age of sixteen, Carly has already had a profound impact on those affected by autism.

Of the thousands of questions, words of support, and comments from Carly's followers and readers through various social media channels, there seem to be several recurring themes. It has been Carly's mission to help debunk the myths and share the truths about life with autism. Here are some of the observations I thought you might find compelling.

When it comes to the unusual behaviors exhibited by many who have autism, sometimes there is a method to their madness.

Q: dillon @CarlysVoice *Hi Carly, i have written to you before, My question for you is this, My children have often overheard people say to us, oh you poor dears, we dont feel that way we feel very lucky. How do you as one who has autism feel when you hear this? I would like to have an idea how our boys feel at these times, as they dont speak but thru sign.*

A: I hate when that happens my moms friend just had a tragic accident happen and she had one of her two autistic sons pass away and people told her its for the best. It's really sad the way society views the importance of life just because he was different does not mean he did not have any importance or any things to teach us. We all have feelings even if we don't often show it at times.

Q: kevin @CarlysVoice *I have a 16 yrs who has a fascination with cards, numbering as like the clock on a VCR. Do you have any thoughts why?*

A: Repetition is always a good way for us to stim. Visually stims like seeing numbers & repeating it in our head/out loud are always great.

Q: SgtMgt @CarlysVoice *My 6yrold son gets sad and cries often, & I cant figure out why. Do U have any suggestions how I can figure out what is wrong?*

A: It could be many things. Is he on any medication I have had lots of extreme mood changes like crying and being angry for no reason. It was because of the medication It could be things that are happening earlier in the day or days that he is just processing through now.

Q: SgtMgt @CarlysVoice *When you are w/your family in public and someone seems curious, how do you prefer your family to address your situation?*

A: To tell you truth I never really have had a talk with my family about that. If I am with my mom she will either tell them what is going on or tell my dad what morons they are. My dad just looks away from them and tries to move us on if he can. I think the real way to handle it is just to go up to them and tell them I am Autistic and answer any questions they might have. But sometimes I cant do that because I am to worked up.

Q: Bonnie1018 @CarlysVoice *you mentioned you would miss a few things about being autistic . . . what would you miss? #Autism*
A: I would miss spelling to some one 4 the first time & seeing there face. Setting a goal that every on thinks is to high and braking it.

Q: Momtweets @CarlysVoice *What thing about being autistic do you like? What's the worst thing about being autistic?*
A: I like when I shock people because they think just because I'm autistic I am not smart. The worst thing is not being able to control my self even though I know what I am doing is wrong.

Q: caringchild @CarlysVoice *Whats it like being a silent observer of things going on around U? When you found your voice did it open the world to U?*
A: Being able 2 hear things that people don't know I hear or I'm in the room but don't think I hear them is cool some times. But some time you don't want to hear things that you do. Spelling has helped open some of the world to me.

A person who cannot speak may still have plenty to say.

Q: manly7678 @CarlysVoice *My 5yo daughter has #Autism & is non-verbal, but she has a definite spark in her eye. Your story fills us with hope.*
A: I go to school every day with kids that are Autistic And some of them are non verbal but I have no doubt in my mind that they all have inner voices and they just need to find away to get there inner voice herd. So if you have a feeling your daughter has a inner voice don't give up till she is heard.

Q: bearclaw @CarlysVoice *At what age did u feel you had a breakthrough, even if u couldn't voice it yet? #Autism*
A: I think when I was around nine I really was able to audio filter what my sister had to say and I wouldn't believe it.

Q: chag61 @CarlysVoice *Please explain how you can organize your thoughts and type but you cannot speak . . is this a possibility for all who are autistic.*
A: We all have the ability to spell. Work on simple words and make sure we are always around words. We are looking at things all the time.

Q: aaronr @CarlysVoice *How did u learn 2 communicate so well on your PC & can low functioning kids w/ #autism be taught likewise? Thx!*
A: We all have a inner voice that needs to come out and we just need some one to believe in us and push us to get it out.

Q: Devina @CarlysVoice *My brother has autism and he doesnt communicate with us in ways we understand. Any ideas/tips on what we can do? Thanks!*
A: When I was younger I started talking with pictures. It was a great starting point on learning 2 spell bcs the pictures had labels on them.

Q: anne @CarlysVoice *yes I have a question Carly. Do you think facilitated communication can be taught to anyone?*
A: I don't use facilitated communication so I really don't know. I spell on my own with out any holding my hand or whispering in my ear.

The five senses are anything but independent of one another, especially for many living with autism.

Q: Tammy @CarlysVoice *Carly, I almost don't want to bother you because you seem like you will be busy for days answering all the questions we people have for you, but I hope you don't mind me asking you anyway. You can take days to* *answer if you want. Take your time, no rush. Here is my question. My 14 year old is always using her hands like a puppet and talking to them. Besides humming, hand flapping, etc . . . what kind of environment or activities calm you the best? She reinacts a lot of the movies she sees with her hands speaking to them as if they were people. She holds her hands up in front of her face, almost like she were talking to someone. She does it all the time. I'm not sure what it's about. Is this stimming? Is their a way to stop it? Should I stop it?*

A: It sounds like your daughter is audio filtering. This is actually a good thing and don't let any therapist or doctors tell you it isn't. As she gets better at it her hands will stop moving and she will be able to understand your words and things around her better. Tell her I say keep it up girl friend.

Q: PatZ1 @CarlysVoice *Besides humming, hand flapping, etc . . . what kind of environment or activities calm you the best?*
A: Flapping and humming and rocking does not calm me down it helps me cope with stuff around me. #Autism

Q: DCxQueen @CarlysVoice *My cousin has autism, she doesn't like clothes at all, have you had trouble with that? Is there anything what could help?*
A: I use to hate the feeling of clothing rubbing and tuching my body. Especially if they got wet. Get rid of tags. I like wearing shirts a lot better since I started wearing a bra. Feeling is still hard to put up with but i am getting use to it.

Q: Myseth @CarlysVoice *Are you aware of dangerous situations like crossing the street and what you would need to do if a car was coming.*
A: Yes, but that is really hard. 2 many sounds to take in & sights & smells & it gets over whelming thats why we have a hard time waiting.

Q: toni @CarlysVoice *my little boy only eats toast. He will smell the food and not try it at all. He is nearly 4. I will try forever but why?*
A: Lots of food can be over powering. See if you can find a dip he likes. Add it to different food even if its grouse to you.

Q: Tileguy12 @CarlysVoice *Do you hum or spin? If so do you know what makes you do that? My son does it all day. Thanks.*
A: Its a way 2 shut down all my other senses & just focus on one. Huming normaly is followed by covering your ear to change sounds. Its masking.

Q: Cjboy09 @CarlysVoice *what kind of music do you listen to? calming jazzy type? pop? Etc.*
A: I like lots of different music but it also depends on how I am feeling. I like stuff that has a beet or base when I need to stim. I find music at night that has calming voices helps me sleep and stay a sleep.

Q: DailyDose @CarlysVoice *My 5yr old often stares off to the side not turning his head just using his eyes wide eyed and almost straining. Why?*
A: When I was young I couldnt stare directly at things. I was looked out the corner of my eyes and even though U think hes not looking he is.

Q: DailyDose @CarlysVoice *What do you mean when you say "i take over a thousand pictures of a persons face when i look at them"?*
A: It's the way I describe how we see. All the images come at us at once. It is so overwhelming.

Q: pressdough7 @CarlysVoice *When stimming, what is going on? Is it relaxing, a need, defense mech., centering (proprioceptive) . . ? I'll be watching in Aug.*
A: Drs. have the definition of stimming wrong. Stims are when you make or create output to block sensory input or over load.

Q: jhannah5 @CarlysVoice *Am i the only person with a child who dips pizza in hummus? Danny's autistic so i guess that makes it OK, LOL!*
A: Its funny you should say that. A lot of times when autistic children and adults eat food, we have a hard time with textures and smells. It can be a little over barring some times. We block these things out buy adding dips to mask the problem. I like dipping my pizza in mustard and at camp I dip my food in ranch dressing.

Q: Momtweets @CarlysVoice *You talk about audio filtering, how did you learn to audio filter?*

A: I am glad you asked that question. I learned how to audio filter on my own. However I did pick up different techniques from therapists, even though they did not know they were teaching me. I have been getting better at audio filtering in the last 2 to 3 years. It has helped me be able to understand better and communicate with others.

Q: Lena @CarlysVoice *Carly, when you were younger- did you like to watch the same cartoons over and over again? Our son does this. Thanks.*

A: No, I had a hard time audio filtering t.v for the longest time. But I know why your child does it. Its easier to process sounds that we here over and over again when we are audio filtering.

Q: Lena @CarlysVoice *do sounds seem amplified to you. My daughter's weakness is loud noises, fire alarm, especially thunder.*

A: I take in lots of sounds and some times sounds that are loud for you are even louder for me. I also Find sounds like the dish washer set my ears ringing.

Q: Iifffkne @CarlysVoice *my daughter is 3 & she's non verbal. She cries alot cause certain sounds bother her. I don't know why.. Do u maybe know why?*

A: I my self hear a hundred sounds a minute. Lots of noises that other people tell me that they can not hear. We take in many sounds all at once. For some of us certain sounds are much louder then others.

Q: tifffkne @CarlysVoice *Was it hard to learn meditation? My daughter also has extreme anxiety and sensory challenges. I feel so helpless!*

A: My OT and my Therapist Howie introduced me 2 meditation and I was shocked at how fast I was able 2 learn it and how affective it works. I recommend meditation 2 any one who has high anxieties.

Having autism does not preclude a desire for friendship, love, and affection.

Q: Shannon @CarlysVoice *do you have a lot of best friends?*
A: I have a couple best friends and before some one twitters me yes one some are autistic. But not all.

Q: Shannon @CarlysVoice *How old were you when you understood love & felt how very much your parents love you. I've heard it can be a hard concept.*
A: I don't know how old I was but from a young age I always new my mom and dad loved and cared for me. I wasn't able to tell them I loved them back or sometimes even hug them back but I still loved them.

Q: caringchildren @CarlysVoice *Who do you like hanging out with more? "typical children" or "Autistic children" Why?*
A: I like hanging out with typical children because it pushes me to control my behaviors and find different stims that look more suitable. But it is not easy. I get judged for sounds and noises I make. However this summer I did walk away with lots of friends and emails. I do hang out with autistic children as well and like that too. I have many friends in L.A who spell like me. Its fun to hang out with them because I don't have to explain anything to them, they just get it.

Don't think of those with autism as victims or view them with pity.

Q: klou4 @CarlysVoice *what kind of job do you want when you grow up?*
A: I would like to work for Borack obama in four years as a I think its called ambassador for autism and get #Autism out in the open.

Q: oprahclub @CarlysVoice *If you went on oprah what would you talk about???*

A: I would tell people ignorance is caused by lack of #knowledge so lets #educate our selfs. #Autism needs to be talked about.

Q: pamsfan1 @CarlysVoice *So many people don't understand autism. We have been advocating for our son since he was diagnosed.*
A: A lot of times its not that they don't under stand its that know one has educated them.The only time an autistic person is on the news is when something bad happens.Or one day a year to raise awareness for autism. But autism day should be every day. People like larry king oprah and news stations around the world should publicize it every day. That's the only way we will get people to learn.

Q: zen @CarlysVoice *Hi Carly! what can we do to help you promote your cause! Wonderful amazing blog You are an inspiration!*
A: I just want to explain the truths and secrets of autism. So you can help me by asking questions and getting others to do the same.

Some helpful tips

Q: *I am a massage therapist, planning to work with children with autism, any ideas on how to provide a space where the child will feel comfortable?*
A: I have had a massages and enjoyed them as for a space make sure the oils or cream you use is ok with the child and the smell of them isn't over whelming. We can still smell certain sense after you have used them on other people in the room. Make sure fans and even air-conditioners are off. Some times sounds overwhelm us when we are experiencing increase of sensory input like a massage.

Q: *How do you feel about your therapists/aides? What can I as a therapy aide do to make a kid's time with me a positive experience?*
A: I like therapists in fact I am friends with a lot of mine. The best thing u can do is go with your gut not the book. If you think something will work try it. And always believe in your child. They will feed off of that.

Q: Jeff @CarlysVoice *How do you feel about gluten-free, dairy-free, casein-free and wheat-free diets? what do you eat?*
A: I tried it when I was younger. It never made me feel different. If it works 4 some people that is great. but I haven't spoken to many that actually say its helps and not alot of kids are still on it that i no of that are my age.

Q: Jeff @CarlysVoice *What would you tell siblings of a Autistic kid on how to better deal with Autism?*
A: That we don't mean to steal the attention form them and we are sorry when we brake things and we do care for them.

Q: AnthonyH @CarlysVoice *Would you recommend (or discourage) any devices/ apps ideal for kids with autism. Eg iPod Touch or Nintendo DS?*
A: I like using proloquo2go on my ipod it helps me communicate when I don't have a computer around and look like all the other kids with it.

Q: ferrista @CarlysVoice *I am a teacher for kids like you. If you were my student what one thing would you like me to know?*
A: That we are all teachable you just need to think out side of the box. Never give up.

Q: jubilee @CarlysVoice *if you didn't live at home what technology would you want in your apartment?*
A: I would need my Ipod my laptop and a free chip vending machine. I would really like a t.v that I could hook my laptop into so people dont look over my shoulder to see what I am saying/spelling. I like to listen to t.v with wireless head-phones sometimes. They help me block out the other overwhelming sounds and can helps me focus.

Q: Healher @CarlysVoice *When you can't control yourself even when you know it's wrong, what is the best support a person can give you when this happens?*

A: I know people want me 2 say they can help control some of our behaviors but alot of times. Some of our behaviors are to stop other behaviors. I was hitting my hands and the doctors thought it was self aggressive behavior. In fact I was hitting my hands to stop another behavior. I could not walk by paper or bags with out feeling the need 2 rip or shred them. So I would hit my hands to stop it. Sometimes when people interject they end up making things worse. But sometimes it can be great help.

Q: GreenDilly @CarlysVoice *my younger brother has autism, he sometimes gets very frustrated and hits himself, what is the best way to calm him down?*
A: First of all we hit ourself for many reasons. I hit my self 2 stop me from doing what I no is wrong. So if that is the case don't stop it. Best way to help is to read us when we our getting frustrated and try to calm us down be for we get to that point.

A Look Forward

Carly's input to her Grade 10 Individualized Education Plan, Fall 2011

Area	From Student's Perspective
Main Learning Goals What are the most important things you want to learn this year?	I would like to learn how to improve my writing styles. I also want to learn how to get the knowledge that is in my head out on paper faster so I am not behind on my work. I find I finish an assignment a few minutes after it is handed out but getting it from my head to the computer takes a lot of time and effort.
Areas Of Strength What do you do well?	I have a photographic memory that allows me to look at a image or a page of a book and memorize it in seconds. I have an exceptional command of the English language and therefore I am able to write elaborate papers or assignments that make teachers and other students think.
Areas Of Need In what areas do you have difficulty or show limitations?	I am slow with typing because of my autism so it is hard to answer questions right away in class and even participate in class discussions. Math is very difficult for me to do not because I don't understand it but because it takes hours for me to write out the answers. I have difficulties in anything that involves fine motor or gross motor control.

Disability/Medical Conditions

Can you provide us with any resources or additional information about yourself like disability/medical condition?

I have Autism, Apraxia, O.C.D. and good lookingness syndrome. My autism is not really an issue however I do stim, flap my hands, cover my ears, make deep sounds and twiddle paper and leaves. My apraxia prevents me from getting the message from my brain to the muscles of my mouth and therefore stops me from speaking and being heard right away. I am still able to think the same way a typical teenager thinks but I am not able to show you in the same amount of time. My O.C.D. is just like every case you might have heard of. Like Donald Trump or Howie Mandel, I have impulses to do things in certain ways. I need to wash my hands with soap on the back and then the front two times or else I feel like I'm being stabbed in my side.

Special Equipment

Is there any special equipment that you will use at school, e.g. walker, stander?

I use an iPad to communicate with an app called Proloquo2go. I also use a program called Kurzweil to take notes on my computer. I use a program called iPrompt to help with my O.C.D. and I also use a computer program called "read please" to read my assignments to my class.

Engagement

How do you learn best?

I am a visual and auditory learner who likes it when teachers write notes on the board or give handouts to the class. I find that when teachers lecture the class, I learn a lot. However, it's hard for me when other kids are talking or making noise while the teacher is talking.

Avoidance

What frustrates, distracts, or disengages you?

I have a hard time learning when the teacher wants me to answer questions right away in class. I have a hard time completing in-class assignments that are due during class time. I have a hard time doing art or artistic projects such as drawing a diagram or making a picture to do with the subject.

Independence

In what areas would you like to see yourself demonstrate more independence?

I would like to see myself demonstrate more independence in the classroom by sitting by myself and less with my aid. I would like to be more independent on pushing myself to complete the work on time.

Safety/Vulnerability

Are there any issues unique to you that we should be aware of?

I have Autism/O.C.D. and that brings up a lot of safety issues. I have a hard time controlling my impulses and I have a hard time controlling my body. I do have trained workers that know how to deal with these issues and they have been successful in the past.

Response To Inappropriate Behaviour

What are the best strategies to use when you have inappropriate behaviours?

The best response is to tell me what I am doing, e.g. if I am making noise because sometimes I don't even know I am doing it. If it's something serious that has to do with my autism or my O.C.D., the best thing to do is let my aids deal with me and assist them if they ask you too.

Social Interaction

How do you relate to other students in one-to-one, small group, and large group situations?

I have made lots of friends last year and I am trying to make more this year. I have completed two small group projects this year and felt I do well getting my voice heard and listening to others.

Literacy

Listening, Speaking, Reading, Writing

What do you do well?

What do you have difficulty with?

I do well at Listening, Reading and Writing. I do have problems with speaking. I might not talk out of my mouth however I do speak on my computer or iPad. It's really slow and I find it hard to talk to teachers because they tend to cut me off before I finish my thought.

Numeracy

Concepts, Computation, Problem Solving

What do you do well?

What do you have difficulty with?

I do well at Concepts, Computation, Problem Solving but have a hard time showing or explaining it due to time limitations. It is hard to write equations due to limitations with software or programs on the iPad/computer.

Transition Plan

14 years of age and older

What actions need to be considered now in planning for your life upon leaving secondary school?

My goal is to go to UCLA and get my BA or Doctorate like my idol, Temple Grandin. I am also thinking of applying to Caltech to learn about computer programming. My goal is to visit the universities in March and meet the Deans and Professors.

Key Information

Is there any additional information that you would like to share that you feel it is important we know?

That I am eager to learn and that even if I am not looking at you, I am still listening and paying attention.

Acknowledgments

When referring to raising Carly, we have often evoked the African proverb that it takes a village to raise a child. Though in our version, we elevate the *village* to an *army*. Without the following people in our lives, my family and I would still live under a cloud of darkness.

We would not have gotten to really know our daughter Carly if not for Barb Nash-Fenton and Howard Dalal. This magical duo saw Carly's potential—even before she did—and never gave up guiding her forward. They have done more for our family than we could have ever asked or ever done for ourselves.

While there are numerous medical professionals to whom we are indebted, the commitment and wisdom of Dr. Wendy Roberts, Carly's "Cool Doctor," has been a beacon for us. We also feel enormous gratitude to Dr. Morton Goldbach, Dr. Diane Superina, and Dr. Rose Geist for helping us through the most chaotic years and working tirelessly to improve the quality of Carly's life. The team of doctors, specialists, and nurses at the Hospital for Sick Children in Toronto are too many to mention by name, too important to ever forget. The patience and counsel of Dr. Sharon Marcovitch helped guide us in planning Carly's education and understanding the intellectual milestones Carly has achieved.

Years of excellent, scientifically backed therapy are at the root of helping Carly thrive. From the outstanding programming and dedication of the team at the Behaviour Institute led by Dr. Nicole Walton-Allen, Donna Chenney, and Kendra Gayadeen and Audrey Meisner at New Haven Learning Center, to the ABA teams that preceded them led by Elizabeth Benedetto-Nasho and Shayna Guenther, these people have taught Carly every skill she possesses. Autism affects the ability to learn, but not necessarily a person's innate intelligence, and through the creativity, focus, and discipline of these wonderful ABA providers and therapists, Carly has shown us that her disability needn't be her prison.

While many therapists and support workers joined us for a period of time before moving on to other callings, some are a part of our life years later: Joanne Alexander, Dina Kalales, Melissa Perri, Colin Campbell, and, more recently, Katie Czich and Sheila Duggin (whose first "teaching position" was to work with Carly at school and which required her to do things never taught in teachers' college). Carly's team in recent years has expanded to include Barb Muskat, who provides Carly with a confidante and counselor. Ashleigh Eccles, Carly's occupational therapist, has helped Carly reach personal goals that many of us take for granted and, on occasion, achieve an inner calm many of us would love to find. Running our crazy household would have been impossible without the dedicated support of Shiela, our nanny of seven years.

Thank you to Paul McCormack, Steve Noonan, and Brenda Scott for your never-ending support to our family. You have always had our back.

We have been fortunate to have family in our lives—in particular, Tammy's sister Carol; a better aunt does not exist. But friends have frequently been an extension of our family, and I don't know where we would be without Mary Eberts, a legal champion for the cause of families living with autism, and a loyal friend. David Corbett and Jonathan Strug also stood by us in court when that was the only forum available to ensure our own voices were heard. Chip and Ruthie Bailey, whose door is always open to us, and who opened doors *for* us when we sought out Ellen to read Carly's bat mitzvah speech. Similarly, those generous of time and patience who supported us and tried to understand the incomprehensible nature of our life include the Collies, Kibels, Seldons, Shepherds, Smiths, and Wellses, and friends from our youth who endured the test of time: Brian Saber, Randi Stern, and Karen Willsky.

Sometimes, autism brings new friendships (despite being known as a condition that inhibits social ability) and in more recent years, we've been blessed with introductions to the Valners, Portia Iversen, and Jon Shestack, who, while we don't see them often enough, we think of all the time. Carly's story could never have been told without our friend Beverley Brock, who was tenacious in recommending Dana Dalal to us as a therapist when Carly was four; and to Dana for her commitment to Carly and, even more important, for bringing us her brother, Howard. Our list of friends would not be complete without acknowledging Holly and Rodney Peete and their kids, who generously awarded Carly a Youth Champion award and welcomed us into their home and their lives.

As Carly continues to open doors for herself, there have been teachers and educators who march in front, helping her along the way. To those at the fictitiously named "Western Secondary," including Varla Abrams, Ron Felson, Linda Swales, Leonilla Liko, Jennifer Molloy, and Michelle Pinet, we are thankful that you were willing to take a chance and see in Carly what many could not.

Carly would not be able to achieve her mission of sharing "the truth and mysteries of autism" without the dedicated and supportive following of her audience on Facebook and Twitter. And her story would not have been told so powerfully without the help of news professionals Alan Goldberg of ABC and Avis Favaro and Elizabeth St. Philip of CTV, who took the time to tell it with insight and integrity.

Many of us can identify pivotal moments in our lives. For Carly, the pace and depth of her communication accelerated exponentially with her introduction to Ellen DeGeneres. Ellen has been generous with her time and empathy, something we'll treasure forever. Contacting Ellen was only possible through the efforts of Steve Levine, who answered the cold-call email that would ultimately change Carly's life. Julie Silver, Mary Connelly, and my sister-in-law, Ruth Fleischmann, helped amplify this request and ensure that Ellen heard it loud and clear. And Craig Peralta, who implored Ellen to read Carly's introductory letter, and has subsequently made us feel wanted and welcome.

I never dreamt of telling Carly's story in printed word, and likely would not have if not for the mentorship and support of my agent, Linda Loewenthal of David Black Literary Agency. She saw the story in *Carly's Voice* before it was a story and patiently helped me bring it to life. And it would have remained an "inner voice" without the guidance, persistence, and wisdom of my editor, Sally Kim, at Touchstone/Simon & Schuster. I was lucky to not have one great editor but two, and I thank Trish Todd at S&S for going above the call of duty in providing me a first-read edit, which formed the basis of the final manuscript. I am grateful for the leadership and heavy lifting of the entire team, including Stacy Creamer, David Falk, Meredith Vilarello, Marcia Burch, Allegra Ben-Amotz, and Cherlynne Li.

But of course only my immediate family really understands what it has taken to live this story and what it means to tell it. Matthew, thank you for your maturity and righteousness. You are an old soul who will have great impact on the world. Taryn, your humor makes me smile; your unconditional love for your twin sister makes me proud. Carly, I learn from you every day and cannot think of a hero I admire more. Tammy, you never think your efforts are sufficient, but in fact no one who walks this earth could move it the way you have for your family. I love you all, and believe because of you, regardless of our challenges, that I am one hell of a lucky guy.

That we have this impossibly large, passionately engaged team supporting us is the miracle of Carly.